# SPECIAL FORCES

This edition published by Parragon Books Ltd in 2015 and distributed by

Parragon Inc.
440 Park Avenue South, 13th Floor
New York, NY 10016
www.parragon.com

Cover design by Talking Design
Inside front & back cover images © Shutterstock

Designed, produced and packaged by
Stonecastle Graphics Limited

Designed by Paul Turner and Sue Pressley
Text by Chris Chant
Edited by Philip de Ste. Croix

ISBN 978-1-4748-0455-4

Printed in China

# SPECIAL FORCES

### History › Roles and Missions › Training
### Weapons and Equipment › Combat Scenarios

Bath · New York · Cologne · Melbourne · Delhi
Hong Kong · Shenzhen · Singapore · Amsterdam

# CONTENTS

▲ U.S. Special Operation Forces soldiers in combat.

# INTRODUCTION

# special forces

Ever since May 5, 1980, when elements of Britain's Special Air Service Regiment stormed the Iranian embassy in London to free hostages held by terrorists, special forces have captured the world's attention.

Special forces, sometimes known as special operations forces, are small, high-quality, elite military units with the skills, physical capabilities, and mental strength to be tasked with the performance of missions which conventional units cannot undertake. Two of the key factors that characterize special forces operations are the high tactical value of the objective, and the high level of risk involved—a danger that can be offset, in part at least, by the extreme professionalism of the members of the special forces teams. Members of any special force unit possess, as primary attributes, immense mental commitment and resolution, considerable physical strength, robustness, and resilience. They have the cast of mind that endows them with the realistic confidence, considered bravery, and a combination of military and personal skills that enables them to operate either individually or in small teams (and almost always in isolation from supporting units) deep in enemy territory, and usually in areas of geographical and/or climatic challenge.

▲   *Members of the Brazilian marine corps' Comandos Anfibios (amphibious commandos) clear a house, using tactics exchanged with U.S. Navy SEALs during a joint combined exchange training exercise in 2010.*

▼   *Masked men of the Lawan Keganasan (Anti-Terror) 11 Rejimen (Grup Gerak Khas) of the Malaysian Army use a rigid-hull inflatable boat during a demonstration.*

▲ Spanish Army paratroopers exit a Boeing CH-47 Chinook helicopter at Bala Murghab FOB (forward operating base) in Afghanistan during an ISAF (International Security Assistance Force) mission in 2008.

▲ Men of the Chilean navy's Comando de Fuerzas Especiales, armed with 9-mm Heckler und Koch MP5N sub-machine guns, train for the type of undertaking that may be needed in antipiracy operations.

In overall terms, then, special forces are small units which are expensive to train and maintain. However, they provide very considerable military value because they can fulfil difficult tasks and thus yield a high return on the associated investment in men, training and equipment. Special forces therefore represent a high-value tactical asset, which can offer a significant operational-level advantage. As such, they are often controlled directly from the operational, and sometimes strategic, levels of the military command structure.

Military history is littered with examples of what would now be termed special forces, although in the past they operated on a more limited and extemporized basis than is now deemed appropriate. What has not altered, however, is the fact that special forces, both early and modern, were created specifically to provide support to the larger military establishment, though not necessarily on the primary battlefield. Special forces around the world have created, and indeed continue to deliver, an added tactical dimension through the employment of additional skills and commitment. Some of these skills, in the form of tactics and specialized combat techniques, remain of value principally to special forces, but others have proved to be suitable for subsequent dissemination to more conventional units.

◀ *Men of the South Korean Army's Special Warfare Command take part in a sea infiltration drill against possible threats from North Korea in 2009.*

▼ *A SEAL of the Thai navy heads toward the bridge of a U.S. Military Sealift Command roll-on/roll-off container ship after fast-roping onto the flight deck.*

Special forces have played an important role throughout history at times when it was deemed important to disrupt an enemy's dispositions and rear areas by "hit and run" raids and sabotage, thereby paving the way for decisive attacks by conventional forces. Other significant tasks have included reconnaissance to provide vital tactical and operational intelligence from the enemy's forward and rear areas, and increasingly in fomenting subversive elements, and supporting their infrastructure and activities in the enemy's rear areas. Special forces of the modern kind started to develop in the first part of the twentieth century, and there was a major acceleration of this trend in World War II. Earlier developments, such as the emergence of light and rifle units to provide mobility and aimed firepower (in the reconnaissance and skirmishing roles) superior to those of conventional infantry units (which were ponderous in maneuver and armed with the musket more suitable for volley fire than aimed fire) marked a start of the process in the late eighteenth century.

A more pronounced shift toward the deployment of special forces became evident from the later nineteenth century as mainstream forces started to adopt, in adapted form, tactics pioneered in the field against them by irregular forces, such as those of the Boers in South Africa. This tendency continued during the first part of the twentieth century, and certainly "caught on" in a major way during World War II, when forces such as the British Commandos were raised specifically to take the war to the Germans in a limited fashion at a time when more conventional assaults on a larger scale were impossible.

▲  *Dutch commandos of the Maritime Special Operations Forces (merged mountain leader reconnaissance, Interventie Mariniers, and combat diver units) are trained in counter-terrorism tactics.*

▼  *In the Gulf of Aden a Danish visit, board, search, and seizure team trains by boarding a U.S. Navy guided missile cruiser.*

Thus, there emerged a practical basis for special units whose capabilities came to include all the factors that now characterize properly structured special forces. These capabilities include reconnaissance deep in the enemy's rear areas (the deep battlespace), training other nations' military units, offensive action, preparation of the battlespace for operations by conventional forces, support of counter-insurgency in enemy-held territory by engaging the support of the local population, support of counter-terrorism operations, and tactically important disruption of the enemy's lines of communication in the deep battlespace.

So far as the British were concerned, it was the Second Boer War (1899–1902) that provided compelling evidence that highly specialized units were an urgent necessity. Scouting units, such as the Lovat Scouts, a Scottish Highlands regiment renowned for its sharpshooting skills, were raised to fulfil this task and, after the war, they became the British Army's first dedicated sniper unit. Another unconventional warfare unit of the same vintage was Bushveldt Carbineers, a British mounted infantry regiment again raised during the Boer War.

In World War II, the Germans led the way with Regiment "Brandenburg," originally created as a special forces unit by the Abwehr (intelligence service) to undertake infiltration and deep reconnaissance during the invasions of Poland, France, and the U.S.S.R. between 1939 and 1941. Later in World War II the 502nd SS Jägerbataillon also conducted many special operations under the leadership of Otto Skorzeny who, in December 1944, planned a special operation in which German troops, in U.S. uniforms and driving Jeeps, infiltrated the U.S. lines at the beginning of the "Battle of the Bulge" in France and caused a fair degree of confusion behind the Allied lines by misdirecting convoys.

In Italy, frogmen and "human torpedoes" of the 10a Flottiglia MAS sank or damaged many Allied ships in the Mediterranean. After the surrender of Italy in September 1943, those men who continued to fight alongside the Germans retained the original name, while those who switched to the Allied side became the Mariassalto. Another Italian special forces unit was the air force's Arditi Distruttori Regia Aeronautica, which made raids on Allied air bases and rail communications in North Africa in 1943.

◀ A man of the Wojska Specjalne Rzeczypospolitej Polskiej (Polish special forces) secures the perimeter while French helicopters train for a hostage rescue.

▼ Men of the French 1er Régiment de Chasseurs Parachutistes train for the regiment's imminent departure for Afghanistan as part of a "joint tactical group."

In the U.K. during 1940, the first Commando units came into being in response to Prime Minister Winston Churchill's demand for "specially trained troops of the hunter class, who can develop a reign of terror down the enemy coast." The men were volunteers from existing servicemen, and the process was then developed to create a number of other high-quality units, including the Parachute Regiment, the Special Air Service, and the Special Boat Service. In the U.K., No. 10 (Inter-Allied) Commando comprised sub-units of men from occupied France, Belgium, the Netherlands, Norway, and Poland, and the survivors provided the core of their own national special forces after the war. Comparable units that came into being in the North African theater were the Long Range Desert Group and Popski's Private Army (a unit founded in Cairo in 1942 by Lt Colonel (then Major) Vladimir Peniakoff), and in Burma an altogether larger division-size formation, the Chindits, was raised for long-range penetration operations deep behind the Japanese front.

◀ Commandos of the British Royal Marines board a Boeing Chinook helicopter at Bagram air base in Afghanistan as they prepare for deployment into the field as part of Operation "Condor," an offensive sweep in search of al-Qaeda fighters in southern Afghanistan during 2002.

▼ A man of the British Royal Marine Commandos patrols a ridge line in eastern Afghanistan, aware that there could be an enemy anywhere.

▲ British Army and Royal Marine Commandos were among the pioneers of the modern type of special forces in World War II. This is their memorial near Spean Bridge, Scotland.

The United States formed its Ranger and Marine Raider battalions in 1942. The U.S.A. and Canada jointly raised the 1st Special Service Force ("Devil's Brigade") for sabotage operations in Norway, but this was used mainly as a high-grade infantry unit, specializing in mountain operations, in the Italian campaign. The 5307th Composite Unit (Provisional), otherwise known as "Merrill's Marauders," was an American counterpart of the Chindits and took part in similar operations in northern Burma. Late in November 1943, the 6th Army Special Reconnaissance Unit, otherwise known as the "Alamo Scouts," was created for reconnaissance and raider work in the Southwest Pacific under the personal command of Lt General Walter Krueger, commander of the 6th Army. It was planned that the Alamo Scouts would operate in small teams of specially trained volunteers, deep behind Japanese lines, to provide intelligence-gathering and tactical reconnaissance in support of planned 6th Army landings.

From the mid-1950s, special forces rose to greater prominence as the world's armed forces and their political masters realized that specialized tasks can sometimes be accomplished just as effectively by small and specialized teams as by larger, more costly, and more politically controversial, conventional units whose deployments generally attract greater public attention and scrutiny. Special forces have further confirmed their utility in the Kosovo and Afghan campaigns, in which they were (and indeed still are) significant in the coordination of military undertakings by local resistance forces working in combination with air power: local resistance forces are often used to tackle enemy forces, thereby encouraging them to change position, when they may be spotted by special forces, who are communicating via unmanned reconnaissance drones and reconnaissance satellites, and so be attacked by tactical warplanes.

▲   *Men of the U.S. Army's Ranger force parachute from a U.S. Air Force Boeing C-17 Globemaster III heavy transport during "Ranger Rendezvous" over the Fryar drop zone at Fort Benning, Georgia, on August 3, 2009. More than 1,000 Rangers assigned to four Ranger battalions from across the U.S.A. participated in this training exercise for large-scale tactical airborne deployment.*

▲   *U.S. Army Rangers provided support for the African Land Forces summit in May 2010. The men also served as exemplars for local forces.*

▲ An MQ-9 Reaper unmanned aerial vehicle flies a reconnaissance and attack combat mission over southern Afghanistan. Difficult to spot visually and aurally, drones add to special forces capabilities.

◄ A ScanEagle UAV sits on its catapult before launch to provide low-observability intelligence, surveillance, and reconnaissance capabilities in western Iraq. The UAV is perfect for forward operating forces.

◄ U.S. soldiers of the 1st Battalion, 75th Ranger Regiment, patrol the streets of a mock city before evacuation in a Boeing CH-47 Chinook helicopter during a training exercise at Fort Bragg, North Carolina, in April 2009.

▲ An American soldier of the 2nd Battalion, 75th Ranger Regiment, provides overwatch security in the area of a tactical objective during a mission in Iraq in the course of 2009.

▲   An intelligence sergeant of the U.S. special forces assigned to Special Operations Task Force–South clambers over the ruins of an abandoned compound during a 2011 patrol in the Panjwai district of Kandahar province, Afghanistan. The SOTF–South team undertakes regular patrols in order to secure known abandoned compounds against the possibility of their use for the storage of explosives.

◄   In 2010, a member of the Australian Special Operations Task Group takes a sight picture of insurgent positions from the relative safety of a compound in northern Gizab, Afghanistan. The Taliban was ousted from Oruzgan and local government restored as a result of a community uprising supported by Australian special forces and their Afghan partner, the Provincial Police Reserve.

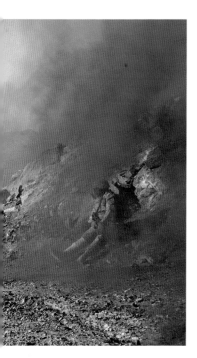

◀ *Two men of the Provincial Reconstruction Team Ghazni secure the landing zone for the arrival of Polish medical personnel to aid a "wounded" third man during an Afghan exercise in 2009.*

From 1965 special forces have been used in a host of paramilitary and conventional theaters of war, such as the Vietnam War, the Third Indo-Pakistan War, Portuguese colonial wars, the Falklands War, Northern Ireland's "Troubles," the First and Second Gulf Wars, Afghan, Bosnian and Kosovan campaigns, the First and Second Chechen Wars, Sri Lankan campaigns against the Liberation Tigers of Tamil Elam and the U.S. raid on Osama bin Laden's compound in Pakistan. They have also been called into action to assist in various types of civilian crises, such as the Iranian embassy siege in London, the Moscow theater hostage crisis, the Japanese embassy hostage crisis in Peru, and numerous situations in which civil aircraft have been hijacked.

▼ *Men of the Australian Special Operations Task Group maintain watch of an Afghan valley. Partnered with indigenous security forces, the Australians cleared a Taliban insurgent stronghold in northern Kandahar province during 2010.*

The U.S.-led invasion of Afghanistan in 2001 has seen the involvement of many special forces elements from most of the members of the coalition seeking to defeat the Taliban and create a democratic country. These coalition special forces have included the U.S. Special Operations Forces, U.K. Special Forces, Italian 9º Reggimento d'Assalto Paracadutisti "Col Moschin," Australian Special Air Service Regiment, New Zealand Special Air Service, French Commandement des Opérations Spéciales, Canadian Joint Task Force 2, Danish Jægerkorpset, the Polish Grupa Reagowania Operacyjno-Manewrowego, German Kommando Spezialkräfte, Dutch Korps Commandotroepen, and Norwegian Forsvarets Spesialkommando and Marinejegerkommandoen.

# CHAPTER 1

▲ American troops of Merrill's Marauders and the Chinese march side by side down the Ledo Road in Burma.

# THE EARLY HISTORY

# THE BRANDENBURGERS

Special forces of the type which have become so important to the pursuit of modern military operations had their immediate origins in the elite units that were raised in World War II.

The first of these, already in existence at the start of the war in September 1939, was the prototype of the German force known as the Brandenburgers, which increased in size from a battalion to a division during the war. The Brandenburgers fought in almost all of Germany's campaigns (Poland, Denmark, Norway, France, U.S.S.R., Finland, mainland Greece, Crete, Romania, Bulgaria, and Yugoslavia), and smaller elements were tasked to infiltrate Afghanistan, India, Middle Eastern countries, and South Africa. The Brandenburgers achieved great success during Germany's early campaigns by seizing strategic bridges, tunnels, and marshalling yards in advance of the main German forces.

▲  *Special forces, such as the "Brandenburgers," greatly aided more orthodox German forces, typified by these officers of the "Grossdeutschland" Division, in areas such as the Romanian campaign of 1944.*

▶  *Admiral Wilhelm Canaris, Abwehr leader for much of World War II.*

▶  *Otto Skorzeny (tallest) was a major German exponent of special forces operations.*

◀  *Formal and informal special forces provided the German forces on the Eastern Front with invaluable reconnaissance and tactical information.*

The unit was conceived by Hauptmann Theodor von Hippel who, after having his idea rejected by the traditionalist Reichswehr, approached Admiral Wilhelm Canaris, commander of the Abwehr, the German intelligence service. Raised at the behest of the Abwehr's 2nd Department but controlled by the armed forces high command, the resulting Bataillon "Ebbinghaus" served as a commando unit during the war's early years, and initially was composed mainly of former German expatriates fluent in other languages. Typical of the type of operation which the unit undertook was that on the eve of the Polish campaign that started World War II, when small groups of German special forces, in civilian clothes, crossed into Poland to seize strategic points before dawn on the day of the planned invasion.

One example of such an undertaking was the capture of the railway station at Mosty. Commanded by Leutnant Hans-Albrecht Herzner, this group had to capture the railway station in the Jabłonków Pass to prevent the destruction of a railway tunnel. During the afternoon of August 26, Herzner's group took the railway station. However, without communications with his superiors, Herzner was unaware that, during the previous evening, after the British and French hinted at further appeasement of Adolf Hitler's demands, the German leader had postponed the invasion. It was not until 9:35 a.m. on the following day that the Abwehr finally managed to get through to Herzner and order him to release his Polish prisoners and return.

▲ *Men of the "Grossdeutschland" Regiment in training during the winter of 1940-41. Nothing could prepare the German special and conventional forces for the real rigours of the Russian winter of 1941-42.*

▼ *Another theater in which the Brandenburgers were active was Yugoslavia in the extraordinarily bitter campaign against Tito's partisan forces. This is the damaged Neretva River bridge.*

When the invasion of Poland began, the Bataillon "Ebbinghaus" greatly distinguished itself by causing untold confusion in the Polish rear areas through the seizure or destruction of major road and rail junctions, also aiding the German advance by the capture of vital bridges and other strategic targets. Despite its success, the Bataillon "Ebbinghaus" was disbanded immediately after the campaign, only to be revived on October 25 as the Lehr und Bau Kompanie zbV 800, whose troops were for the most part Poles, Slavs, and men of other ethnic groups willing to fight for Germany. Up to the latter part of 1942, the new unit's roles were essentially similar to those that its predecessor had performed in Poland, but from that time onward the ever more numerous Brandenburgers were used primarily as high-grade infantry, and they came under full army control in September 1944. During this time the Brandenburgers were the Lehr-Regiment "Brandenburg" zbV 800, Sonderverband "Brandenburg," Division "Brandenburg" (mot) and, from September 15, 1944, Panzergrenadier Division "Brandenburg" that fought on the Eastern Front. After the war, many ex-Brandenburgers worked as advisers to several foreign governments.

# German and Italian Elite

A unit with comparable tasks in the Waffen-SS was the SS-Jägerbataillon 502, formed in June 1943 under the command of Otto Skorzeny at Friedenthal just north of Berlin. It consisted originally of the 300 men of the former Sonderlehrgang zbV Friedenthal. In November 1944, the battalion became the SS-Jagdverband "Mitte" and expanded to an eventual total of five battalions. The SS-Jägerbataillon 502's first undertaking was the September 1943 rescue of the ex-Italian leader Benito Mussolini, who had been incarcerated in a hotel in the Gran Sasso massif in the Abruzzo region of central Italy. The battalion was later meant to participate in several operations that were subsequently cancelled, including the kidnapping of the Vichy French leader Marshal Pétain, and the assassination of Josef Stalin, Winston Churchill, and Franklin D. Roosevelt at the Tehran conference of November–December 1943. An operation that was launched, but failed, was an attempt to capture the Yugoslav partisan leader, Josip Broz Tito. A successful operation was the kidnapping of the son of Admiral Miklós Horthy, the Hungarian leader, to pressure him into ending surrender negotiations with the Soviets and to stand down as head of state. Like the Brandenburgers, Skorzeny and his men found ready employment after the war as specialist advisers.

▶ *These three images show the deposed Italian dictator Benito Mussolini after his rescue by Otto Skorzeny and his small German commando force, from the Campo Imperatore Hotel, a ski resort on Gran Sasso, Italy, on September 12, 1943.*

◀ *Skorzeny organized the "underground railway" that helped Germans escape at the end of the war.*

The most celebrated and successful Italian special forces unit was the 10a Flottiglia MAS, which was an Italian commando frogman unit of the Italian navy. The unit was notably active in the course of the Battle of the Mediterranean during World War II , and was involved in several courageous raids on Allied ships. Some of these operations used surface boats (such as the sinking of the British heavy cruiser HMS *York*, which was struck by an explosive-filled motor boat), manned torpedoes (such as a raid on Alexandria in which two battleships were sent to the bottom, and one destroyer and one tanker were damaged), and frogmen (against British naval and mercantile ships in Gibraltar). In overall terms, the 10a Flottiglia MAS undertook more than 12 operations, which sank or damaged five warships and 20 merchant ships totalling 130,000 tons.

▲  *Miklós Horthy, the leader of Hungary, was forced to end negotiations with the Allies and also to resign by Skorzeny's kidnapping of his son in October 1944.*

▼  *The British heavy cruiser HMS York was sunk by an explosive-filled motor boat of the Italian commando frogman unit at Suda Bay, Crete, in March 1941.*

# ALLIED SPECIAL FORCES

On the other side of the battle lines, the British were the first of the Allies to raise special forces, initially in the form of the Commandos. They were established in June 1940 at the behest of Churchill who wanted a force to launch pinprick raids on coastal targets in German-occupied Europe. The Commandos at first recruited from British soldiers who volunteered for special service, but gradually came to include men of all branches of the British forces and numbers of foreign volunteers from German-occupied countries. Reaching a wartime strength of over 30 individual units and four assault brigades, the Commandos served in all theaters of war from the Arctic Circle to Europe and from the Middle East to Southeast Asia. Their operations ranged from small groups of men landing from the sea or by parachute to a brigade of assault troops spearheading the Allied invasions of Europe and Asia.

The Commandos' first raids in Europe were attacks on the Lofoten islands off Norway in March and December 1941, and this area continued to be the focus of raids, as too did the German-occupied Channel Islands (seven raids) and France (36 raids). The increasing size and skills of the Commandos meant that they were steadily tasked with the support of more conventional forces in operations such as those against Dieppe in August 1942 and the Normandy Landings (June 1944), and in numerous operations in the Italian theater. The Commandos also saw extensive service as amphibious troops in the Netherlands to clear the approaches to Antwerp, and in Burma.

▲ Men of No. 41 (Royal Marine) Commando lay charges on a railway used by the communist forces for demolition during a raid 8 miles (13 km) south of Songjin in Korea, on April 10, 1951.

▲ In March 1945, British Commandos move forward with extreme caution as they encounter sniper fire in a shattered wood near Wesel during the Allied conquest of western Germany.

◀ British Royal Marine Commandos take control of the railway station at Osnabrück as the Allies advance deeper into Germany in March 1945. By this time commandos were used largely as elite infantry.

Another, but smaller, special forces element of the British Army in World War II was the Special Air Service, which was formed in July 1941 by Lt. Colonel David Stirling as "L" Detachment, Special Air Service Brigade. It comprised five officers and 60 other ranks. The unit was formed in order to undertake small-scale operations behind the Axis lines in North Africa. The first SAS mission took place in November 1941 and was a disastrous parachute-launched support for the Operation "Crusader" offensive, which aimed to relieve the Siege of Tobruk: one third of the men were killed or captured. The second mission was successful: transported by the Long Range Desert Group, the SAS party attacked three airfields in Libya, destroying 60 aircraft without loss. In September 1942, the unit became the 1st SAS, consisting at that time of six squadrons (four British, one Free French, and one Greek) and the Folboat Section (named for a type of folding canoe used in raids).

▲   *Training in Scotland in the early days of British Commando development in 1940–41. A British Commando demonstrates the method of attacking and killing an enemy from behind, using a combat knife.*

▲   *In 1953–54, during the Malayan Emergency, men of the Special Air Service are delivered by a Westland Whirlwind helicopter into a jungle clearing before moving off in search of Communist "bandits."*

In January 1943, Stirling was captured. He was succeeded by Lt. Colonel "Paddy" Mayne, and three months later the 1st SAS became the Special Raiding Squadron, with the Special Boat Squadron under the command of Major the Earl Jellicoe. The Special Raiding Squadron fought in the Sicilian and Italian campaigns of 1943 in company with the 2nd SAS, formed in North Africa in part by the renaming of the Small Scale Raiding Force. In 1944, the SAS Brigade was formed from the British 1st and 2nd SAS, the French 3rd and 4th SAS, and the Belgian 5th SAS, and undertook parachute-launched Jeep operations behind the German lines in France, and then performed basically the same role in support of the Allied advances through Belgium and the Netherlands, and thence into Germany. At the end of World War II, the British foresaw no need to retain the SAS, which was disbanded on October 8, 1945. In the following year, though, it was decided that a long-term deep-penetration commando unit was in fact needed, and a new SAS regiment was required as part of the Territorial Army. The Artists Rifles became the 21st SAS Regiment (V) on January 1, 1947. The requirement for an SAS regiment in the regular army was recognized in 1952, and the 22nd SAS Regiment came into being, and from 1960 it was based at Hereford. In 1959, a second Territorial Army unit was raised as the 23rd SAS Regiment.

# SPECIAL BOAT SECTION

The Special Boat Section was created in July 1940 by Captain Roger Courtney. It was initially comprised 12 men and a number of folding kayaks and was known as the Folboat Troop, which became No. 1 Special Boat Section early in 1941. It was then attached to the Layforce commando unit and moved to the Middle East. The SBS undertook beach reconnaissance on Rhodes, evacuated troops left behind on Crete in June 1941, and also launched a number of small-scale raids. Courtney returned to the U.K. in December 1941 and established No. 2 SBS, while No. 1 SBS was attached to the SAS as its Folboat Section. In June 1942, the Folboat Section raided Cretan airfields and, in September of the same year, made raids on two airfields on Rhodes. Because of its losses, after the Rhodes raids the SBS was absorbed into the SAS. But in April 1943, the 1st SAS was divided, and 250 men (from the SAS and the Small Scale Raiding Force) became the Special Boat Squadron under Major the Earl Jellicoe. The SBS then operated in the Dodecanese and Cyclades islands and, during August 1944, worked with the Long Range Desert Group in operations in the Adriatic, Peloponnese, Albania, and Istria.

▼◄   *Bill Sparks was one of only two survivors of Operation "Frankton," a canoe raid by 12 men of the Royal Marines Boom Patrol Detachment, led by Major Herbert "Blondie" Hasler, against shipping in the German-occupied French port of Bordeaux in December 1942. Several limpet mines caused severe damage to the port. The unit involved in the raid became known as the "Cockleshell Heroes."*

▲   *Men of "L" Detachment, Special Air Service, return from a three-month operation behind the Axis lines in their heavily armed vehicles, laden with fuel and water cans, during the North African campaign of 1942. "L" Detachment had much in common with the Long Range Desert Group.*

Throughout the war, No. 2 SBS did not use the Special Boat Squadron name but instead retained the name Special Boat Section. After service in the Mediterranean, No. 2 SBS detached Z SBS to Ceylon for collaboration with the Special Operations Executive, Force 136 and finally Special Operations Australia. The rest of No. 2 SBS became part of Southeast Asia Command's Small Operations Group during the later stages of the Burma campaign. In 1946, the SBS, of Commando or SAS parentage, was disbanded, and its title was adopted by the special forces element of the Royal Marines.

Other British special forces of World War II included the Long Range Desert Group, and Popski's Private Army.

▲   Some time in 1943, a group of Chindits cross a river on their march into Burma where they carried out attacks on lines of communication deep in the rear of the occupying Japanese forces.

▲   British Chindits relax at a jungle base. At the size of a full division, the Chindits were the largest Allied special force of World War II, and operated behind the Japanese lines in northern Burma under the command of Major General Orde Wingate.

▼   A New Zealand patrol of the Long Range Desert Group. This mobile force of small parties of men, operating in heavily armed vehicles, covered many thousands of miles in the Sahara Desert.

# U.S. ARMY RANGERS

Early during the period of U.S. involvement in World War II, Colonel Lucian K. Truscott came to appreciate the value of the British Commandos, and addressed to his superiors in the United States a recommendation for the raising of a comparable U.S. Army force. Approved by General George C. Marshall, the Army chief-of-staff, the concept paved the way for the creation of the U.S. Army Rangers, a name selected for its association with the early part of the colonization of North America.

It was decided that the first new battalion, commanded by Lt. Colonel W. Orlando Darby, would be raised from U.S. Army troops already in Northern Ireland, and many thousands of soldiers applied. Most of these were men of the 1st Armored and 34th Infantry Divisions. After the men of the new battalion had been selected and undergone strenuous training under the supervision of Commandos at Carrickfergus in Northern Ireland, the 1st Ranger Battalion was activated on June 19, 1942. Together with the following 3rd and 4th Ranger Battalions, the 1st Ranger Battalion first fought in northwest Africa and then Italy. However, in the Battle of Cisterna in central Italy on January 29, 1944, most of the men of the 1st and 3rd Ranger

▲ *General Dwight D. Eisenhower, the Allied commander in Europe, waves from the back of a Jeep with General George C. Marshall, U.S. Army chief-of-staff, in June 1945, shortly after the end of the European war.*

◀ *In 1944, men of the U.S. 1st Air Commando Group are seen during a briefing near Mawlu behind Japanese lines during Operation "Thursday," the second Chindit undertaking behind the Japanese lines in Burma. The 1st Air Commando Group provided the British Chindits with all manner of logistical and tactical air support during this grueling campaign.*

▲   *Relief forces reach the U.S. Rangers and their German prisoners of war following the attack on the Pointe du Hoc on June 6, 1944. The U.S. flag had been spread out to prevent fire from friendly tanks approaching from inland.*

Battalions were captured. The survivors were incorporated into the U.S. and Canadian 1st Special Service Force led by Brigadier General Robert T. Frederick. This force played an important part in the fighting for and around the Anzio beachhead.

The Rangers greatest claim to fame came on June 6, 1944 with their attack on the Pointe du Hoc during the D-Day invasion of France. In an extraordinarily difficult undertaking, the 2nd Ranger Battalion scaled the 150-ft (46-m) cliffs of the Pointe du Hoc, a few miles to the west of "Omaha" Beach, to destroy a six-gun battery. Under constant fire during their climb, the Rangers encountered only a small company of Germans on the cliffs, while the artillery were withdrawn some 550 yd (500 m). The guns were later destroyed, and the Rangers cut and held the main road for two days before being relieved.

The 98th Field Artillery Battalion was formed on December 16, 1940 and activated at Fort Lewis in January 1941. On September 26, 1944 the battalion was converted to a light infantry unit. This 6th Ranger Battalion led the U.S. invasion of the Philippines and performed a daring raid at Cabanatuan, when they worked with the Alamo Scouts and Filipino guerrillas to rescue 489 Allied prisoners of war as well as 33 civilians. The 6th Ranger Battalion continued to fight with distinction until the end of the war, and was deactivated on December 30, 1945..

◀   *U.S. soldiers of the 6th Ranger Battalion and Filipino guerrillas return from the mission during which they freed Allied POWs from the Japanese prison camp at Cabanatuan in the Philippine islands. Many of those freed were survivors of the Bataan "Death March," which had been the transfer of 75,000 prisoners of war over 60 miles (97 km) by the Imperial Japanese Army and had resulted in the deaths of many thousands of prisoners.*

# U.S. MARINE RAIDERS

The Marine Raiders comprised a number of special forces units created by the U.S. Marine Corps during World War II to operate as high-quality light infantry in the amphibious warfare role, and most particularly in using rubber boats to land and then operate behind the Japanese lines. "Edson's Raiders" and "Carlson's Raiders" (1st and 2nd Marine Raiders Battalions) are generally regarded as the first U.S. special forces to enter combat in World War II.

Four Marine Raider battalions saw service, but all were disbanded on January 8, 1944 when the U.S. Marine Corps decided that the Marine Raiders no longer possessed a role in their original remit as the nature of the war in the Pacific theater had changed to large-scale amphibious assaults against well-defended islands in place of the previous tactic, in which small specialized units could attack Japanese forces deployed only in limited numbers.

◀ *Lt. Colonel Harry B. Liversedge was a Marine Raider leader (3rd Marine Raider Battalion and 1st Marine Raider Regiment), and in 1945 took part in the grim fighting for Iwo Jima as commander of the 28th Marines. He is pictured here following his 1948 promotion to Brigadier General.*

However, most combat operations saw the use of the Marine Raider battalions as conventional infantry and, in combination with general USMC resentment that the Marine Raiders were an unnecessary elite within an elite force, this led to the disbandment of the Marine Raiders. On February 1, 1944, the 1st Raider Regiment became the 4th Marine Regiment, and the men of the Raider Training Center were reallocated to the new 5th Marine Division. The 4th Marine Regiment proved itself an excellent unit in the assaults on the Pacific islands of Guam and Okinawa, and at the end of the war joined the occupation forces in Japan.

◀ *Men of a U.S. Marine Raider battalion train for landing off the U.S. coast near San Diego in 1942.*

▶ *U.S. Marine Raiders and their dogs, used for scouting and message delivery, start off for the front in the jungle fighting on Bougainville Island in 1943.*

▲ Marine Raiders in operation at Makin Island in the Gilbert Islands during its seizure in November 1943.

▼ Rightly possessing a reputation for skilful jungle fighting, these U.S. Marine Raiders pose in front of a Japanese dugout at Cape Torokina on Bougainville Island, in the Solomon Islands group, which they helped to take in November 1943.

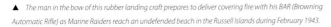

▲ The man in the bow of this rubber landing craft prepares to deliver covering fire with his BAR (Browning Automatic Rifle) as Marine Raiders reach an undefended beach in the Russell Islands during February 1943.

# SPECIAL FORCES IN VIETNAM

The first U.S. special forces operations in Vietnam took place in 1957, when the 1st Special Forces Group trained South Vietnamese soldiers at the Commando Training Center in Nha Trang, and special forces were deployed into Laos as Mobile Training Teams in 1961. As the U.S. became actively involved in the war, the role of the special forces was enlarged and they trained guerrillas, gaining valuable knowledge required for counter-guerrilla actions (the so-called Foreign Internal Defense role). The 5th Special Forces Group often led South Vietnamese units, such as Montagnards and lowland Civilian Irregular Defense Groups. A raid on Son Tay, in an effort to recover U.S. prisoners of war, used only men of the special forces as its ground element.

The primary special forces unit in South Vietnam was the 5th Special Forces Group (Airborne), who were significant in the secret multi-service Military Assistance Command Vietnam Studies and Observation Group. Special Forces also watched the border region and infiltration routes, undertook strategic intelligence missions and deployed many groups for special operational tasks. The Vietnam War shaped the U.S. Army's special forces, putting less emphasis on

▲　U.S. Marine Corps' LVTP-5 amphibious tractors move men of the 3rd Marine Division in South Vietnam during 1966, the year after the division arrived to protect Da Nang airport.

◄　A patrol of Montagnard soldiers wades through a jungle stream, led by U.S. special forces Captain Vernon Gillespie during the early years of the U.S. involvement in the Vietnam conflict.

internal strike and more on the creation of a training force to help develop unconventional warfare and counter-insurgency tactics.

A leading U.S. Marine Corps special force in the Vietnam War was the 3rd Force Reconnaissance Company, which despatched a two-platoon detachment to South Vietnam in May 1966 for a combat debut in Operation "Hastings" early in July 1966. The detachment was then attached to the 3rd Reconnaissance Battalion, and boosted by the arrival of another platoon. The detachment patrolled in Thua Tin province until early January 1967, when a special-purpose group made a prisoner rescue attempt. The rest of the detachment moved to Khe Sanh, where it gathered intelligence of a major Communist build-up before an offensive in April 1967. What was left of the three platoons was reunited in April 1966, just in time for the North Vietnamese offensive to seize Quang Tri province.

The combined establishment of 18 teams went on to undertake a zone reconnaissance in the Cobi Than Tan valley, and then moved to Dong Ha early in May. Here the company's commander assumed command of the 3rd Reconnaissance Battalion that patrolled the area between Highway 9 and the Demilitarized Zone until November 1969, when it came under command of the 3rd Marine Expeditionary Force. The force was deactivated in mid 1970.

▲ The U.S. Navy's PCF-38, of Coastal Division 11, patrols the Cai Ngay Canal in South Vietnam during April 1970. Such craft were widely used for the deployment of special forces.

◀ Men of the 3rd Battalion, 1st Marines, question a man suspected of being a Viet Cong guerrilla in Operation "Badger Catch" during January 1968 in Quang Tri province, South Vietnam.

# CHAPTER 2

▲ A shell casing flies out with a trail of smoke from an M4 rifle during a reflex firing exercise.

# ROLES AND MISSIONS

# Paramilitary Tasks

Special forces are highly effective in performing paramilitary tasks, such as the rescue of hostages and the retaking of hijacked aircraft and ships. Both of these operations might properly be deemed to fall within the responsibility of the police, as hostage-taking and vehicle hijacking are criminal acts, but the police may not be legally entitled to operate outside their own country, and they often lack the specialized training and equipment which are vital for success.

In domestic situations a crisis may arise that is too complex or too difficult for the police to resolve by orthodox police methods. This is the niche in which the special forces excel. Their men are trained to analyze and then react to unorthodox situations, with the equipment the police lack and with a speed which the police can seldom match. The essence of the effective use of special forces in domestic scenarios (which is, in fact, a rare occurrence) lies in reconnaissance by visual, optronic, and electronic means, and then the formulation of a plan that exploits to the full the special forces weapons and technical equipment. Surprise is a key "weapon" in the special forces armory, so a rapid assault and entry with the aid of small explosive charges and stun grenades provide the major shock that often "paralyzes" the hostage takers or hijackers for the precious few seconds that the special forces need to accomplish the first part of their task.

Where the hostage or hijacked airliner or ship is situated in foreign territory or waters, special forces often have the advantage of previous contacts with local elements hostile to the hostage takers and hijackers, who are frequently insurgents working to their own political agenda. Sometimes, though, the perpetrators' motives are largely financial, as is the case with the pirates that have been operating from Somalia in the first part of the 21st century.

▶ *A man of an Argentine joint service special forces team maintains a security watch while "hostages" are extracted during a multi-national amphibious beach assault training exercise in Ancon, Peru, on July 19, 2010. International collaboration is an increasing feature of special forces training and operations.*

▶ *Members of the Brunei special forces prepare to storm the bridge of the U.S. Navy's "Arleigh Burke" class missile destroyer Howard. Special forces must train for a host of contingencies, including the capture of warships as well as civilian vessels.*

◀◀ *Men of the Chilean navy's special forces, armed with 9-mm (0.36-in) Heckler & Koch MP5N sub-machine guns simulate a maritime interdiction operation during Exercise Panamax 2006. Panamax is a multi-national training exercise tailored to the defense of the Panama Canal.*

▼ *Men of the Guatemalan navy's special forces conduct a room clearance exercise. Only constant training can provide the level of concentration and capability required for such undertakings, which demand exceptionally fast reaction times and first-time "kill" capability.*

# VIP PROTECTION

It is clearly better to prevent hostage taking in the first place, rather than having to deal with a situation in which a rescue attempt can result in injury to, or even the death of, the hostage. Thus, many special forces undertake the close protection (bodyguard) role, especially after the 1974 event in which Britain's Princess Anne and her husband Mark Phillips were attacked in their Rolls-Royce in what appeared to be an armed kidnap attempt. The abduction attempt failed, but the fact that it had been attempted highlighted failings in the equipment and thinking of the police's Royal Protection Group (RPG) and, by extension, of the police guarding important political and diplomatic figures. The Special Air Service Regiment's Counter-Revolutionary War Wing was brought in to evaluate and improve the police procedures and to train the men of the RPG.

Special forces also undertake the bodyguard role for political, diplomatic, and senior military personnel when they are traveling abroad in dangerous (or potentially dangerous) circumstances. This is a task that calls for various different bodyguard techniques in response to differing political considerations, as well as for practical reasons.

◀ *A bodyguard of the Bundeskriminalamt, the German federal body whose responsibilities include close protection of members of Germany's constitutional bodies and their foreign guests of state. The BKA uses highly trained officers with special equipment and vehicles.*

Overt military protection is most often seen when VIPs visit war zones, where the strength and military nature of their bodyguards are both deliberately emphasized. Body armor may be worn over normal clothing, and weapons (assault rifles and sub-machine guns) are carried in plain view. This overt profile is intended to serve as a deterrent against attack and to ensure that the close protection personnel can react with maximum firepower and minimum delay.

▶ *Three images from a demonstration by the close protection unit of the Croatian military police at Karlovac in 2009. Defensive and offensive driving techniques (right) are important for the evasion of attempted interceptions and the halting of suspected parties for arrest and the interrogation that can often lead to the later seizure of other criminal or terrorist operatives.*

Low-key overt protection is standard when a lower profile is desirable. The men of the close protection team seek to blend in more with their surroundings. Thus, civilian clothing, usually a suit, is worn, and weapons (pistols and sub-machine guns) are concealed beneath jackets. The close protection team still maintains a visible presence around the VIP, who is free to interact with the public.

Covert protection is the type of cover in which the close protection team is not obviously visible, but nevertheless remains close to the VIP so that it can react swiftly as and when needed.

▼ ► *In the same demonstration by the close protection unit of the Croatian military police, team members in dark clothing reveal how, after halting the suspects' vehicle, they immobilize and remove the suspects for questioning.*

# MOSSAD AND THE KIDNAP OF ADOLF EICHMANN (MAY 11, 1960)

One of the major organizers of Germany's attempted destruction of the Jewish race in World War II, Nazi Adolf Eichmann escaped to Argentina after the war. His capture was made one of the primary tasks of the Mossad, the new state of Israel's official intelligence agency after its establishment in 1949. In 1954, Simon Wiesenthal, a dedicated Nazi hunter, received a postcard from an associate living in Buenos Aires saying that Eichmann was in Argentina. In 1957, further information was provided by Lothar Hermann, a Jew who had survived Dachau and emigrated to Argentina. In the 1950s, Hermann was living in Buenos Aires with his family. His daughter Sylvia became romantically involved with Eichmann's son, Klaus, who boasted about his father's Nazi background and major involvement in the Holocaust.

▲   *A photograph released on June 7, 1960 depicts the house in which the Nazi war criminal Adolf Eichmann lived, in a suburb of Buenos Aires, before his seizure by a team of Mossad and Shin Bet agents on May 11, 1960. To avoid diplomatic problems, Eichmann was then smuggled out of Argentina to Israel to face trial.*

◄   *The Red Cross identity document used by Adolf Eichmann to enter Argentina was made out in the false name Ricardo Klement. The document was issued in 1950 by the Italian delegation of the Red Cross in Geneva, Switzerland.*

In 1957, Hermann realized Eichmann's identity after reading an account of the German war criminals, and soon after this sent his daughter to the Eichmanns' home to learn more. She became suspicious of Eichmann's claim that he was only Klaus's uncle. Hermann began a correspondence with Fritz Bauer, chief prosecutor for the West German state of Hessen. Bauer contacted Israeli officials, who worked sporadically with Hermann over the next several years trying to discover if this was really Eichmann.

In 1959, the Mossad established that Eichmann was definitely living in Buenos Aires under the name Ricardo Klement, and it sought to find his precise location. Surveillance finally persuaded the Mossad that Ricardo Klement really was Adolf Eichmann. The Israeli government then granted permission for a covert operation to capture Eichmann and bring him to Jerusalem for trial as a war criminal. It was to be a joint operation carried out by the Mossad and Shin Bet (Israel security agency). The Israeli services maintained their watch of Eichmann into the first months of 1960, completed their capture plans, and awaited the right moment.

It was on May 11 that a combined Mossad and Shin Bet team, which had arrived in Argentina during the preceding month, seized Eichmann in a suburb of Buenos Aires. Knowing that he worked as a foreman at the Mercedes-Benz factory in the Argentine capital, the team decided to ambush Eichmann as he walked from the bus stop to his home after work and bundle him into a car with forged license plates. The Israeli team almost abandoned its plan after Eichmann did not board his usual bus home, and tensions in the Israeli team rose steadily as passing pedestrians asked if they could aid the disguised Mossad agents who were pretending to repair their broken-down vehicle. Almost half an hour later Eichmann got off a bus. A Mossad agent accosted him, asking him in Spanish if he had a moment. A frightened Eichmann tried to flee but was blinded by the headlights of the team's car, whereupon a pair of Mossad agents felled him and rushed him to the car.

Once at the Mossad safe house, Eichmann was tied to a chair and interrogated. He was given a choice between death on the spot or trial in Israel, and opted for the latter. The agents kept Eichmann in a safe house until they judged that he could be taken to Israel without Argentine detection. Drugged to make him appear drunk, and dressed as a flight attendant, Eichmann was smuggled out of Argentina on board an El Al flight from Argentina to Dakar and thence to Israel on May 21, 1960. Tried and convicted, Eichmann was hanged on May 31, 1962.

▼ *Adolf Eichmann faced the Israeli court in Jerusalem from a protective glass booth flanked by Israeli police during his trial in June 1961. The evidence against Eichmann, a leading figure in the Nazi program to achieve the extermination of Jews in German-occupied Europe, was compelling, and after being convicted and sentenced to death, Eichmann was hanged on May 31, 1962.*

# COUNTER INSURGENCY

A major function of special forces is the support of counter-insurgency operations undertaken either by conventional units of their own nation's armed forces, as has taken place in Iraq and Afghanistan, or by the armed forces of friendly nations. A classic example of the latter is provided by the support afforded by the Special Air Service Regiment to the Sultan of Oman's armed forces between 1970 and 1976 in tackling the Communist-inspired insurrection in the nation's southwestern province of Dhofar.

The SAS was among the British units involved in training the Omani forces in the arts of irregular and counter-insurgency warfare, and also took a direct part in operations where the quality of the counter-insurgency forces clearly outmatched that of the insurgents. This direct combat role sometimes arose from attacks by the insurgents on bases in which the SAS was training the local forces (as in the Battle of Mirbat), and on other occasions when helicopters delivered small SAS parties to areas in which they could interdict the insurgents' lines of communication and reconnoiter local conditions.

▲   *Men of the Iraqi special forces, assigned to the 1st Marines, patrol cautiously and clear every house on their way through Fallujah during Operation "Al Fajr." Use of local forces greatly boosts available local knowledge.*

▲   *In the Iraqi town of Suwayrah, U.S. Army special forces, supported by Iraqi Army elements, conduct an air assault on their way to attempt the capture of terrorists of a known insurgent force onSeptember 9, 2007.*

◀   *Two Iraqi soldiers with the 36th Commando Battalion, Iraqi Special Operations Forces Brigade, with their 7.62-mm (0.3-in) AK-47 assault rifles. The battalion conducts joint Iraqi-coalition forces combat operations and is composed of experienced men who have undertaken many raids and located dozens of weapons caches.*

One of the keys to the success of the SAS in Oman was the "five fronts" campaign created by Lt. Colonel Johnny Watts, commander of 22nd SAS. The five fronts consisted of the establishment of an intelligence cell; the creation of an information cell to inform the population about the government's civil aid program, and to counter the propaganda of Aden-launched radio broadcasts against the Omani government; availability of medical officers backed by SAS medical personnel; availability of a veterinary officer to treat animals owned by local Omanis; and raising local Dhofari troops to fight for the sultan. Implementation of this plan allowed the training of the Omanis in the above five tasks, eventually allowing local forces to perform all of the functions themselves.

▲ At Camp Courageous in Iraq on August 3, 2007, men of the U.S. Army special forces undertake familiarization training with the Carl Gustav M3 recoilless antitank and anti-bunker weapon during Operation "Iraqi Freedom."

◄ Australian special forces soldiers and Afghan police await extraction in Afghanistan's Uruzgan area. The Australian-Afghan combination severely degraded the insurgency in central Uruzgan, largely by the capture of three key leaders in separate missions.

# ANTITERRORIST OPERATIONS

Special forces train to undertake antiterrorist operations against all types of threat and involving any number of target types. In the SAS, antiterrorist teams are known as Special Projects teams, and there are comparable designations in most of the world's special forces. Such teams provide the capability to rescue hostages from airliners, trains, coaches, and buses in what are generally termed "tubular assaults," from buildings ranging from small houses to large nuclear power stations and oil refineries, and from ships. In the latter case, operations against docked ships are generally allocated to land-based special forces, and against ships at sea to naval special forces.

Special Projects teams undertake a constant round of training to improve and then maintain their levels of skill and readiness. In the case of the SAS, a special training house, equipped with movable rubber walls, is used to facilitate training with live ammunition. The Special Projects team comprises command, sniper, and assault

▲ Men of the U.S. special forces undertake "shoot-house" training at Fort Carson, Colorado, the home of the 10th Special Forces Group, in the course of 2009. Constant high-pressure training under realistic conditions and with live ammunition is essential and literally vital to success in combat.

▲ A team of SEAL trainees prepares to breach a room during qualification training. The essence of a successful breaching is complete tactical surprise, using noise and speed, to confuse the enemy before they can kill hostages.

◀ Men of the Iraqi Army clear a room during close-quarter battle house training at Forward Operating Base "Duke." Pioneered in the U.K. by the SAS, such training has been steadily exported to special forces across the world.

elements. The command and control element is usually set up close to the cordon around any area held by terrorists. It is generally equipped with computers containing blueprints of the "stronghold" (terrorist-held area) and secure communications to all members of the sniper and assault teams, as well as to higher political control elements. All intelligence gathered on-site is sorted and evaluated. The strategic decision to hand over control of the operation from the police to the Special Projects team is taken at the political level.

Snipers are generally the first Special Projects element to deploy around the "stronghold." Working in pairs, the sniper teams usually cover all sides of the target building. Snipers are naturally excellent marksmen, but they are also very skilled observers and can

▼ *A group of Chilean navy special forces operatives during a maritime drill. The Comando de Fuerzas Especiales (Special Forces Command) has two components: the Buzos Tácticos de la Armada (Tactical Divers of the Navy) and the Equipo de Intervención Rápida (Rapid Intervention Team) optimized for underwater and surface action, respectively.*

▲ *A two-man sniper team of the Trinidad and Tobago special operations force at the Fuerzas Comando exercise in El Salvador during 2011. Firing a suppressed rifle with a scope providing only a narrow field of vision, the firer receives information from a spotter using a telescope offering a wider field of view.*

therefore feed a steady stream of intelligence back to the on-site commander. Snipers provide surveillance of the terrorists and the hostages, constantly monitoring their patterns of movement, of sleep, and of levels of morale. When an assault is ordered, the snipers shoot any terrorist they can target accurately. Many snipers are also cross-trained as assaulters, and can supplement the assault team if needed. Some hostage situations can be solved entirely with a coordinated sniper assault.

The assaulters are trained to enter the "stronghold" and then rescue any hostages and neutralize any terrorist threat, usually at close quarters. In "silent" assaults the assaulters infiltrate the "stronghold" carrying noise-suppressed weapons and hoping to catch the terrorists without warning. The more usual approach is the "noisy" assault, in which the assaulters blow their way into the "stronghold" with explosives and stun grenades, in the expectation of so shocking the terrorists that they can offer no effective resistance.

# THE BATTLE OF MIRBAT
## (JULY 19, 1972)

A small town on the southwestern coast of Oman, Mirbat was the scene in 1972 of a classic battle, which fully demonstrated the military skills and personal courage of the Special Air Service. Here a small SAS detachment and its Omani allies battled some 250 Communist insurgents.

In 1970, several small SAS teams ("British Army Training Teams" or BATTs) were sent to Oman to use a "hearts and minds" policy and train *firqat* (local Dhofari irregular units), resulting in increasing levels of success against the *adoo* (insurgents of the People's Front for the Liberation of the Occupied Arabian Gulf and Dhofar Liberation Front). To weaken the garrison of Mirbat, an *adoo* group let itself be seen on a nearby escarpment, and this resulted in the detachment of 60 *firqat* soldiers on a search. During the night of July 18–19, the insurgents surrounded the town and its fortified perimeter. The now-besieged garrison was considerably outnumbered. The nine-man BATT, of 8 Troop, B Squadron, 22 SAS, was led by Captain Mike Kealy. Some 30 armed tribesmen held the Wali Fort and 25 armed police occupied the Gendarmerie Fort, beside which was a 25-pounder (11.3-kg) howitzer in a gun pit.

At about 5:00 a.m. shots were heard from the Gendarmerie Fort as the *adoo* cautiously approached the perimeter. Kealy ran up to the roof of the "Batthouse" (BATT headquarters) to assess the situation. The keys to the battle were the Gendarmerie Fort and the 25-pounder. Over the short-range radio Fijian Trooper Savesaki informed Kealy that Trooper Labalaba had been wounded and that the fort was in danger. He requested permission to get medical aid to his fellow Fijian by running over the fire-swept ground between the "Batthouse" and the fort. With Kealy's agreement, Savesaki pelted over the exposed ground, and reached the gun pit unharmed. The 25-pounder continued to fire and by 7:00 a.m. the first crisis had passed.

As the fighting continued, no response came from the gun pit to Kealy's radio calls. Deciding to investigate, Kealy and Trooper Tobin made for the Gendarmerie Fort. Taking a more circuitous route than Savesaki, they too reached the fort safely. The badly wounded Labalaba reported that Savesaki, though hit in the back, was covering the northwestern side of the fort. At this moment the *adoo* broke through the wire and advanced on the fort, so precipitating the battle's second crisis. Labalaba continued to man the 25-pounder until killed by small arms fire. Tobin took over, but he too was soon hit fatally.

Kealy radioed the "Batthouse," some 1,400 ft (425 m) to the southwest, to pour mortar and machine-gun fire onto the Gendarmerie Fort in an effort to drive off the fast-approaching *adoo*. Kealy heard over the radio that Omani warplanes were on their way to assist. Only moments later, BAC Strikemaster light attack aircraft arrived and blasted the *adoo* with machine-gun fire. The *adoo* started to pull back, and by this time the *firqat* from the town were also in action. The situation was still serious, but reinforcements had arrived as helicopters landed 23 men of G Squadron, 22 SAS, on the coast to the southeast of Mirbat. Under cover of a barrage of fire, the reinforcements advanced toward the battle, forcing the *adoo* to retreat. Mirbat had been relieved.

The SAS had lost two men killed, and another two men had been badly wounded. More than 30 *adoo* dead were found on the battlefield, although many more later died of their wounds. Mirbat was a turning point in the war, for its defense vindicated Sultan Qaboos's policies and led to violent disagreement within the guerrilla movement.

◄ *A small town on the southern coast of Oman, Mirbat was the scene of a celebrated SAS victory. Here, in July 1972, nine men of the SAS and some Omani soldiers fought off an attack by some 250 men of the Popular Front for the Liberation of Oman, a rebel organization funded and supported by Communist Aden.*

▶ *The nine-man SAS team was based in the Batthouse, so called as it was the headquarters of the British Army Training Team. It was from here that the SAS soldiers sortied to aid the local gendarmerie attacked in the fort some 300 yd (275 m) to the northeast.*

▼ *The fort was held by about 25 men of the local gendarmerie, and outside it in a pit was an elderly 25-pound gun/howitzer that proved a decisive weapon in the fighting for the fort. The battle was a serious reverse for the Popular Liberation Front, which is thought to have lost more than 80 men.*

# Reconnaissance

One of the primary tasks of special forces on the modern battlefield, especially that of the low-intensity type of war fought in areas such as Iraq and Afghanistan, is reconnaissance deep in the battlespace where the enemy has his command and logistic centers. The role demands the use of four- or six-man long-range surveillance teams operating well to the rear of the enemy's front line, and thus far in advance of more conventional reconnaissance elements operating just ahead of their parent units. The length of time a deep-battlespace reconnaissance team can operate effectively depends on the equipment and quantity of supplies the team can carry, the distance that has to be covered to and from the team's operational area, and the nature of any resupply effort. Depending on the weather and terrain, long-range surveillance teams generally operate for a period of up to seven days without resupply.

◀ A member of a U.S. Seabee Engineer Reconnaissance Team, a concept pioneered in the Iraq War for an improved battlefield engineering capability.

▼ A soldier of the U.S. Special Operations Task Group maintains a tactical surveillance during a patrol in southern Afghanistan.

Such teams are necessarily well armed, since they may have to defend themselves if they are detected before they can be evacuated. Despite the inherent risk of doing so, long-range surveillance teams sometimes operate out of uniform. They may use motorcycles, four-wheel-drive vehicles, or multiple helicopter lifts in their area of operations, or have mountain or underwater capability. Most long-range surveillance teams are trained in advanced helicopter movement and at least basic parachuting, and some also have high-altitude/high-opening and high-altitude/low-opening parachute skills.

The men also carry long-range communications equipment, and often use specialized signals intelligence and other ways to collect technical intelligence. The team generally includes at least one medical technician capable of more than basic first aid. The teams must be able to remain undetected in enemy territory for several days, based in dugout hides and working to the "hard routine" of no talking, no smoking, no cooking, etc.

▲ Marines of an armored reconnaissance unit focus down-range during live-fire training. Mounted on LAV-25 (Light Armored Vehicle 25) eight-wheel fighting vehicles armed with a 25-mm (1-in) cannon and two 7.62-mm (0.3-in) machine guns. Such marines can undertake several mission roles, including reconnaissance, artillery direction and "hit and run" missions.

▲ A U.S. Army soldier assembles an RQ-11 Raven unmanned aerial vehicle in order to conduct a short-range tactical reconnaissance of insurgents in the area of Taji, Iraq, during 2005.

◀ U.S. Marines of the elite Force Reconnaissance unit assigned to the 22nd Marine Expeditionary Unit at the start of parachute delivery into their designated operational area.

# TACTICAL OPERATIONS

Because of the emphasis on the intense multi-role training of high-quality personnel as members of the special forces, it makes sense to employ small teams of such personnel to undertake offensive action against high-value targets. Though expensive to train and maintain, special forces offer an excellent cost/benefit ratio as the value of the destruction and damage that small teams can inflict is generally out of all proportion to the team's size.

Modern warfare, even at the low-intensity level, is still highly dependent on the ready availability of power and of modern communications. Roaming deep in the enemy's rear areas, special forces teams provide a huge tactical benefit to their conventional comrades by destroying infrastructure, such as oil and gas pipelines, electricity pylons and telephone masts, and by blowing dams to flood the areas downstream of them. As a more direct aid to their front-line counterparts, the teams also sometimes ambush convoys of technical vehicles and technical personnel, either destroying them entirely or at least damaging and delaying them significantly. Generally, the cost to the enemy is far greater than the cost of assembling and despatching the special forces team.

▲  *British Commandos of the Royal Marines take part in Operation "Sond Chara," the clearance of the Nad-e Ali district of Helmand province in southern Afghanistan. Though lacking in some of the specialist skills of the SAS and SBS, the Royal Marines are excellently trained for more conventional warfare.*

◀  *A U.S. Marine, armed with a 5.56-mm (0.219-in) M249 Squad Automatic Weapon (SAW), mans a forward field position during TRAP (Tactical Recovery of Aircraft and Personnel) training at Fort Magsaysay, Philippines.*

▶▶  *A staff sergeant of the U.S. Army scans the terrain during training at Camp Atterbury, Indiana. His unit was assigned to the 2nd Battalion, 152nd Airborne Cavalry Reconnaissance and Surveillance Squadron.*

▲   A vehicle-carried combat patrol of Afghan troops and men of the U.S. special forces moves cautiously through the Gayan valley of Afghanistan.

◄   During tactical warfare training, the SEAL in the foreground carries a field radio and Colt Model 653 carbine fitted with an M203 grenade launcher.

# OPERATION "THUNDERBOLT" – THE ISRAELI RESCUE OF FLIGHT 139 (JULY 4, 1976)

Air France Flight 139 with a crew of 12 and 248 passengers, bound from Tel Aviv in Israel to Paris in France, lifted off from Athens in Greece at 12:30 p.m. on June 27, 1976. Soon after take-off, the airliner was hijacked by two Palestinians of the Popular Front for the Liberation of Palestine and two West Germans of the German *Revolutionäre Zellen* (Revolutionary Cells) and diverted to Benghazi in Libya. The airliner remained on the ground for seven hours and was refueled. After departing Benghazi, the airliner landed at Entebbe in Uganda at 3:15 p.m. on June 28. Here the four hijackers, led by Wadie Haddad, were joined by at least four more terrorists with the support of the pro-Palestinian forces of Idi Amin, the Ugandan president. The terrorists demanded the release of 53 Palestinians held in captivity, and threatened to kill the hostages if the demands were not met by July 1.

The hijackers divided their hostages into Israeli nationals and other nationalities, and moved them into the transit hall of Entebbe airport. As the deadline approached, the Israeli government approved a rescue mission, Operation "Thunderbolt, " under the command of Major General Yekutiel Adam, with Matan Vilnai as his deputy and Brigadier General Dan Shomron as the ground commander. Speaking with released hostages in Paris, Mossad agents were able to piece together a picture of the hostages' location, their numbers and weapons, and the involvement of Ugandan troops.

After days of planning by the deputy of the attack force's commander, Lt. Colonel Yonatan Netanyahu, four Israeli Lockheed C-130 Hercules transports flew secretly to Uganda. The route took

▲ *As in many other successful special forces operations, the workhorse of "Thunderbolt" was the Lockheed C-130 Hercules tactical transport that delivered men and equipment to Uganda, and then flew out the Israeli commandos and the rescued hostages.*

◄ *The leader of the Israeli commandos on the ground at Entebbe in "Thunderbolt" was Dan Shomron, seen here at a press conference after the conclusion of this very daring, but highly successful, rescue undertaking.*

the task force first over Sharm el Sheikh in eastern Egypt and along the international route over the Red Sea at an altitude of less than 100 ft (30 m) to avoid detection by radar. Exiting the Red Sea, the transports turned south and passed Djibouti and thence flew on to a point northeast of Nairobi in Kenya before turning west across the Rift Valley and Lake Victoria.

▲ An Israeli hostage is greeted by family and friends on her return to Israel on July 3, 1976.

◄ One of the Israeli hostages is carried to a waiting ambulance by Israeli soldiers.

▼ The Israeli defense minister, Shimon Peres (right), addresses Israeli paratroopers after the completion of "Thunderbolt," which spent only 53 minutes on the ground in Entebbe.

The C-130 carrying the assault force landed wholly unannounced at Entebbe at 11:00 p.m. Its cargo bay ramp had already been lowered, and the transport now disgorged a black Mercedes-Benz limousine and accompanying Land-Rovers, suggesting that the Israeli troops were in fact Amin and his escort returning from an international visit. The Mercedes and its escorts headed for the terminal and the commandos burst into where the hostages were being held in the main hall next to the runway. The commandos shouted in English as well as Hebrew that they were Israelis, and told the hostages to lie down. The hostages managed to indicate that the other terrorists were in a room off the hall, and the Israelis lobbed grenades into it before entering and shooting dead the other three hijackers. The hostages were secured.

Meanwhile, the other three C-130s had landed and unloaded armored personnel carriers to provide defense in the hour scheduled for refueling, the destruction of the Ugandan jet fighters that might otherwise have attacked the Israeli aircraft as they departed, and to gather intelligence. The assault team returned to the aircraft and began loading the hostages. Ugandan soldiers opened fire, but the commandos returned a more effective fire and inflicted a number of casualties on the Ugandans. Israel's sole fatality was Netanyahu, who was killed by a shot in the chest, and at least five other commandos were wounded.

The entire operation lasted 53 minutes. All seven terrorists and between 33 and 45 Ugandan soldiers had been killed, and some 11 MiG-17 fighters destroyed on the ground. Of the 106 hostages, three had been killed, one had been left in Uganda, where she was later murdered on Amin's orders, and about ten had been wounded.

# BEHIND ENEMY LINES

Special forces teams are trained to operate behind the enemy's front lines for several days at a time, or longer if they can be supplied by air, and so they are ideally placed to exploit their intelligence discoveries by direct action. Such teams always include at least one man skilled in demolition work, and this allows the team to target vital lines of communication and elements, such as rail lines, bridges, viaducts and tunnels, as well as high-value fixed targets such as command bunkers, communications centers, supply dumps, and airfields.

Such undertakings knock the enemy off balance, and this process can be further reinforced by harassment attacks. Using their ability to remain concealed when they need to, and then moving rapidly to and from a target area, special forces teams can ambush convoys of vehicles and animals, kill enemy couriers traveling by motorcycle or other vehicle, and constantly harass troops with hit-and-run attacks, especially at night, that make it difficult for the troops to rest properly.

▲ These snipers of the 2nd Regiment of the Foreign Legion are using a 12.7-mm (0.5-in) PGM Hécate II heavy anti-matériel rifle and a 7.62-mm (0.3-in) FR-F2 rifle in Afghanistan during 2005.

◀ This special forces Ops A two-man sniper team (sniper and spotter) of the U.S. Army Rangers is pictured during a shooting competition. The sniper is armed with a 7.62-mm (0.3-in) M24 SWS rifle.

▶ *A SEAL carries his 5.56-mm (0.219-in) Colt Commando assault rifle through the woods during a field training exercise. Though light and handy, the Commando lacks longer-range killing and anti-matériel capabilities.*

▼ *Clad in semi-desert clothing, this special forces soldier looks down the scope of his 5.56-mm (0.219-in) Mk 12 sniper rifle, a weapon developed by the Naval Surface Warfare Center Crane Division.*

Associated conceptually with sabotage and harassment attacks is another task that can be successfully undertaken by the most highly trained special forces teams, namely the kidnapping or, when necessary and indeed possible, the assassination of high-ranking enemy personnel, both military and civilian. The killing of such people, generally by explosive charge, missile attack, or sniper fire as deemed most applicable to the specific tactical situation, can bite deeply and decisively into the enemy's chain of command, and can therefore result in at least a temporary interruption in the enemy's capacity to provide effective command and control of his own front-line forces.

Kidnapping provides the same short-term advantages, as well as the welcome and tactically advantageous possibility of seizing marked maps, written orders, and computer media. It also allows skilled interrogators to extract information that may, in turn, open the way to more successful overt and covert military undertakings. Kidnapping is inherently more dangerous than assassination, however, because the person kidnapped must be kept quiet and under tight supervision while the team returns to its own lines with the kidnap victim secure in their possession.

# air power

Modern warfare at every level emphasizes the importance and utility of air power in the tactical and operational arena. Tactical warplanes now carry a mass of specialized navigation, target acquisition, and targeting equipment that provides them with a high degree of acquisition and targeting autonomy. However, there are many valuable targets that are either mobile or extremely well concealed, which means that they are largely proof against discovery, even by modern sensors.

▼ *A Lockheed AC-130U "Spooky II" gunship of the 4th Special Operations Squadron releases flares to defeat heat-seeking SAM. The air-to-surface armament is one 105-mm (4.7-in) howitzer, one 40-mm (1.57-in) gun, and one 25-mm (1-in) cannon.*

◄ *Wherever possible, the efforts of U.S. Air Force close-support aircraft are controlled from the ground by a tactical air controller (known since 2004 as a joint terminal attack controller) by radio to call fire down on exactly the right target.*

It is here that special forces can aid the air effort by locating mobile targets and passing on their coordinates for a rapid air attack, or by designating the target with a ground-based laser designator whose beam is invisible to the naked eye but "paints" a precise point against which a laser-guided bomb or missile can home after its release. Most special forces teams include a man with forward air controller skills and the right equipment to call in a tactical warplane and vector it into the attack with "dumb" as well as "smart" ordnance. Increasingly, moreover, the attack can be delivered by an unmanned air vehicle or drone rather than a manned warplane.

An example of this capability occurred when special forces called in air attacks on "Scud" ballistic missile launchers during the First Gulf War of 1991 and against Serb armor operating in Bosnia during the 1990s. They continue to perform this function against Taliban and al-Qaeda positions in the mountains of Afghanistan.

▲ *A sensor operator of the U.S. Air Force's 4th Special Operations Squadron performs all the requisite pre-flight system checks on his equipment before his AC-130U "Spooky II" gunship takes off on a mission.*

◄ *The KAB-500-OD is an optronically guided Russian fuel/air explosive bomb designed against targets such as fire emplacements and manpower hidden in mountains.*

► *The detonation of a U.S. BLU-82 "daisy cutter," a weapon developed to create helicopter landing zones in dense jungle during the Vietnam conflict.*

# OPERATION "FEUERZAUBER" – THE RESCUE OF LUFTHANSA FLIGHT 181 (OCTOBER 13, 1977)

At 11:00 a.m. on October 13, 1977 Lufthansa's Flight 181 lifted off from Palma de Mallorca for Frankfurt a.m. Main with 86 passengers and five crew led by Jürgen Schumann, with Jürgen Vietor as his co-pilot. About 30 minutes later as it passed over Marseilles, the Boeing Model 737-200 was hijacked by four "Commando Martyr Halime" terrorists (the Palestinian Zohair Youssif Akache and Suhaila Sayeh, and the Lebanese Wabil Harb and Hind Alameh). Their leader, Akache, instructed Schumann to fly to Larnaka in Cyprus. He was informed that the airliner lacked the fuel for such a trip, and would have to land in Rome to refuel.

The airliner landed in Rome and, at this stage, in concert with the Siegfried Haisner Kommando (a Red Army Faction group) that had kidnapped a West German industrialist, Hanns Martin Schleyer, some five weeks earlier, demanded the release of ten RAF terrorists held in Stuttgart-Stammheim prison as well as two Palestinian compatriots held in Turkey and US$15 million. Despite West German protests, the Italian authorities allowed the airliner to be refueled and it took off at 5:45 p.m. en route to Larnaka, which it reached at 8:28 p.m.

After landing permission had been refused by several Middle Eastern countries, Akache opted for Bahrain where, after a number of alarms, the airliner landed at 1:52 a.m. After Akache had threatened to shoot the co-pilot, the airliner was again refueled and took off for Dubai, which the authorities sought to close by blocking the runway with vehicles, only to relent on being told that the airliner was running out of fuel. The hijacked airliner landed at 5:40 a.m.

Meanwhile, Hans-Jürgen Wischnewski, the West German minister responsible for handling the hijacking, and Colonel Ulrich Wegener, commander of the elite German antiterrorist squad GSG 9, had arrived in Dubai to try to get the government to agree to let GSG 9 commandos into Dubai to storm the aircraft. However, time was lost in preparations and at 12:20 p.m. on October 17 the airliner took off and headed for Salalah in Oman, where landing permission was once again refused, and then Aden in South Yemen, where the airliner would yet again have exhausted its fuel.

At Aden, the airliner had to make an emergency landing on a sand strip as the two main runways were blocked. Not certain of their aircraft's ability to take off from this strip, the pilots said they needed

◄ *Men of the 400-strong Grenzschützgruppe 9 of the West German federal police practice fast-roping to the ground from a hovering Bell UH-1 helicopter. This technique is widely used for getting a modest party of troopers onto the ground rapidly and safely.*

▲ Hans-Jürgen Wischnewski and the members of the GSG 9 team return to Cologne/Bonn airport on October 18, 1977 following the team's successful liberation of the hostages held by terrorists in a hijacked Lufthansa airliner at Mogadishu airport in Somalia.

▲ A member of the GSG 9 special police unit of the West German state with the kit and weapon typical of this unit.

to make an exterior examination of the landing gear. Schumann was given permission, but delayed his return and was shot in the head as he re-boarded the airliner. Once again refueled, the airliner took off at 6:00 a.m. and headed for Mogadishu in Somalia, where it touched down at 6:22 a.m. local time.

The hijackers informed Vietor that he was free to leave, but the co-pilot opted to remain with the rest of his crew and the passengers. The hijackers now issued an ultimatum for the RAF prisoners to be released by 4:00 p.m. or the airliner would be blown up. The ultimatum was then changed to 2:30 a.m. on October 18.

Meanwhile, a team of 30 GSG 9 commandos, under their deputy commander, Major Klaus Blatte, had assembled at Hangelar in West Germany. The commandos took off on the morning of October 17 to fly to nearby Djibouti, but while transiting over Ethiopia the GSG 9 team was informed that it could land at Mogadishu, which it did at 8:00 p.m. without lights to avoid detection.

Wegener and Blatte finalized their assault plan, scheduled to start at 2:00 a.m. They decided to approach from the airliner's blind spot to the rear with six teams and use black-painted aluminum ladders to gain access through the escape hatches under the fuselage and via the doors over the wing. Just before 2:00 a.m., Somali commandos lit a diversionary fire 200 ft (60 m) ahead of the airliner. Akache and two

of the other three hijackers rushed into the cockpit. At 2:07 a.m. the GSG 9 commandos climbed noiselessly up their ladders and opened the emergency doors. Wegener, leading one group, opened the forward door, and two other groups clambered onto the wing and opened both emergency doors simultaneously. Shouting in German for the passengers and crew to hit the floor, the commandos shot and killed Harb and Alameh, and wounded Akache and Sayeh, who was hiding in the lavatory; Akache died of his injuries shortly afterward. Three passengers and a flight attendant were slightly wounded.

◀ Werner Maihofer, the West German interior minister, welcomes Hans-Jürgen Wischnewski on the tarmac at Cologne/Bonn on October 18 1977. Wischnewski played a key role in the negotiations that led to GSG 9's successful storming of the hijacked airliner at Mogadishu airport.

# LINES OF COMMUNICATION

All armed forces are reliant on their lines of communication for the delivery of reinforcements, weapons, ammunition, fuel, and other supplies to the front line, and for the evacuation of casualties and damaged equipment to rear-area hospitals and maintenance facilities. This is especially true of large forces employing a high degree of mechanization and advanced weapons systems, but is still true to a lesser extent of small and more lightly equipped forces, such as the insurgents fighting in Afghanistan. These smaller forces rely on animals and human porters, as well as light vehicles, to move their supplies, and within the context of a low-intensity war it is just as important to target and destroy these assets as it is to sever the supply lines of more technically advanced armies.

Given the light weight and unsophisticated nature of the supplies on which insurgents are reliant, they are ideal targets for interdiction by special forces teams, especially in difficult terrain where the ambush and destruction of the lead and rear vehicles can trap a convoy in a mountain defile or other area that it is difficult to leave.

◀  *A man of the U.S. Marines Special Operations Command leads his mule. In some terrains draft animals offer major advantages over wheeled or tracked vehicles.*

▼  *U.S. Army soldiers provide security in the Masamute valley as other elements cordon off and then search the village of Bala in Laghman province, Afghanistan.*

Insurgents are generally equipped with nothing heavier than an optically sighted heavy machine gun, with which it is difficult to locate and destroy a carefully concealed special forces team at any distance. All the special forces team needs is a well-trained sniper firing a full-bore rifle fitted with a telescopic day sight, or an infrared or image-intensification night sight. Part of a two-man team (firer and spotter), the sniper can readily immobilize vehicles with shots into their engines, leaving the trapped convoy for piecemeal destruction by the rest of the special forces team.

Behind the front line of a higher-intensity battlefield, of course, there are more valuable lines of communication targets, but on the other side of the tactical coin the quality of the opposition is usually superior—larger, more highly trained and better equipped forces will be deployed to search for the special forces team and potentially destroy it.

▲   *A MARSOC operator with the 2nd Marine Special Operations Battalion engages his target in the course of a shooting drill.*

▶   *A sergeant (left) with men of his special forces team and members of the Northern Alliance west of Konduz in Afghanistan.*

▼   *A long-range patrol vehicle convoy of a special operations task group moves across terrain typical of one of Afghanistan's desert, or "dasht," regions.*

# "Hearts and Minds"

Since the 1960s, special forces are frequently asked to share their expertise with friendly nations through the provision of information and by taking on the training of their local special forces and bodyguards in a variety of skills and capabilities. Such collaboration and training must, of course, be authorized by the national government, which gains diplomatic and financial rewards for the assistance of its special forces, but which also boosts the reputation of the special forces used for the training mission. The training effort also provides the special force with the chance to gain insights into its host nation's military capabilities and also the nature of its terrain and climate. All of these could be useful in the future.

Special forces training teams concentrate on the military aspects of their mission, but often also take the opportunity to try to inculcate in the minds of their hosts the overriding importance of winning the "hearts and minds" of the local civilian population, whose support is essential to the longer-term viability of the armed forces and the government at their head. Something that can be scaled up and down according to requirement, this "hearts and minds" concept is related to the "five fronts" effort devised for the later part of the Omani campaign against insurgents in Dhofar between 1962 and 1976.

▲ A U.S. Marine laughs with Iraqi children as the Marines, Iraqi soldiers, and Iraqi police work to provide better security for the civilians of Fallujah.

◀ A U.S. Army soldier jokes with Iraqi children and so helps to bring them into the allied fold.

▶▶ U.S. troops move to embark in a Sikorsky CH-53 Stallion heavy-lift transport helicopter.

The idea of the "hearts and minds" initiative arose in Malaya during the early 1950s. It was the brainchild of Brigadier J. M. Calvert and served as a cornerstone of the campaign that the British waged to defeat a Communist insurgency (1948–58). "Hearts and minds" is centered on the vital task of winning the trust of the local population by learning its language and customs, and sharing its pattern of life. As a consequence, the local population is not alienated by the military presence. They may even become firmer supporters of the government, and aid the counter-insurgency effort by physical support of the troops operating in their area and also by providing intelligence of a timely and accurate nature. The policy generally requires extra training on the part of the special forces. Medical staff, for instance, may have to learn something of midwifery and dentistry, and the serving men have to learn at least the rudiments of the local language. Above all else, though, the "hearts and minds" effort demands the employment of sensitivity, tact, courtesy, and patience.

▲ A member of the U.S. special forces conducts SAT (Security Assistance Training) of members of the Philippine Army's 1st Infantry.

◄ As with other elements of the Afghan forces, Afghan commandos work in a situation in which distrust of the authorities is often compounded by tribal and religious antipathies.

# CHAPTER 3

▲ Soldiers participate in log and rifle PT at Camp MacKall, North Carolina, the setting for primary training to become a member of U.S. Army Special Forces.

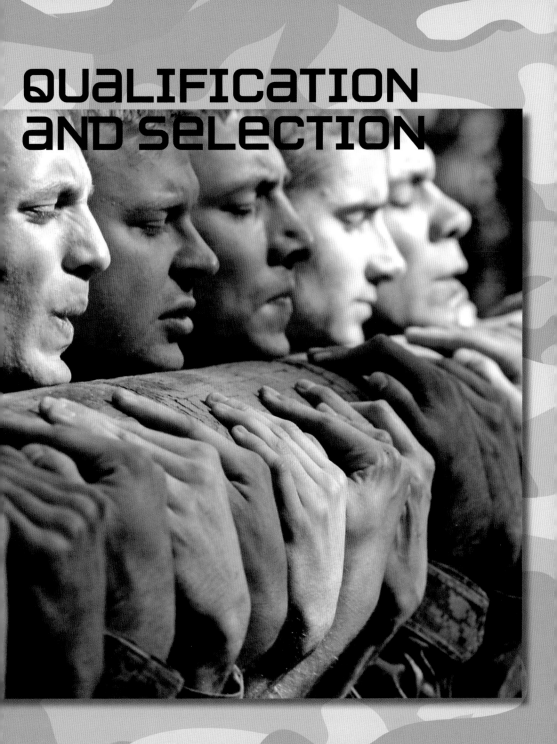

# QUALIFICATION AND SELECTION

# SELECTION PROCESS

The training process described here, which has subsequently been adopted as a model by many other special forces, is that developed in the U.K. as the first step in the selection and training for soldiers and other members of the armed forces wishing to join the three special forces units, namely the 21st Special Air Service Regiment, the Special Boat Service, and the Special Reconnaissance Regiment. Those wishing to join the SAS and SBS undergo a standard selection process up to the award of a sand-colored beret to SAS troopers. At that point, those wishing to join the SBS then undergo a further selection process to qualify as swimmer canoeists, while those accepted for the SAS undergo further specialist training. The selection process for the SRR has never been revealed.

In the period before the late 1990s, candidates for the SAS and SBS underwent separate selection processes devised, implemented, and controlled by their prospective units. The two separate processes were then merged to create a standardized selection process that offered efficiency savings and—a very useful by-product—encouraged and facilitated a greater degree of interoperability between the units.

▲ *Special forces selection assesses candidates' ability to function effectively under all conditions. These U.S. Army personnel are seen during a water confidence course.*

▲ *Physical fitness, endurance and agility are all primary requirements for special forces candidates. This is a U.S. Navy chief petty officer selectee scaling a wall with the help of his teammates at the Fleet Marine Force Challenge.*

◄ *The endurance and mental strength of special forces candidates, such as these U.S.A.F. personnel, are measured in a forced march under adverse time, terrain and climate conditions.*

The British selection process is believed to be the single most demanding military training course in the world, and though exact figures have not been revealed, it is thought that the pass standard is so high that only one in ten candidates achieves it. The selection process is a very arduous physical, emotional, and intellectual examination of each candidate's fitness, strength, endurance, and resolve in terrain and climatic conditions as diverse as the bleak cold and driving rain of the Brecon Beacons and Elan Valley in Wales, and the heat and high humidity of the lush jungle of Brunei. The process takes about six months.

Selection for the SAS and SBS takes place twice each year (once in summer and once in winter), and continues regardless of the prevailing conditions. It is impossible to enter the SAS and SBS directly, and each candidate has to wait for his call to the selection process. An absolute prerequisite even for application to the selection process is current or previous service in the regular armed forces or the reserve forces. Regular troops must be no older than 32 years and still have at least 39 months of service remaining on completion of selection. In general, candidates are in their mid-20s. Candidates are limited to a maximum of two attempts at selection, and those who fail are immediately returned to their units.

▼▲ *Endurance is not an end in itself, but allows the special forces soldier to move far and fast, yet still be capable of combat at the end of this. Here, soldiers begin a tough training exercise on the southern edge of Dartmoor.*

# FITNESS TEST

Designed to weed out those not suited to proceed to further special forces training, the selection process is specifically designed to find men with the right qualities: physical and mental toughness, self-reliance, and the ability to analyze and solve a problem regardless of the circumstances and conditions. The procedure is divided into several phases, and starts with a briefing course that takes place several weeks before the start of selection. The briefing course lasts one week, and in this preliminary phase the potential candidates receive a detailed instruction about the employment of the special forces and also on the nature of the physical and mental elements of the selection method. Candidates undertake a map and compass test, a swimming test, a first-aid test, and a combat fitness test. There are also numerous "Directing Staff walkabouts" and runs in the hills. Candidates are told privately of their likelihood of success or failure, and are also given a rigorous training program to help them build up their strength and stamina for the exceptional rigors of what they are about to experience.

The first phase of the selection process proper is the four-week fitness and navigation element. The men are based at Sennybridge Training Camp in Wales, which exposes them to the Brecon Beacons and the Elan Valley, where the typical weather conditions are both problematical and often highly unpredictable. The first element of the

▶  *Exposed, and often very cold and wet, the Brecon Beacons in Wales provide the taxing conditions needed to test SAS candidates to their very limits.*

tests is basically similar to British Army general training. This involves the personal fitness test, in which each man must perform at least 44 press-ups and 50 sit-ups before completing a 1.5-mile (2.4-km) run in less than 9 minutes 30 seconds.

The test, which occupies the first week of selection, comprises a series of day and night runs and marches in the Brecon Beacons, up and down hills with a loaded Bergen (backpack). At first they are undertaken in pairs, and then by each man individually. A candidate is given a Bergen, map, and compass, and then told the grid reference for the first rendezvous (RV). He sets off in the knowledge that he must complete the course as quickly as possible, although only the members of the directing staff actually know the time limit that has been fixed. It is only on reaching his first RV that the candidate is told his next RV, and so on. This uncertainty helps to induce the type of stress which the soldier must conquer if he is to succeed. The candidate is also aware that he is being watched and assessed continually during the selection process.

▼ *Combat capability and survival depend on very great physical fitness as measured in trials such as the U.S. Marine Corps combat fitness test.*

◄ *Sprinting within the run portion of the U.S. Marine Corps combat fitness test proves the candidate's ability to step up his effort when needed.*

▲ *The endurance and commitment required for consideration as a special forces soldier are evident in the face of this U.S. Marine.*

# EGYPTIAN AL-SA'IQA UNIT AND THE LARNAKA DISASTER (FEBRUARY 19, 1978)

Late on February 18 two Palestinian terrorists had assassinated Youssef Sebai, editor of a major Egyptian newspaper and a friend of Egypt's President Anwar Sadat, at a convention in the Hilton hotel in the Cypriot city of Nicosia. The terrorists then seized as hostages 16 Arab delegates (including two Palestinian Liberation Organization representatives and one Egyptian national) and demanded transport to Larnaka airport. They also demanded an airliner, and were allocated a Douglas DC-8 of Cyprus Airlines. The terrorists flew out with 11 hostages and four crew. The DC-8 was refused landing permission in Djibouti, Syria, and Saudi Arabia, however, and was thus compelled to return to Cyprus.

Sadat asked President Spyros Kyprianou of Cyprus to mastermind the rescue of the hostages and seizure of the terrorists for

▼ *The Larnaka disaster began at the Hilton hotel in Nicosia, Cyprus, with the terrorist seizure of a number of Arab hostages.*

extradition to Egypt. Kyprianou agreed, and traveled to the airport to supervise matters personally. Apparently, at much the same time Sadat dispatched an elite antiterrorist force, the Al-Sa'iqa (Thunderbolt) Unit to Cyprus on a Lockheed C-130 Hercules transport aircraft, informing the Cypriot authorities only that "people are on the way to help rescue the hostages" without any detail of their numbers, nature, and plans. Immediately after landing at Larnaka, the Al-Sa'iqa Unit began its assault: one Jeep with three men aboard headed toward the DC-8 followed by 58 (according to other sources 74) men on foot.

As the Egyptians moved on the DC-8 and the Cypriot national guard forces surrounding it, the Cypriot forces feared that the new arrivals might be terrorist reinforcements and ordered them to halt. The men in the Jeep and the national guardsmen then exchanged fire, despite the fact that the Egyptians had absolutely no cover out on the open tarmac. The Jeep was hit by both gunfire and a rocket-

▲ *The terrorist murder of Youssef Sebai was seen as a direct threat to President Anwar Sadat of Egypt.*

▶ *With its capacious hold and good range, the C-130 was used by the Egyptian special forces team.*

▼ *The Cypriot national guard was well armed, but had only limited experience in counter-terrorist operations.*

propelled grenade, all three Egyptians being killed. As the Jeep slowed to a halt, the Cypriots and the main Egyptian force confronted each other at a range of less than 330 yd (300 m), and the two forces exchanged fire. The Cypriots also fired an antitank rocket at the C-130, which was hit on the nose. All three members of the Egyptian crew were killed.

With their transport aeroplane destroyed, the Egyptians continued to exchange fire with the Cypriots for almost one hour on the open tarmac, though some of the Egyptians took cover in a nearby Air France airliner, which was empty. When the firefight finally ended, the Egyptians had lost 12 commandos killed as well as the three-man aeroplane crew. It is also estimated that another 15 commandos were taken to hospital in Larnaka with gunshot

wounds. The Cypriots, who had the inestimable tactical advantage of cover, suffered no casualties.

It was only after this fatal fiasco that it emerged that the surrender of the two terrorists had already been arranged at the time of the failed Egyptian attack. The two men were later extradited to Egypt, where they received death sentences, later commuted to life imprisonment. On February 20, Egypt recalled its diplomatic mission and requested that the Cyprus government should do the same. Egypt and Cyprus severed political ties until the assassination of Sadat in 1981.

The episode also led, later in the same year, to the establishment of Unit 777 as Egypt's elite antiterrorist and special forces unit.

# TEST WEEK

By test week, which is the last phase of this initial selection process, the numbers on the course will have dropped considerably from the initial 200 or so men, some leaving of their own accord and others being "binned" and therefore returned to their units. In addition, the weight of the Bergens is steadily increased from 24 lb (11 kg) to 55 lb (25 kg), to which must be added the candidate's food, water, and personal weapon. Each man has to carry his weapon unsupported: thus, the soldier must keep his rifle in his hands as he climbs slopes and scrambles down again. The exacting nature of the runs and marches is further complicated by navigation and map-reading exercises. Navigation runs in small groups in woodland areas, and night "tabs" (forced marches carrying a heavy load) then follow without any real break. The object of this first period of selection is to impose an ever-increasing mental and physical load on the candidate.

▲ *For selection into the SAS training program the candidate must pit himself against the clock while crossing the Pen-y-fan mountain under adverse conditions, carrying a sizable load, and fighting against his own ever-increasing exhaustion.*

The final element of the "hills" phase of selection is known as "Test Week," and this comprises six marches of steadily increasing length on consecutive days with ever-heavier Bergen weights. The penultimate day involves a cross-country march of 22 miles (35 km) guided by a hand-drawn sketch map rather than a printed map. The last day is devoted to the "Long Drag" or "Fan Dance," which is a solo 31-mile (50-km) timed navigation exercise named after Pen-y-fan, the highest elevation in the Brecon Beacons. The candidate must complete the exercise, which passes over some of the highest peaks in the Brecon Beacons, in no more than 20 hours; the time limit to scale and descend Pen-y-fan is four hours. By the end of the hill phase the candidate be able to run 4 miles (6.4 km) in 30 minutes and swim 2 miles (3.2 km) in 90 minutes.

◀ *As well as his own physical and mental limitations, the SAS candidate faces the threat of ever-changing conditions on Pen-y-fan, where dry warmth can change without notice to the cold wetness of driving rain or snow.*

▶▶ *The SAS selection procedure demands that the candidate moves fast, far, accurately in areas such as the Elan Valley while carrying his personal weapons and a very heavily loaded pack.*

◄ *Pen-y-fan mountain in the Brecon Beacons presents a major challenge to the heavily laden SAS candidate not only for its physical demands, but also for its rapidly changing and often dangerous weather conditions.*

# Basic SaS Training

The candidate who has survived to this stage, probably no more than one out of every five men who embarked on the selection process, is now committed to a four-week period of initial continuation training, in which he learns basic SAS and SBS skills to enable him to become an effective member of the standard four-man patrol. He is taught standard operating procedures for the four-man unit, such as how to move through hostile territory, the arcs of fire of each patrol member, and how to conduct contact drills. Each candidate is also instructed in signaling, which is a vitally important skill for long-range patrols operating deep in hostile territory. Each man must achieve the regimental signaler standard, which includes the ability to transmit and receive messages at the required rate. Training is also given in SAS field medicine, which combines the use of advanced drugs with more basic medical knowledge.

▼   *Clean weapons and equipment, together with the ability to sleep wherever and whenever the opportunity presents itself, are primary SAS survival requirements.*

▲   *SAS trainees form a human chain to load filled sandbags into the back of a truck at Battle Camp farm.*

After learning these skills, which are the foundation of the special forces trooper's ability to survive and operate in adverse conditions of terrain and climate, the candidate then moves on to combat training (including weapon handling, vehicle handling, demolitions, and small unit patrol tactics) all under the watchful eyes of the SAS and SBS personnel running the course, and to survival training, where he learns the many skills required to remain alive in all kinds of hostile environments. Among these latter skills are the construction of shelters, finding food and water, lighting fires, and laying traps.

Those who successfully complete this phase are deemed to have passed their continuation training, and move forward to the six-week jungle-training phase, which is usually carried out in the thick rainforests of the island of Borneo but also, on occasion, in Belize or Malaysia. Candidates are allocated to four-man patrols, each patrol supervised by a member of the directing staff. Humidity, rain, heat, and general fatigue are standard elements of this jungle-training phase, and assessment is made continuously of each candidate's state of morale, and also his ability to take care of himself, as well as his weapon, in conditions in which bruising, broken skin, cuts, blisters, and insect bites raise the very real threat of major infection.

▲  *Training in the Brecon Beacons creates the collaboration essential to the efficiency of the standard four-man patrol.*

▼  *The availability of exterior facilities, such as Battle Camp farm, provides the vital element of reality necessary to tactical training that might become standardized if undertaken only in the specially prepared conditions of a fixed base.*

▲  *The Brecon Beacons are used not only for physical challenges, such as the "Fan dance," but also for basic and advanced tactical training.*

# OPERATION "STORM-333" — THE KILLING OF PRESIDENT HAFIZULLAH AMIN (DECEMBER 27, 1979)

Operation "Storm-333" was the Soviet designation of the special forces operation which, on December 27, 1979, presaged the Soviet invasion of Afghanistan on the same day. In the course of the "Storm-333" assault, Soviet special forces attacked and stormed the Tajbeg Palace in Kabul, the capital of Afghanistan, and killed President Hafizullah Amin and his 200 personal guards. Several other government buildings were seized during the operation, including those of the ministry of the interior, internal security organization, and general staff (Darul Aman Palace).

Involved in the operation were 30 men of the "Grom" (Thunder) unit of the Alpha Group, 30 men of the "Vympel" Group and 30 men of the "Zenit" (Zenith) Group. All three of these forces had been raised by the KGB (Soviet state security organization) for counter-terrorism, deep penetration and covert operations. The Alpha Group (otherwise Group "A") was more specifically a special forces (Spetsnaz) and special operations unit attached to the KGB, and had been created on July 28, 1974 within the First Chief Directorate of the KGB on the orders of Yuri Andropov, then chairman of the KGB. It was intended for counter-terrorism operations to give the KGB the capacity to respond within the U.S.S.R. to such incidents as the Palestinian massacre of Israeli athletes at the 1972 Olympic Games in Munich.

▶ *Shrapnel damage at the ruins of the Tajbeg Palace in Kabul.*

▲ *The ruins of the Tajbeg Palace (or Queen's Palace), which was built in Kabul during the 1920s by King Amanullah Khan for his queen. This was the site of the Soviet assassination of President Hafizullah Amin in 1979.*

◀ *A Spetsnaz special forces unit in Afghanistan in about 1980, the year after such a unit was involved in the killing of Hafizullah Amin.*

▼ Masked members of the special forces of the "Vympel" unit in a mock antiterrorist exercise near Moscow in 1994. Also known as Vega Group or Spetsgruppa V, "Vympel" is a Russian counter-terrorism unit.

Operation "Storm-333" also employed 520 men of the 154th Separate Spetsnaz Detachment (known as the "Muslim Battalion" as it comprised only men from the southern republics of the U.S.S.R.) of the Soviet ministry of defence, and 87 men of a company of the 345th Guards Airborne Regiment. These support troops were not issued with body armor or helmets, whereas the three KGB units had bullet-proof body armor and helmets. This was a critical factor as Amin's personal guards, totaling some 2,500 men, were armed only with sub-machine guns, whose comparatively low-velocity rounds could not penetrate the Soviet body armor.

The Soviet forces approached their target buildings in a convoy of vehicles, many of them armored personnel carriers that were already in the country as part of the Soviet military and technical support for the Afghan government in its fight with a major Muslim fundamentalist insurgency in several parts of the country. By the time of Operation "Storm-333," however, the Soviets had become suspicious of Amin's loyalties and longer-term objectives, and decided to replace him with a more compliant Communist president.

As the vehicles approached their targets, they were met with ineffective small arms fire and showers of grenades. ZSU-23-4 Shilka armored anti-aircraft vehicles, each armed with four 23-mm (0.9-in) cannon, responded with devastating effect, killing many of the Afghan guards and setting fire to many vehicles. After disembarking from their vehicles, the Soviet forces sprinted to their target buildings as the palace guards continued to fire from the roof and windows. Protected by their bullet-proof armor and helmets, the Soviet special forces quickly entered the buildings.

Once inside, each group knew its task and had been fully briefed on the buildings' interior layouts. Grenades were thrown, followed by small-arms fire, as each group broke into its assigned room and cleared it. Resistance soon petered out, and the commandos approached Amin's suite. Amin had earlier been seen, half-dressed, shouting at his wife to bring Kalashnikov assault rifles. He was behind a bar, apparently dressed in Adidas trunks, when the Soviet troops entered, and the first officer into the room shot and killed him.

Operation "Storm-333" cost the Soviet forces 19 killed and about 50 wounded, the former comprising two men of the "Alpha" Group, three men of the "Zenit" Group, nine of the "Muslim Battalion" and five of the paratroopers. The Afghan losses were in the order of 200 killed, 200 wounded, and 1,700 captured.

# SPECIALIZED TRAINING

Jungle training concentrates on the candidate's ability to survive as an effective member of his patrol, and also involves instruction in patrol techniques, navigation, boat handling, camp and observation post techniques, building a shelter, finding food and water, contact drills, and, of course, medicine. The last test of this phase encompasses all these skills, where all things that have been learned must be applied correctly in a tactical environment.

Finally comes the four-week survival, evasion, resistance, and extraction phase. After a period of specialized training, the candidate performs an evasion exercise, wearing a greatcoat to restrict movement, and operating in a small group. A "hunter force" provided by the Special Forces Support Group tries to locate and seize the small group as it seeks to reach its designated objective without being detected. All candidates, including those who reach their objective, then experience tactical questioning. Removed to an interrogation center, they undergo a 24-hour resistance-to-interrogation test. In this

▲   *Many aspects of small arms training are undertaken at Battle Camp farm. Here an SAS trooper stands guard with a general-purpose machine gun.*

▼   *An essential element of SAS training at Battle Camp farm is the exploitation of the range and hitting power of weapons such as the GPMG.*

▲ *Another vital skill, when an enemy may be using tunnels and other such ways of concealing himself, is the almost arcane science of trench clearing.*

▼ *For the attack, the SAS soldier must become a skilled exponent of the concept of tactical fire and movement using typical patrol weapons.*

they are subjected to various forms of stress, all designed to make them reveal information to their interrogators. Many men crack at this stage, and are rejected and returned to their units.

If they manage to complete the whole selection process successfully, candidates for the SAS are awarded the sand-colored beret and petrol blue stable belt of the SAS Regiment, while SBS candidates move to the SBS headquarters at Royal Marines Poole to undergo further selection assessments.

The 21st and 23rd SAS (Reserve) Regiments of the Territorial Army undergo the same selection process, but as a part-time program over a longer period in the form of nine weekends of endurance training, one week of endurance training in the Brecon Beacons, and one week for an assessment, also in Wales. There follows Standard Operational Procedure (SOP) Training, in the form of nine weekends of patrol SOPs (including surveillance and reconnaissance), one week of live firing (including patrol contact drills and troop offensive action), nine days of battle camp (comprising live-firing assessment and field training exercise) to test the skills learned throughout selection, and conduct after capture training.

# U.S. FORCES SELECTION

There are two ways for U.S. soldiers and civilians to volunteer to attend the equivalent Special Forces Assessment and Selection (SFAS) procedure. An enlisted man in the U.S. Army with the rank of corporal/specialist or higher, and an officer with the rank of 1st lieutenant or captain can apply. The alternative is direct entry, in which an individual who has either left the service or has no previous military service can apply directly. On approval, the candidate starts on the Special Forces Qualification Course. In this, the first phase is the 24-day Special Forces Assessment and Selection at Camp Mackall, North Carolina. This taxing course is designed to see if the soldier has the 12 "Whole Man" physical and mental attributes to continue in Special Forces training and then progress to service with one of the 12-man Operational Detachments "Alpha." The 12 required attributes are intelligence, physical fitness, motivation, trustworthiness, accountability, maturity, stability, judgement, decisiveness, teamwork, influence, and communications. The men who complete the course must then be selected by the final selection board.

▲    Harsh drill instruction (here at the Officer Candidate School) helps to inculcate discipline, but not drive out the initiative of the special forces soldier.

▲    During "Hell Week" surf drill training, a U.S. Navy SEAL instructor assists students from the Basic Underwater Demolition/SEAL part of the course.

▶    The students of a Basic Underwater Demolition/SEAL course must develop additional team spirit, strength, and stamina through "Log PT" efforts.

▶ *Basic Underwater Demolition/SEAL students low crawl during a field training exercise simulating a combat scenario. Too high a body position in combat invites the enemy's small-arms fire.*

▼ *Shoreline evidence, should such be needed, that the endurance training element of the Basic Underwater Demolition/SEAL course places the utmost demands on the trainees' bodies and minds.*

Elements of the SFAS include several long-distance land navigation courses by day and night under heavy loads of equipment, in any and all weather conditions and in rough, hilly terrain. Land navigation is performed on an individual basis, has a time limit that is steadily shortened and always covers courses of 12 miles (19 km) or more. The weights carried also increase during the assessment period. Instructors evaluate candidates by means of obstacle courses, 12-man team events including the movement of heavy loads through sand, a physical fitness test, a swimming assessment, and a battery of psychological tests. Successful Active Duty candidates then usually return to their previous units to await a slot in the Special Forces Qualification Course.

# OPERATION "EAGLE CLAW" – THE ABORTIVE TEHRAN RESCUE MISSION (APRIL 24-25, 1980)

Operation "Eagle Claw" was a disastrous U.S. undertaking ordered by President Jimmy Carter in an effort to end the Iran hostage crisis by rescuing 52 Americans who had been held at the U.S. embassy in Tehran since November 4, 1979, when Iranian students seized the embassy in support of the Iranian Islamic revolution.

Diplomatic efforts having failed, Carter opted for a military solution based on a complicated two-night mission. On the first night a small U.S. Army Delta Force was to occupy a small staging site inside Iran, near Tabas, as "Desert One." This was to be used as an airstrip for three USAF Lockheed MC-130E "Combat Talon I" special operations penetration/transport aircraft and three EC-130E Hercules aircraft, each of the latter equipped with a pair of collapsible fuel bladders containing 6,000 gal (22,710 litres) of jet fuel. "Desert One" would then receive eight U.S. Navy Sikorsky RH-53D Sea Stallion

▼ *Sikorsky RH-53D Sea Stallion helicopters of the U.S. Navy are readied for "Eagle Claw" aboard the aircraft carrier Nimitz (below). Six RH-53D helicopters of the HM-16 squadron pass ahead of the Nimitz in the Arabian Sea as they prepare for "Eagle Claw" in April 1980 (bottom).*

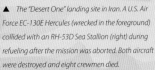

▲ The "Desert One" landing site in Iran. A U.S. Air Force EC-130E Hercules (wrecked in the foreground) collided with an RH-53D Sea Stallion (right) during refueling after the mission was aborted. Both aircraft were destroyed and eight crewmen died.

◄ U.S. Navy RH-53D Sea Stallion helicopters fly near the carrier Nimitz in preparation for "Eagle Claw." The operation was a complete fiasco.

minesweeping helicopters. In fact flown by U.S. Marine Corps personnel from the carrier *Nimitz* in the Indian Ocean, the Sea Stallions would then transport the rescue team to Tehran. The entire operation was covered by fighters from *Nimitz* and *Coral Sea*.

After an inbound flight below the Iranian radar, the C-130s were to offload men and equipment and refuel the helicopters. These were to deliver the special forces to "Desert Two," near Tehran, during the same night, and remain concealed. On the second night the rescue force was be transported, under CIA leadership, by truck to the embassy, overpower the guards and escort the hostages to the Shahid Shiroudi stadium, where the helicopters would land to recover all the Americans, civilian and military.

The embassy assault was to be preceded by the cutting of all electrical power in the area to disrupt an Iranian military response. AC-130 gunships were to patrol overhead to provide supporting fire as required. The helicopters were to transport the rescuers and hostages from the stadium to Manzariyeh air base outside Tehran, which was to be seized by a force of U.S. Rangers so that Lockheed C-141 StarLifter transports could land ready to move all the Americans to safety under a fighter screen.

The delivery of the rescue force, equipment, and fuel by the MC-130E and EC-130E aircraft proceeded as planned. Meanwhile, the eight Sea Stallions were having a more eventful time of it as they

transited southern Iran. One helicopter was forced to land when its pilots suspected a cracked rotor blade, and its crew was collected by another of the helicopters. The seven surviving helicopters then unexpectedly encountered a local weather feature, known as a *haboob* (fine particles of sand suspended in the air after a thunderstorm). One of the helicopters entered this phenomenon but turned back to *Nimitz* after instrument errors made it impossible to continue without sight of the ground. Thus, the six surviving helicopters straggled into "Desert One" between 50 and 90 minutes behind schedule. One of the helicopters was abandoned at "Desert One" with malfunctioning hydraulics.

With only five Sea Stallions remaining to transport the men and equipment to "Desert Two," the commanders were in a quandary, and after the helicopters had been on the ground for 150 minutes, President Carter ordered the mission to be aborted. But as one of the helicopters was being moved, it collided with an EC-130E, and in the explosion and fire that followed, five U.S.A.F. aircrew in the C-130 and three U.S.M.C. aircrew in the RH-53 died, only the helicopter pilot and co-pilot surviving with severe burns. During the frantic C-130 evacuation that now took place, the helicopter crews attempted to retrieve their classified mission documents and destroy the helicopters, but Delta Force commander Colonel Charlie Beckwith ordered them to embark in the C-130s or be left behind. The helicopter crews complied, and thus five RH-53 helicopters were abandoned largely intact.

# CHAPTER 4

▲ Students from Basic Underwater Demolition/SEAL (BUD/S) class 284 participate in a land navigation training exercise in the third and final phase of their training.

# TRAINING

# PERSONAL WEAPONS

Though the world's special forces often use the standard personal weapons of their own nations' armed forces, their particular nature and the diversity of the roles they have to perform has frequently been reflected in their use of other weapons more suitable for specialized tasks. Special forces thus train with a wide assortment of weapons to maximize their familiarity with a host of weapon types. They also become fully conversant with the weapons used by potential opponents. This last skill is important so that they can appreciate the capabilities of weapons that they may have to face. It also allows them to "live off the country" in the event that they run out of ammunition, for they can seize and use the enemy's weapons, which are likely to be in abundant numbers and well supplied with ammunition.

▲ The 7.62-mm (0.3-in) M24 bolt-action sniper rifle with the PVS-10 Day+Night Vision Sniper Scope is used by the U.S. special forces and is accurate to 900 yd (825 m).

◄ A U.S. Marine uses the M2A1 reflex sight of his M32 Multiple Grenade Launcher, a South African weapon that can deliver all six 40-mm (1.57-in) grenades in less than three seconds.

▶ *This U.S. Marine of a SOC (Special Operations Capable) element mans a "50-cal" (0.5-in) M2, the western world's standard heavy machine gun.*

▲ *A U.S. Marine loads the end of a belt of 7.62-mm (0.3-in) ammunition into an M240G air-cooled medium machine gun before firing.*

▶ *A custom-built M4A1 compact assault carbine with the RIS/ RAS foregrip, tactical handguard, crane stock, and red-dot sight.*

▲ *A U.S. Marine with an AT-4 recoilless antitank rocket launcher. The spent cartridge cases are not from the AT-4.*

Apart from heavier weapons, such as antitank rocket launchers used for bunker busting as well as attacks on armored vehicles, special forces use the standard types of personal weapons, although often in suppressed forms to reduce their acoustic signatures and so avoid ready detection in closer-quarter undertakings. The weapons habitually operated by special forces include the 12.7-mm (0.5-in) belt-fed heavy machine gun, which is generally used only in vehicle-mounted applications; the 7.62-mm (0.3-in) belt-fed medium machine gun, which is commonly used in relatively static operations; the 5.56-mm (0.219-in) belt- or magazine-fed light machine gun, which is the "standard" support weapon as both it and its ammunition are relatively light; the 7.62-mm sniper rifle for long-range killing of key personnel and destruction of vehicle engines and electronic equipment; the 7.62-mm (0.3-in) or 5.56-mm (0.219-in) assault rifle (carbine) for closer-quarter combat and urban operations; the combat shotgun for specialized tasks, such as the breaching of doors and fighting inside buildings; the 9-mm (0.354-in) sub-machine gun for close-quarter fighting; and the pistol for self-defense and operations inside buildings.

# WEAPONS TRAINING

Weapons training is designed to make the special forces soldier completely comfortable with the nature and capabilities of all the weapon types he is likely to use and come up against. The soldier needs to be able to handle and use his weapon almost instinctively so that it functions virtually as an extension of his mind and body. He should also be able to field-strip and reassemble the weapon quickly and accurately—even sight unseen—under all climatic and geographical conditions, by day or night, and also to diagnose and repair simple failures.

Much basic weapons training, designed to accustom the soldier to his weapon and teach him to fire with extreme accuracy (important in itself and as a matter of conserving ammunition) can be carried out on the firing range. This is of course a wholly unnatural situation for the soldier, however, and has to be matched by extensive and more realistic weapons training in the various types of conditions likely to be encountered in real operations. The special forces soldier can expect to operate in conditions as varied as the extreme cold of the

▲   *U.S. Marines of a U.S./Australian joint task force train during a patrol exercise at the Shoalwater Bay Military Training Area, Queensland, Australia.*

*U.S. Marines train aboard the U.S. Navy's Harpers Ferry, lead ship of the four-strong "Harpers Ferry" class of dock landing ships. The ship can land 402 marines (504 under austere conditions) in its two air-cushion landing craft, and constant training ensures that the marines or a special forces team are ready to enter combat as soon as the ship reaches its objective.*

Arctic and extreme heat and aridity of the equatorial desert, the intense humidity of the jungle, the heavily vegetated terrain of coastal jungles or temperate forests, and vegetation-free deserts, mountains and plains, and even marshes and swamps. Special forces soldiers, marines, and sailors tasked with operations in coastal and riverine conditions have also to be capable of swimming with full equipment over possibly long distances in often turbulent water, and potentially in conditions where visibility is virtually nil. The soldier must then emerge to fight on land just as efficiently as his wholly land-based counterpart.

The special forces role perhaps best known to the public is counter-terrorism. In the case of the Special Air Service Regiment, at any one time one of its four "Sabre" (combat) squadrons undertakes the counter-terrorism role, which is rotated through the squadrons every six months. After catching up with counter-terrorism techniques, the designated squadron is divided in half. One continues training at the various SAS training facilities and is on standby for immediate response to a terrorist incident, while the other takes part in exercises and is on 24-hour warning to respond.

◄◄ *U.S. Navy Basic Underwater Demolition/SEAL (BUD/S) students wade ashore on San Clemente Island, California, with their assault carbine personal weapons and other equipment, during an "over the beach" landing exercise.*

▲ *An Australian soldier returns fire with his 5.56-mm (0.219-in) F88S-A1 Austeyr assault rifle fitted with an M204 grenade launcher and PEQ-2 night-aiming device, during a joint exercise with U.S. forces.*

# THE IRANIAN EMBASSY SIEGE
## (APRIL 30–MAY 5, 1980)

On the morning of April 30, 1980, six terrorists of the Democratic Revolutionary Front for the Liberation of Arabistan (a region of Iran) invaded the Iranian Embassy in London and seized 26 hostages, including PC Trevor Lock of the Metropolitan Police's Diplomatic Protection Group. Within minutes, the five-story building had been cordoned off by the police, soon reinforced by members of the police's own D11 marksman, C13 antiterrorist, Special Patrol Group, and C7 technical support units. In addition, SAS soldiers in plain clothes arrived during the afternoon to assess the situation.

The terrorists demanded the immediate release and delivery to the U.K. of 91 Arabs incarcerated in Iranian jails, and asked Arab ambassadors to mediate on their behalf with the British government. The deadline for these demands was 12:00 p.m. on the following day. Non-compliance would result in the killing of the hostages and the destruction of the embassy. As negotiations continued beyond the deadline, an SAS Special Projects Team had arrived as part of Operation "Nimrod" after the SAS had been ordered to readiness by Prime Minister Margaret Thatcher.

At the Blues and Royals barracks in London's Regents Park, the men of the SAS studied a model of the building and assessed intelligence from C7, which had placed a number of microphones and surveillance devices in the chimneys and walls of adjacent buildings. Thermal imagers were also used to determine which rooms were occupied. The SAS plan was straightforward: one four-man team was to abseil down the building's rear to the level of the ground and first floors, and another team would enter the building at the front. Tactically, the teams would use frame charges to make their entries and hurl in stun grenades to disorientate the terrorists. The members of both teams would wear black one-piece suits, bullet-proof jackets, respirators, and be armed with Browning High-Power automatic pistols and Heckler & Koch MP5 sub-machine guns.

By the morning of May 5, the situation in the embassy was deteriorating, especially after the government's refusal to concede anything had persuaded the terrorists that the police could not be trusted. At 6:50 p.m., the terrorists shot an embassy press officer and dumped his body in front of the building. The negotiators then contacted the terrorist leader with the offer of safe conduct for all the terrorists to an aircraft that would take them out of the country.

◀ *Caught by the camera during the last stages of the Iranian Embassy siege in London on May 5, 1980, a counter-terrorist soldier of the SAS, well armed and wearing specialist clothing, prepares to enter the Iranian Embassy through a first-floor balcony after a frame charge had detonated and opened his way to toss stun grenades and storm in.*

▶ *When terrorists of Iran's disaffected Arab minority shot and killed two of the 19 hostages they had seized in the Iranian Embassy in London, tear gas and stun grenades paved the way for the men of the SAS to storm the rooms in which the hostages were being held, and kill the terrorists.*

▼ *The burning first floor of the Iranian Embassy, shortly after a bomb had exploded inside. In a short and sharp action, the SAS team killed five of the Arab terrorists and liberated the surviving hostages, who stumbled out of the building stunned but unhurt. It was a classic undertaking, and catapulted the SAS onto the world stage.*

Meanwhile, the "Pagoda" Troop, as the SAS assault party was codenamed, stormed the building. Two SAS soldiers abseiled down to the first-floor balcony and another pair to the ground. The men on the balcony were unable to detonate their frame charge because one of their comrades was dangling above them, entangled in his rope. Thus, both teams were forced to use sledgehammers to gain entry. Stun grenades were thrown in and then the SAS men stormed into the building. At the front, the SAS team blew in the window with frame charges, threw in stun and CS gas grenades, and then went inside. The electric power to the embassy had been cut immediately before the assault, to aid the SAS. The building quickly filled with smoke and tear gas.

The terrorist leader was killed on the first-floor landing as the SAS men made their way to the telex room on the second floor where, as a result of C7 surveillance, they knew the hostages were being held. The three terrorists holding the hostages killed one of their captives and wounded two more before the SAS men burst into the room, killing two of the terrorists and seizing the third. All six terrorists had now been neutralized, as one had been killed in the hallway near the front door and another in an office at the back of the building. The entire operation had been completed in 17 minutes. The hostages and one remaining terrorist were quickly evacuated from the burning building, and the SAS men, who had suffered no casualties, left in two vans.

# CLOSE QUARTER BATTLES

Counter-terrorism is most usually associated with situations unfolding in urban buildings or public vehicles, and the special forces place great reliance on realistic training in specially constructed facilities typical of the type of structure that they may be called upon to assault. In the case of the SAS this is the so-called "killing house" or, more formally, the Close Quarter Battle building constructed at its base near Hereford in the U.K. The U.S. Delta Force uses a comparable building nicknamed the "House of Horrors." Originally developed for training in bodyguard skills, the SAS "killing house" was later used to develop and improve counter-terrorist tactics, most specifically those needed for the rescue of hostages. During the six-week close-quarter battle shooting course, each soldier fires at least 5,000 rounds per week, though the stand-by special projects team shoots far more.

The close-quarter battle techniques practiced in the "killing house" include rapid changes of magazine, the clearance of jams, firing accurately on the move and from unconventional positions, rapid acquisition of the right target, exact placement of any shot, and targeting of the head to ensure a swift kill. The course is designed to ensure that all of these skills become instinctive.

▲◄ *U.S. Navy SEALs undertake a close quarter combat training exercise in a simulated home at the U.S. Training Center, Moyock, North Carolina. The training facility is a private enterprise, and caters for law enforcement and civilian training, as well as the needs of the U.S. special forces.*

◀ *This multi-purpose structure at the Alliance Home Station Training Area in Belgium is used by many nations for exercises such as hostage recovery and information gathering.*

▼ *Spain maintains several special forces units including that of the Guardia Civil, as well as separate air force (one), army (one), and marine corps (two) elements. All are notably well trained and well equipped for the full gamut of special forces operations.*

The "killing house" initially comprised a single room representing a typical situation in which hostages might be held. Inside the room were live "hostages" (SAS men) and dummy "terrorists." To add to the realism the room was often kept in darkness. The team in training had to burst in and, in less than four seconds, identify the terrorists and hostages and "kill" the former without harming the latter. The use of live ammunition added an extra dimension of realism. The system worked successfully until 1986, when an SAS "terrorist" moved at the wrong moment and was killed instantly by a head shot.

The "killing house" now has movable partitions—rubber-coated walls which absorb live rounds—and extractor fans to clear out the gun fumes. It can be laid out to simulate a number of differing scenarios. Here room-entry techniques are perfected, soldiers learn how to make effective use of stun grenades, tear gas, explosive charges to breach doors and walls, and shotguns firing hinge-busting Hattan rounds. These are all designed to provide an edge to the assault team in siege-busting operations. Only after the members of the team have developed the necessary disciplines do they start to train with live ammunition.

One room contains the "terrorists" and "hostages," while the assault team makes its attack on another duplicate room. The two rooms are connected by a sophisticated camera system, which relays real-time coverage of events taking place in one room to a life-size wraparound screen in the other, and vice versa: thus, the assault team fires at images of the terrorists projected onto bullet-absorbent walls, and the "terrorists" also fire back at their screen. In addition, the whole sequence is recorded on video to allow post-exercise debriefings and examination.

The SAS also uses a multi-story building nicknamed "the embassy" in which to practice assaults. Terrorists take hostages on board trains, buses and coaches, and special forces soldiers practice assaults on such targets. The SAS, for example, has a stretch of railway track and carriages on which it rehearses the storming of hijacked trains, and also a dummy airliner.

▲ *A U.S. Navy SEAL advanced training instructor engages targets with his automatic pistol during a close-quarter defense hooded-box drill at the Naval Special Warfare Advanced Training Center in California.*

# HAND-TO-HAND COMBAT

In addition to his skills with firearms, the special forces soldier has also to develop a capability for hand-to-hand combat. This involves lethal or non-lethal physical combat between two, or perhaps more, persons within grappling distance of each other without the use of firearms or, indeed, other distance weapons. While the phrase "hand-to-hand" would seem to indicate unarmed combat, the term is in fact generic and can include the use of striking weapons, such as knives, sticks, batons, or even improvised weapons, such as entrenching tools.

In the U.S. armed forces, for example, the U.S. Army adopted the Modern Army Combatives hand-to-hand combat training program during 2002, and in 2008 the U.S. Air Force also adopted this. In 2002, the U.S. Marine Corps adopted the Marine Corps Martial Arts Program as successor to the LINE (Linear Infighting Neural Override Engagement) combat system in 2002.

◄  A counter to a frontal bearhug during a U.S. Marine Corps Martial Arts Program Gray Belt Course.

▼  Guidance and supervision for "hands-on" training for Bangladesh Army personnel during a non-lethal weapons seminar. The advantage of such combat is silence.

Among the exponents of hand-to-hand combat, the Russian (ex-Soviet) Spetsnaz is perhaps the service which places greatest emphasis on the techniques. The two favored weapons are the knife and the entrenching tool. In knife fighting it is hard to anticipate an opponent's actions as the number of possible moves is very large. The knife fighter practices constant motion, trying to secure a position that offers an advantage in the attack, and he also uses feint movements designed to entice the opponent to engage. It is not enough to know the basic techniques of knife fighting to beat an experienced enemy, so the knife fighter must be able to combine several elements into the so-called "bunch" of fighting combinations, and use them instinctively according to the situation. Improvisation is important in any fight, but extemporized tactics should be derived from experience and practical knowledge.

◄ *Members of the Jamaica Defense Force practice hand-to-hand/close-quarter combat. Though used by many armies, such techniques are notably important to special forces.*

▼ *A foam pad provides protection in a knee-strike demonstration. U.S. Marines and sailors attend such courses to learn the right techniques for defending themselves.*

# THE RAID ON PEBBLE ISLAND
## (MAY 14, 1982)

During the 1982 war that resulted from the Argentine seizure of the Falkland Islands, Argentinian forces established an airstrip on Pebble Island off the north coast of West Falkland. Small and improvised, this airstrip nonetheless posed a limited threat to the ships of the British naval task force operating off the islands, and it would have posed a more significant threat if the light ground-attack aircraft based there could be deployed against the British ground forces once they had landed on East Falkland. The Special Air Service was thus instructed to destroy the Argentine aircraft. The ships involved were the aircraft carrier *Hermes*, frigate *Broadsword* providing air defense for *Hermes*, and destroyer *Glamorgan* for shore bombardment.

Members of the Boat troop of the 22nd SAS's D Squadron landed by canoe on the island before the raid to reconnoiter the airstrip. The original plan was for the SAS assault team to destroy the aircraft, their ground crews, and the garrison on the island but, after strong headwinds had slowed *Hermes*'s approach to the flying-off point, the SAS team was left with only 30 minutes for its attack, not the 90 minutes that had first been scheduled. Thus, it was the Argentine aircraft that were the SAS team's first priority. The helicopters used to

▼   *British special forces about to be lifted from the carrier* Hermes *by Westland Sea King HC.Mk 4 helicopters. One of the keys to British success in the Falklands War was the great cooperation between the various forces involved.*

◀ *A Westland Sea King HC.Mk 4 assault helicopter of the Royal Navy. This was a key "weapon" in mobility, the delivery of supplies and reinforcements, and the evacuation of the wounded.*

▼ *A light, single-shot and breech-loaded grenade launcher fired from the shoulder, the M203 was used on Pebble Island, and can fire a 40-mm (1.57-in) grenade out to 380 yd (350 m).*

transport the men to Pebble Island had to be back on *Hermes* before full daylight so that the carrier and her escorts could be well to the east of the island, to minimize the threat of daylight attacks by Argentine antiship warplanes operating from the mainland away to the west.

On the night of May 14–15, the Westland Sea King HC.Mk 4 helicopters of the Fleet Air Arm's 846 Squadron carrying 45 members of D Squadron, together with a Royal Naval gunfire observation team, lifted off the carrier. The helicopters landed on Pebble Island about 4 miles (6 km) from the airstrip. The plan was that the men of the Mountain Troop would attack the aircraft while those of the other two troops sealed the approaches to the airstrip and formed a reserve. As the SAS party prepared to move off, more than 100 bombs for the 81-mm (3.2-in) mortar, explosive charges and 66-mm (2.6-in) Light Anti-Tank rockets were unloaded from the helicopters.

The SAS party, each of whose men carried two mortar bombs, was guided to the target area by a member of the Boat Troop, whose other men created a protective screen for the mortar team. The attack on the airstrip was led by Captain John Hamilton. When the troops reached the perimeter they opened fire with small arms,

M203 grenade launchers, and 66-mm LAWs. *Glamorgan's* para-flares lit up the entire area, aiding the SAS men as they placed explosive charges on their aircraft targets. Taken wholly by surprise, the Argentines managed to return only a notably inaccurate fire, which caused the SAS party only one minor casualty.

AS the SAS party withdrew, six FMA IA-58 Pucará light attack, four Beech Turbo-Mentor armed trainer/light attack, and one Shorts Skyvan transport aircraft had been destroyed, and the SAS party had also demolished a large dump of Argentine ammunition. Thus, the airstrip on Pebble Island had effectively been removed from the Argentine side of the equation when the British made their amphibious landing in San Carlos Water six days later to begin their land reconquest of the Falkland Islands.

# SPETSNAZ SOLDIERS

The combat training of Spetsnaz soldiers stresses the importance of hand-to-hand combat and of using hand-held weapons of many types. Among the latter the humble entrenching shovel is important as it is a standard item of equipment and constitutes a formidable close-quarters combat weapon. It can be lethal in the hands of a trained fighter. Its effectiveness stems from the fact that it is almost as wieldy as a knife but offers greater striking power and effective reach. The knife adds more than 8 in (20 cm) to a fighter's reach, but the entrenching shovel doubles this and, when the hand is moved closer to the shovel blade, it is still effective at very short distances and in confined spaces. It is arguable that the shovel, when held at the far end of its handle, is unequalled by other cold steel weapons. It is light and wieldy, and it is highly effective for close, middle, and long range hand-to-hand combat.

▲   *The special forces of the Russian Federation are notably adept in the skills of intensive unarmed combat and close-quarter fighting.*

▼   *A key element of the type of unarmed combat practiced by the special forces of the Russian Federation is a high level of physical agility.*

Also a soldier can use the shovel to throw soil or sand in his opponent's face from a distance of up to 16 ft (5 m) and exploit the resulting confusion to close the distance and deliver a telling blow. The entrenching shovel is also an excellent throwing weapon: a specialist can throw the tool accurately out to a distance of 33 ft (10 m) or more.

When conducting a combat mission in the enemy's rear, a sudden close-quarter engagement is quite probable. Hand-to-hand combat can take place in conditions of limited visibility: at night, amidst smoke, etc, in forests or woodland, in destroyed buildings, trenches, underground command and communications centers, and incomplete military installations. During such engagements the enemy generally outnumbers the special forces team, so hand-to-hand combat skill against several

▼ *The defense is as critical as the offensive move in unarmed combat, for it allows the combatant to pull back and prepare another attack.*

▲ *Another primary element of Russian unarmed combat techniques is the use of legs and feet, as well as hands and arms, to deliver a telling blow.*

opponents is an important element in the training of the special forces soldier.

As well as knife and shovel combat, close-quarter combat techniques emphasize hand-to-hand combat without any weapon other than the hands themselves. The hand-to-hand combat specialist must be able to put his opponents out of action despite their superior numbers and weapons, and in the least possible time and with the minimum expenditure of effort. The techniques therefore include directing a large number of different blows at vital points, joints, and other vulnerable spots on the body, suffocating, using body locks and the breaking of joints, neck, spine, etc to kill, or at least incapacitate, the opponent.

It is virtually impossible for a close-quarter fighter to prevail over an armed and trained opponent with just his bare hands, so the primary objective is to take a weapon from one of the attackers and turn it on them all.

# SURVIVAL TECHNIQUES

Any member of the world's special forces must be able to survive as an effective fighting man under all geographical and climatic conditions with the bare minimum of equipment brought into the operational area. This last requirement is dictated by the fact that the special forces soldier, even when operating in a well-equipped vehicle, must be capable of continuing on foot if the vehicle breaks down or is destroyed. In such circumstances weight is an all-important factor; a man may be able to move while carrying an 80-lb (36-kg) load on his back, but his mobility will naturally be compromised and his endurance undermined.

Items that cannot be safely omitted from the special forces soldier's personal load include his weapon, ammunition, medical kit, navigation items, and communications equipment. All of these are comparatively heavy, so little weight allowance remains for items that can generally be garnered from enemy territory. Hence, the emphasis is placed on what might be regarded as "value-added" items, such as water-purification tablets, concentrated food items, part of a shelter for use in combination with others, a knife, a length of cord, a method of making fire, and a miscellany of smaller items, such as fishing hooks.

▲ *U.S. Navy SEAL trainees involved in a long-range navigation exercise high in the mountains of Alaska, where survival is as important as the completion of the task in hand.*

◄ *A U.S.A.F. aviation ordnanceman, assigned to Explosive Ordnance Disposal Mobile Unit Five, checks his weapon before heading out to a target area during jungle-warfare training.*

◀ A Sikorsky H-60 helicopter hovers just above the ground in an evacuation exercise as fellow Marine Special Operation Command operators move the marine "casualty" on a stretcher. Rapid treatment is essential to survival.

Just as important as these physical items is the knowledge of how best to use them and also how they can be supplemented from the terrain that the special forces soldier is crossing. This is the key element of survival training. It teaches the soldier, for example, how to make a fire which is smokeless, how to build a shelter from local materials, how to find water, and what plants are likely to be inedible if not actually poisonous in various parts of the world. In tandem with basic physical survival is the ability to endure mentally, and here other elements of the special forces soldier's armory are vital, including a knowledge of basic first-aid techniques, personal hygiene to maintain good health, the identification and avoidance of potentially dangerous insects, and the preservation of a resolute frame of mind.

▲ A U.S. Marine at the Jungle Warfare Training Center, Camp Gonsalves, Okinawa, Japan. Here essential land navigation, small unit leadership, patrol and obstacle maneuvering techniques are taught.

◀ A U.S. sailor of Explosive Ordnance Disposal Mobile Unit Five starts a fire. Fire is perhaps the single greatest "tool" for survival under adverse conditions.

# OPERATION "ARGON"–ATTACK ON THE CABINDA EXCLAVE
## (MAY 20, 1985)

A controversial undertaking during the border war in South Africa, Operation "Argon" involved the South African Special Forces Brigade, generally known as the "Recces," and was designed to establish whether or not the African National Congress and South-West African People's Organization had bases in the area near the Cabinda exclave between Angola and Zaire. Here there were Angolan and Gulf Oil petroleum storage installations, and also a number of large Angolan military bases.

On May 13, 1985, a small naval vessel departed Saldanha Bay on the southwestern coast of South Africa carrying a "Recce" team and a reserve team, and headed north to a point off the coast on Angola near its border with Zaire. The "Recce" team came ashore on the night of May 20–21. Due to a combination of circumstances the "Recce" team landed some three hours behind schedule.

Despite the fact that dawn was now less than two hours away, team leader Captain du Toit decided to press ahead to reach the pre-planned lying-up position in an area of dense jungle. Intelligence and aerial photographs had indicated that this was an essentially uninhabited area, but in fact there were several camouflaged bases of the *Forças Armadas Populares de Libertação de Angola* (People's Armed Forces for the Liberation of Angola) in the area round it. The "Recce" team reached the lying-up position at dawn. This proved to be far from ideal as a hiding place as it was not in fact part of the jungle, but rather an isolated patch of dense vegetation some distance from the edge of the jungle.

▼ *The People's Armed Forces for the Liberation of Angola were supported by Communist countries with training and weapons, including those seen here: sub-machine guns and, for antitank and bunker-busting purposes, recoilless rifles.*

▲ An Angolan with one of the world's classic weapons, the Soviet-supplied RPG multi-role rocket launcher.

Dawn also revealed a well-concealed FAPLA base only about 1,000 yd (900 m) from the lying-up position. A few hours later, the South Africans spotted a small FAPLA patrol following the tracks they had left the night before. At 5:00 p.m., a three-man patrol followed the team's trail directly to the patch of vegetation in which the "Recce" team lay concealed, but halted before reaching them and then turned back to its base. Meanwhile, a second FAPLA patrol approached the lying-up position from the opposite direction, and then opened a heavy fire on the hidden position. As rocket propelled grenades started to land in the position, du Toit ordered his men to pull back, with no alternative but to proceed along the trail they had used the night before. Two South Africans were wounded as they left the cover of the trees.

At this juncture FAPLA troops, some 50 yd (45 m) to the west, opened fire with light machine guns and assault rifles, as well as rocket-propelled grenades. The men of the "Recce" team turned north with FAPLA troops in pursuit, and then discovered another group of FAPLA soldiers flanking them to the west. Thus, the "Recce" team was left with no option but to turn east. Ahead of them was a stand of trees, which offered the possibility of at least temporary protection, but first the men had to cross a large patch of waist-high grass. Captain du Toit and two of his men managed to get through the grass as the rest of the "Recce" team hid in a thicket. The small team drew fire as over 30 troops moved onto the exposed position.

A South African corporal was killed as du Toit and the other soldier fought on. The firefight lasted for 45 minutes before the two men started to run out of ammunition and were both wounded, one dying later and du Toit almost dying.

As the wounded du Toit lay on the ground, FAPLA soldiers approached and began to strip him of his equipment, clearly in the belief that the South African commander was dead. Then realizing that du Toit was still alive, the FAPLA soldiers shot him in the neck. Captain du Toit was eventually taken to Cabinda for medical treatment, and then transferred to a hospital in Luanda, the Angolan capital. The other six men of the "Recce" team picked their way north with extreme caution, and were eventually recovered and returned to South Africa. In a complex prisoner-exchange deal, du Toit was finally released after 837 days of solitary confinement in an Angolan prison.

# JUNGLE WARFARE

Jungle warfare training is undertaken by many special forces either because jungle is a possible combat region within their own countries or because such terrain may be encountered during operations on a worldwide basis.

The U.S. Marine Corps has a Jungle Warfare Training Center (JWTC) at Camp Gonsalves in the north of the Japanese island of Okinawa. This 17,500-acre (7,080-hectare) facility offers 22 helicopter LZs, one water surface for beach landings, four bivouac sites, three outdoor classrooms, one firebase, three third-world village target sites, and one missile target site within rugged, hilly terrain covered by single- and double-canopy forest. The JWTC prepares men for survival and combat in dense jungle, and aims to instil confidence, enhance leadership and provide positive challenges. The six-day jungle skills course trains men in basic jungle combat skills, and includes land navigation, patrolling, rope management and rappelling, and dealing

▲ U.S. Marines on the obstacle course at the Jungle Warfare Training Center.

▼ Jungle movement is especially difficult when manhandling a stretcher.

with jungle booby traps. The jungle skills course culminates with the jungle endurance course.

The jungle leaders' course is designed to develop small unit leadership qualities for combat operations and basic jungle survival skills. It combines the previously taught jungle survival course with basic combat skills, and its object is to improve the capability of team leaders and platoon commanders. This is again a six-day course, and includes patrol orders, patrolling, jungle casualty evacuation, survival skills, and establishment and defense of patrol bases.

The jungle skills course is followed by the jungle endurance course, in which teams up to 18 strong move through 3.8 miles (6.1 km) of dense jungle and rugged terrain. The teams compete against each other to traverse 31 obstacles along the course, in which they face hasty rappels, rope obstacles, water obstacles and the manhandling of a litter to complete the entire course.

For special forces soldiers, the regime is essentially similar, but even lengthier and more arduous.

◄ *A three-strand bridge, typical of jungle conditions including ravines with fast-flowing rivers, at the beginning of the endurance course at the Jungle Warfare Training Center.*

▼ *An instructor with the Jungle Warfare Training Command. Combining practical experience with theoretical knowledge, such men are key elements in imparting survival knowledge to modern special forces soldiers.*

# MOUNTAIN WARFARE

Mountain warfare training is another specialized part of special forces training. Mountain warfare encompasses both arid areas, where the terrain is a major enemy, and wet and cold locations where the hazardous terrain combines with snow, ice, and glaciers. Mountain warfare generally occurs at relatively low altitudes, where the reduced oxygen pressure is still adequate for unconditioned soldiers, but it can also take place at higher altitudes, where even lower oxygen pressure demands the use of specially conditioned soldiers.

Physical fitness is the first prerequisite of mountain warfare training. The effects of the cold and hostile terrain demand a high degree of physical and mental fitness for long-distance climbing and movement. The soldiers must also be trained to wear proper clothing, such as loose-fitting layers and insulated polypropylene clothing that prevents sweat from accumulating close to the body. They must also learn to recognize and treat the symptoms of frostbite. Basic mountaineering and high-altitude skills are vital to develop confidence and the ability to survive in the mountains, and they are also essential in combat. As altitude increases, so does the required level of skills: below 13,000 ft (4,000 m), it may be sufficient for soldiers to understand climbing techniques, mountain navigation, correct route selection, the use of ropes, and procedures to avoid landslides and avalanches, but at higher altitudes, soldiers must learn more complex techniques, such as those required for mountain expeditions.

▲   *A soldier of the Japanese Ground Self-Defense Force with his 5.56-mm (0.219-in) Type 89 assault rifle in a winter patrol exercise.*

▼   *A soldier of the 10th Special Forces Group (Airborne) climbs out of the Worthington Glacier of south eastern Alaska during the U.S. Army Special Forces Command (Airborne) "master mountaineer" course.*

▲   *A Navy SEAL in eastern Afghanistan. Operations in such terrain are daunting even for those with specialized training and the required equipment.*

It is difficult to keep weapons functional at altitude so scrupulous cleanliness and the covering and protecting of weapons and equipment against snow and ice are vital. Batteries may not perform as well as they should, and complex mechanisms, such as those of man-portable surface-to-air missiles, readily malfunction.

Survival and continued operability in the mountains needs more energy than usual: a soldier requiring a daily intake of 3,000 to 4,000 calories under normal circumstances needs 6,000 or more calories in the mountains. This factor is also complicated by the fact that high altitude has an adverse effect on appetite, and care must be taken to ensure that soldiers do not actually eat and drink less, which can result in lowered morale, degraded fighting capabilities, and a greater susceptibility to mountain-related illnesses.

Physiological and psychological demands become steadily more pronounced at altitudes above 8,000 ft (2,450 m), and soldiers must be taught to take preventative measures and be trained to detect signs of illness. Common symptoms of altitude sickness include severe and persistent headaches, coughing, difficulty in breathing, and mental detachment. Other symptoms include swelling around the eyelids, incoherent speech, intolerance, and even outright aggression. The greatest killer in mountain operations is cerebral or pulmonary edema. This is difficult to detect, but often develops if soldiers stay too long at high altitude.

▲ *An instructor monitors SEAL qualification training candidates as they spend a mandatory five minutes in near-freezing water during cold-weather training.*

▼ *A group of U.S. Navy SEALs prepares to cross an Alaskan creek during a joint exercise focused on the detection and tracking of potentially hostile units at sea, in the air, and on land.*

# DELTA FORCE AND THE
# *ACHILLE LAURO* (OCTOBER 7–10, 1985)

On October 7, 1985, four men of the Palestine Liberation Front seized control of the Italian-registered cruise liner *Achille Lauro* off the Egyptian coast as the ship was sailing from Alexandria to Port Said. The seizure happened sooner than the PLF men had planned, for they had been prematurely discovered by a member of the ship's crew and decided to act immediately. With 400 or more passengers and the crew as hostages, the heavily armed terrorists ordered the ship to Tartus, in Syria, and demanded the release of 50 Palestinians then being held in Israeli prisons.

Given the fact that many of the *Achille Lauro*'s passengers were U.S. citizens, President Ronald Reagan of the U.S.A. ordered the deployment by air to Cyprus, off the Syrian coast, of the U.S. Navy's SEAL Team Six and elements of the U.S. Army's Delta Force to plan and, if required, execute the recapture of the liner and the rescue of her passengers and crew. In the event the hijacking ended before the U.S. special forces could be instructed to intervene.

▼ *The* Achille Lauro *was seized by terrorists of the Palestine Liberation Front (PLF), who hijacked the cruise liner off the Egyptian coast and took hostage its 450 passengers (below). Pictures taken from a TV monitor of the four PLF terrorists accused of hijacking the ship (below right).*

After being refused permission to dock at Tartus, the hijackers killed Leon Klinghoffer, a wheelchair-bound Jewish-American passenger, and threw his body and wheelchair overboard. The terrorists then ordered the ship back toward Port Said, and after two days of negotiation with the Egyptian authorities, the terrorists agreed to leave the liner in return for safe conduct and transport to Tunisia on an Egyptian airliner.

President Reagan was furious with what he saw as an Egyptian capitulation to the demands of terrorists, and on October 10 he ordered that the Egyptian airliner should be intercepted by Grumman F-14 Tomcat fighters of the VF-74 and VF-103 squadrons embarked on the carrier *Saratoga*. The aircraft was shepherded across the Mediterranean to land at the U.S. Navy air base at Sigonella, a NATO-declared installation in Sicily. Here Bassam al Asker, Ahmad Marrouf al Assadi, Youssef Majed al Molqi and Ibrahim Fatayer Abdelatif were arrested by the Italian authorities. However, the terrorists' leader, Abu Abbas, was allowed to leave with the other passengers as the airliner was released to complete its flight to Tunis despite the protests of the U.S. government. Egypt also demanded an American apology for the forcing of an Egyptian airliner from Tunis to Sicily.

The arrest of the four terrorists had been made only after the resolution of a major diplomatic dispute between Italy and the U.S.A. Bettino Craxi, the Italian prime minister, was adamant that Italy had territorial rights over the NATO base as it lay on Italian national soil. At Sigonella, men of the Italian air force as well as *carabinieri* (members of Italy's armed *gendarmerie*) faced special forces personnel of the U.S. Navy's SEALs who had been flown into Sigonella in two Lockheed C-141 StarLifter transport aircraft. More *carabinieri* were then despatched from Catania to reinforce the Italian presence at Sigonella. This was the most difficult crisis in modern Italian and U.S. diplomatic relations, and was resolved in favor of the Italians only after a five-hour stand-off.

▲  *The cruise liner* Achille Lauro *departs the harbor of Port Said in Egypt after her hijackers, led by the Palestinian militant Abu Abbas, had left the ship on October 10, 1985 in return for an Egyptian promise of immunity and safe transport to Tunisia.*

▶  *President Ronald Reagan was not prepared to accept this concession to the hijackers, and ordered the interception of the airliner carrying them by Grumman F-14A Tomcat fighters from the carrier* Saratoga. *The airliner was shepherded to Sicily, where the terrorists were arrested.*

# ARCTIC WARFARE

Arctic warfare training is similar to high-mountain warfare training inasmuch as both must teach the special forces soldier to survive and operate under conditions of extreme cold and often very high winds, in which major threats are posed by frostbite, trench foot, and shock. Arctic warfare therefore relies on the use of exactly the right equipment. For survival, troops need warm layered clothing (tough, light, windproof, waterproof and made wherever possible of natural materials, such as cotton, wool, silk, and fur), headgear with flaps to cover the neck and ears, waterproof ski and mountain footwear, and a durable rucksack. The men also require extra-nutritious food, white camouflage overalls, tents with sleeping bags, heaters, and fuel.

Weapons can be fitted with an Arctic trigger, which permits firing while wearing heavy mittens (the standard practice being waterproof outer mittens worn over inner woollen mittens), and individual mobility can be increased by the use of skis, ice cleats, and snowshoes.

▲ *Reservists of the U.S. Marine Corps maneuver a Bv 206 tracked all-terrain carrier through the snow near Aesegarden in Norway. Much of the NATO forces' specialized Arctic training is carried out in northern Norway.*

◄ *A U.S. Navy SEAL starts his free-fall descent from an Austrian C-130 Hercules transport above the Arctic Circle during "Cold Response 2010," a Norwegian exercise open to NATO nations for winter warfare and joint coalition training.*

▲ A U.S. Marine uses his ski poles as an extemporized bipod for his M16A2 rifle during an exercise at the U.S.M.C.'s Mountain Warfare Training Center near Pickel Meadows in the Toiyabe National Forest to the north west of Bridgeport, California.

▲ A U.S. convoy of M998 series multi-purpose wheeled vehicles on the move in a Norwegian exercise. The first two vehicles are equipped with TOW antitank weapons systems and the third has a 12.7-mm (0.5-in) M2 heavy machine gun.

Motor vehicles are often incapable of operating in sub-zero temperatures, though special procedures allowing them to function in such circumstances include continuous running and starting at regular intervals before the coolant and oil can freeze. This is a major drain on fuel, however, and is also noisy. Studded tires or tire chains can be employed to maintain the traction of wheeled vehicles under less arduous terrain conditions, but a better option is the use of purpose-designed tracked vehicles that are also fitted with powerful heaters. Special forces learn about the care and operation of such vehicles, including the Sisu Nasu, BvS 10, and M29 Weasel, during their Arctic warfare training.

◄ A marine of the 11th Marine Amphibious Unit moves out in his white exposure/camouflage suit during an exercise in the Aleutian Islands. Special forces, as well as elite forces such as the U.S. Marine Corps, possess the training and equipment to fight almost anywhere in the world.

# DESERT WARFARE

Desert warfare training is akin to mountain and Arctic warfare training inasmuch as it has to inculcate in the special forces soldier, almost at the unconscious level, the paramount importance of having the right attitude of mind, right equipment, and right clothing to survive and operate effectively in challenging climatic and terrain conditions. While the word "desert" conjures up a picture of heat and vegetation-free sand, it must also be borne in mind that deserts can be very cold at night, and are often constituted not of sand but of unforgiving rock. What does characterize the desert and semi-desert is an almost total absence of running or standing water.

Special forces soldiers committed to desert warfare must understand the importance of conserving water by learning not to breathe through their mouths or working so hard that they sweat profusely, and drinking only sparingly. They must also learn about the importance of wearing the right clothing, which should not expose unnecessary areas of skin and be loose enough to allow the free passage of air. Special boots are also a critically important item of kit.

▼ *Eight-wheeled LAVs (Light Armored Vehicles) of the 3rd Light Armored Reconnaissance Battalion traverse rocky terrain in the Sinjar Mountains while deployed to Ninewa province, Iraq. Special forces are often deployed to such regions.*

▲ *A soldier launches an FGM-148 Javelin antitank missile. Such weapons are used by a number of special forces for tasks such as bunker busting and the destruction of communications centers.*

▼ *Australian special forces soldiers of the Special Operations Task Group on patrol in southern Afghanistan. Theaters such as this have seen much use of highly trained special forces, often brought together in multi-national groupings.*

Whether sandy or rocky, the desert typically contains high levels of fine particulate matter that can all too easily enter the mechanisms of weapons and machinery, causing them to malfunction. Thus, there must be a strong regime of weapon cleaning and attention to vulnerable vehicle parts, such as filters and carburetors.

Personal cleanliness and hygiene to maintain good health is just as important in desert warfare as it is in jungle, mountain, and Arctic conditions. The desert has its own insects and endemic illnesses against which the special forces soldier must be on his guard. He must also possess the right medicines. Other elements of desert training include accurate navigation, often without the aid of readily identifiable landmarks; learning the techniques of crossing sandy areas, which can be hard or almost liquid in their consistencies, with the aid of variable tire pressures and sand channels; and how to locate water or use the leaves and stalks of appropriate fleshy plants to garner drops of moisture.

◀ *A U.S. Marine of the 2nd Combat Engineer Battalion is caught by the camera in the course of combat operations in Now Zad, Afghanistan, during Operation "Cobra's Anger." Special forces often operate on the fringes of such forces to provide time-critical reconnaissance and intelligence.*

# EGYPTIAN UNIT 777 AND THE MALTA FIASCO (NOVEMBER 23, 1985)

At 8:00 p.m. on November 23, 1985, Egyptair's Flight 648 lifted off from Athens in Greece bound for Cairo in Egypt with 92 passengers and six crew. About ten minutes later, three Palestinian terrorists of the Abu Nidal Organization, calling themselves the Egypt Revolution and armed with guns and grenades, hijacked the airliner. Their leader, Omar Rezaq, then started to check all the passengers' passports, and it was at this juncture that an Egyptian agent opened fire, killing one terrorist instantly before himself being wounded, together with two flight attendants. During the exchange of fire the airliner's fuselage was punctured. Because of the resulting depressurization, the airliner had to descend to 14,000 ft (4,265 m) so that the passengers and crew could breathe.

▼ *The last stages of the November 1985 hijacking of an Egyptair airliner by the Abu Nidal Organization unfolded at Luqa airport on Malta.*

The terrorists had planned to fly to Libya, but the airliner lacked sufficient fuel and they therefore ordered a landing at Malta. Despite the fact that the airliner was dangerously low on fuel, suffering pressurization problems, and carrying several wounded passengers, Malta refused landing permission. The terrorists would not accept this and forced the pilot to land at Luqa airport.

Initially, the Maltese authorities hoped to resolve the crisis, and the prime minister, Karmenu Mifsud Bonnici, rushed to the airport to supervise negotiations. He refused to order a refueling and to pull back the Maltese forces, which had surrounded the airliner until all passengers had been freed. As a result 11 passengers and two injured flight attendants were allowed to disembark. Then the terrorists began to shoot hostages, starting with an Israeli woman. France, the U.K., and the U.S.A. offered the services of their special

▼ *Egypt's Unit 777 was trained largely by the U.S. Delta Force, but lacked the experience to cope with difficult operations on the international stage.*

forces to Malta, but were refused. The terrorist leader now threatened to kill one passenger every 15 minutes until his demands were met. His next victim was another Israeli woman, and then he shot three Americans; of the five passengers shot, three survived.

▲ *Had U.S. special forces been allowed to intervene, they would have operated from a nearby Sicilian base using C-130 Hercules aircraft or helicopters.*

Both Egypt and the U.S.A. now pressured Bonnici almost as hard as did the terrorists. Among Bonnici's fears was that Israeli or U.S. forces would appear and seize control of the area—indeed, the U.S. naval air base at Sigonella in Sicily was a mere 20 minutes' flying time distant. After the U.S.A. had informed Bonnici that Egypt had available a special forces counter-terrorism team, trained by the U.S. Army's Delta Force, Bonnici authorized its deployment. The Egyptian Unit 777, under the command of Major General Kamal Attia, led by four U.S. officers, then arrived by air. The Maltese, Egyptians, and Americans reached agreement that the attempt to retake the airliner should be made in the morning of November 25 as food was to be delivered to the aeroplane: soldiers dressed as caterers would jam the door open and the attackers would then storm into the airliner.

Then, totally without consultation and 90 minutes before the agreed time, the Egyptian commandos launched an attack with explosives on the cabin and luggage compartment doors before storming into the cabin. Bonnici later claimed that the explosions ignited plastics in the airliner's interior, resulting in extensive suffocation but, the *Times of Malta* reported that the hijackers, realizing that an attack was under way, threw grenades into the cabin, killing passengers and starting the fire.

The storming of the airliner resulted in the deaths of 56 of the remaining passengers, two crew members, and one terrorist. Injured during the storming, the terrorist leader, Rezaq, discarded his hood, weapon, and ammunition and pretended to be an injured passenger. Egyptian commandos tracked Rezaq to St Luke's Hospital and arrested him there.

Lacking specific antiterrorist legislation, Malta could try Rezaq only on other charges. Convicted, Rezaq was sentenced to 25 years in prison, but was released after only eight years. His release caused a diplomatic incident between Malta and the U.S.A. He was expelled from Malta and arrested on arrival in Nigeria. Three months later Rezaq was delivered to the Americans, brought before a U.S. court and, on October 7, 1996, sentenced to life imprisonment without possibility of any parole.

# DIVERS SCHOOL

Most special forces have some proficiency in combat swimming and diving, and these are of great importance in more highly specialized units, such as the British Special Boat Squadron and U.S. Navy SEALs. Typical of the type of selection and training through which candidates must pass is the U.S. Army's Special Forces Combat Divers School at the Naval Air Station Key West, Florida. The school's objectives are the training of personnel as qualified military combat divers proficient in waterborne operations. Their skills must include day and night ocean subsurface navigation swims, deep dives, an appreciation of diving physics, understanding marine hazards, tides and currents, submarine lock-in/lock-out procedures, and open-circuit and closed-circuit (or rebreather) swims (in the latter case the diver's exhaust breaths are routed back into the breathing set, where the exhaled gas is processed to make it fit to breathe again). Before entering on the course, the candidate must prove that he can swim 1,640 ft (500 m) non-stop on the surface, using only breaststroke or sidestroke, tread water for two minutes continuously with his hands and ears above the water, swim 82 ft (25 m) underwater without breaking the surface with any portion of the body, and recover a 20-lb (9.1-kg) weight from a depth of 10 ft (3 m).

◀ *U.S. Navy SEALs operatives in training. Underwater operations, especially in turbulent or murky waters, offer very difficult challenges surmountable only with the aid of constant training.*

▼ *SEAL Delivery Vehicle Team Two huddle together inside a flooded Dry Deck Shelter mounted on the back of the "Los Angeles" class nuclear-powered attack submarine Philadelphia.*

The course takes slightly less than five weeks. In the first week there are fast 2-mile (3.2-km) runs, conditioning in the pool and instruction in dive equipment and procedures. In the second week there is "ditching and donning," which involves entering the pool, swimming underwater to the 15 ft (4.6 m) deep end, removing the face mask, snorkel, and fins and descending to two air tanks left on the bottom underneath a weight belt. Here the candidate takes one breath of compressed air, surfaces and breathes, goes down once again, puts on the weight belt and other equipment, and starts breathing compressed air. Another exercise is the "harassment dive," in which the candidate enters the water and swims around the edge at the bottom of the pool for one hour, all the while being "harassed" by instructors, who pull at his face mask, remove his fins and air tanks, etc. Failing either of these exercises results in discharge from the course. There is also a 1,640-ft (500-m) navigation dive evaluation.

In the third week there are a number of diving tests by day and night, and a 4,920-ft (1,500-m) navigation dive evaluation. The fourth week is punctuated by more night dives, a team swim, and a 9,840-ft (3,000-m) navigation dive evaluation. This marks the end of the course, and successful candidates graduate. Graduates then proceed to more intensive technical and operational training, including dealing with dangerous marine life, specialized physical conditioning, oxygen tolerance and chamber pressure test, diving physiology and injuries, antiswimmer systems, decompression, regulator repair, tides, waves and currents, altitude diving, use of dry suit, use of open-circuit equipment and buddy breathing, specialized water work and equipment, buoyant ascent, submarine lock-in/lock-out procedures, underwater searches, waterproofing and bundle rigging, ship bottom search, and infiltration techniques.

▲ *Students involved in the Basic Underwater Demolition/SEAL (BUD/S) course, wearing night gear, exchange during the second phase of their training.*

▲ *Basic Crewman Training (BCT) students jump from a dive platform during a training session at the Naval Amphibious Base, Coronado, California.*

▲ *A second-phase Basic Underwater Demolition SEAL(BUD/S) candidate checks his underwater breathing apparatus for ventilation and safety before diving.*

# NAVIGATION TRAINING

Land navigation is a vital tool for all soldiers, but especially so for special forces men, who are operating on their own and often in areas deep behind enemy lines. Maps are often sketchy and/or inaccurate, and the ability to find the right operation area quickly and accurately, and report back the coordinates of enemy positions and other locations of interest are at the core of the special forces soldiers' capabilities.

The first step in the training of the special forces soldier is to ensure that he thoroughly understands the conventions of standard military maps, and can navigate effectively using only the simplest of navigation tools, such as the magnetic compass. There are more advanced navigation tools available, such as lightweight satellite navigation receivers using the signals from the GPS satellite constellation, but like all electronic equipment, even when "ruggedized" for military use, the receivers can break or merely exhaust the power of the available batteries. In such circumstances the special forces soldier must revert to more traditional types of land navigation using his eyes, a compass and, if possible, a knowledge of the night sky.

The principles of land navigation on foot and in a vehicle are essentially similar, the main difference being speed: while it may take a man on foot one hour to cover a specified distance, it may take a man in a vehicle ten minutes or less. When preparing to move, the effects of terrain on navigating vehicles must be taken into account, and during vehicle movement the navigator must learn how to estimate the straight-line distance covered. The majority of military vehicles, and certainly the types of light-wheeled vehicles the special forces

*◀ A Basic Underwater Demolition/SEAL (BUD/S) candidate reads his compass during land navigation training. Skills of this type provide essential back-ups to the advanced technology-based equipment, which is often available to special forces.*

*▼ U.S. Navy SEALs with a laser designator of the type used to "illuminate" a target that can then be hit precisely by a laser-homing weapon.*

*◀ Assembly of a radio antenna during operations in Iraq. Effective real-time communications are important to the utility of special forces.*

generally operate, are limited in the slope they can climb and the type of terrain they can traverse. So while swamps, thickly wooded areas, and deep streams may present the special forces foot soldier with no major problem except for personal discomfort, the same terrain may be impassable to vehicles. The navigator must always have this fact in the forefront of his mind when planning a route, but he must also bear in mind that military vehicles are seldom capable of climbing a slope approaching 60 percent, and then only on a surface that is both dry and firm. Gauging the slope is relatively straightforward using a map: one contour line in any 330 ft (100 m) of map distance indicates a 10 percent slope, two contour lines a 20 percent slope etc. The presence of four contour lines in any 330 ft (100 m) demands that another route is considered. Side slope is also important, and is generally limited to 30 percent in good conditions. Traverse of a side slope demands slow and essentially straight movement.

The navigator must also learn how drastically weather conditions can slow or even check vehicle movement. Snow and ice are obvious dangers, but more significant are the effects of rain and snow on the ability of soil to bear loads. In heavy rain even cross-country vehicles may be limited to road movement. In the event of recent heavy rain, the navigator factors in the possibility of flooded and marshy areas, and modifies the selected route to avoid such impediments.

▲ *Students of a Basic Underwater Demolition/SEAL (BUD/S) course participate in a land navigation exercise as part of their training.*

▲ *A U.S. Marine Corps Mobile Training Team trains soldiers of the Panamanian Army in map reading during land navigation and tactical movement exercises.*

◄ *Checking the channel frequency on a PRC-150 radio during a basic land navigation exercise. The PRC-150 is used by the U.S. Special Operations Command.*

The hours of darkness present their own problems. The basic techniques and principles of night navigation remain essentially unaltered from those of day navigation, but even greater care must be taken in planning the route to avoid obstacles that are a greater hazard by night than by day. However, the use of night vision devices can be a great boon. The basic technique for night navigation is dead reckoning using several compasses if possible, and in some areas navigation using the stars may be possible, though this demands a good knowledge of the constellations and the location of individual stars.

# MOSSAD AND THE CAPTURE OF MORDECHAI VANUNU
## (SEPTEMBER 30, 1986)

Between 1976 and 1985, Mordechai Vanunu was employed as a nuclear plant technician and shift manager at the Negev Nuclear Research Center, a desert facility to the south of Dimona in Israel that was widely believed to have developed and manufactured nuclear weapons for the Israeli forces.

On October 5, 1986, a British newspaper, the *Sunday Times*, published a front-page story headlined *Revealed: the secrets of Israel's nuclear arsenal*. The primary source for the story was Vanunu who,

while in Sydney, Australia, had met the journalist Peter Hounam. Early in September he had flown to London with Hounam, and in violation of a non-disclosure agreement with the Israeli authorities, revealed to the newspaper his knowledge of Israel's nuclear program, including photographs taken clandestinely at Dimona. As the newspaper sought to verify and clarify his claims, Vanunu became impatient and so also approached another national newspaper, the *Sunday Mirror*. As this too sought to confirm Vanunu's reliability, Israel became aware of what was happening

▲ *The Israeli "nuclear spy," or rather whistle-blower, Mordechai Vanunu served 12 years of an 18-year sentence for leaking Israeli nuclear weapons secrets to a British newspaper. He is pictured during a court session in Beersheba in 1998.*

▲ *A part of undisclosed size in the Israeli operation was apparently played by the colorful but dubious figure of Robert Maxwell, owner of the Sunday Mirror newspaper and a self-styled former Israeli agent.*

▲ *The former Israeli nuclear technician Mordechai Vanunu (center) flashes the "V-for-victory" sign as he walks free from the high-security prison of Shikma in the southern Israeli city of Ashkelon on April 21, 2004. Released at the end of an 18-year sentence, Vanunu said he was "proud and happy" to have exposed Israel's nuclear program to the world. Vanunu also said that his treatment was "cruel and barbaric," and insisted that he had "no more secrets" to reveal.*

either indirectly from the newspaper's questions to Israel's embassy in London, or more directly through the paper's owner, Robert Maxwell, who reputedly had links with Mossad.

The Israeli government decided that Vanunu should be seized and brought to Israel for trial. The task was allocated to the Mossad with the provisos that Israel's good relationship with the British prime minister, Margaret Thatcher, was not to be jeopardized and that there was to be no possibility of a confrontation with British intelligence. The decision was taken to persuade Vanunu to leave the United Kingdom voluntarily. The Mossad agent Cheryl Ben Tov, raised in the United States and thus well able to masquerade as an American tourist called Cindy, befriended Vanunu and on September 30, persuaded him to take a holiday with her in Rome. This classic example of the "honeypot" tactic, in which an agent employs seduction to gain the trust of the selected target, effectively removed Vanunu from the United Kingdom.

Once the couple had reached Rome, Mossad agents drugged Vanunu and transported him, still drugged, to Israel on September 30, 1986 in a cargo aircraft. In Israel, Vanunu was tried for treason and espionage in a closed court, convicted and sentenced on February 27, 1988 to 18 years of imprisonment. Vanunu served more than 11 years in solitary confinement before eventually being released on April 21, 2004. Since that time he has lived in Israel, under severe restrictions, after being refused permission to emigrate.

# FINAL TRAINING

A key element of the last stages of special forces training is covered by the acronym SERE (survival, evasion, resistance, and escape). Clearly the best solution for any special forces soldier facing the possibility of capture is to survive and evade being taken or, if captured, to escape as soon as possible. However, if he is captured and held, it is important that the soldier reveals nothing more than that required by international law, which is his name, rank, and serial number. To be prepared for the contingency of forceful interrogation that may involve physical torture, psychological humiliation, and sexual harassment, however, the special forces soldier is taught basic resistance-to-interrogation (RTI) techniques. To this end most soldiers are schooled in the elementary measures to help them resist interrogation, and this is still more important for special forces soldiers, who are inevitably deemed to be in possession of more significant information than the conventional soldier.

Trainees are therefore subjected to real interrogation techniques, such as prolonged hooding, sleep and rest deprivation, time disorientation, enforced nakedness compounded by cold water spraying, sexual humiliation, and deprivation of warmth, water, and food. Most of these techniques contravene international law, but are nonetheless widely used in interrogations when rapid results are required. Only first-hand experience of what he may have to face, even if it is on a less severe scale than would be used by an enemy, can help to prepare the special forces soldier for the realities of interrogation. There is no doubt that previous experience is a great aid in helping special forces soldiers to resist the physical and psychological rigors of brutal interrogation.

▲  Soldiers of the French Task Force "Tiger" patrol one of the many dry and rocky valleys typical of Kapisa province, Afghanistan. Only thorough training allows combatants to operate effectively in such areas and emerge alive.

◀  Colombian Army special forces, probably of the air force's Agrupación de Comandos Especiales Aéreos, make their way into Tolemaida Air Base, Colombia, in the course of a technical demonstration of their skills and tactics.

▲ A U.S. Marine provides security near a Sikorsky CH-53E Super Stallion helicopter of the type often used to deliver and extract special forces.

▲ Men of the Sultanate of Brunei's special forces unit during a visit, board, search and seizure exercise on board the U.S. Navy "Arleigh Burke" guided-missile destroyer Howard while under way in the Pacific Ocean.

◄ A Latvian soldier fires from the standing position during a live-fire exercise. Latvia's special force is the Speciālo Uzdevumu Vienība (Special Tasks Unit).

# CHAPTER 5

▲ A U.S. soldier loading an MK19 (Automatic 40-mm (1.57-in) Grenade Launcher machine gun) with MK281 40-mm (1.57-in) non-dud-producing ammunition.

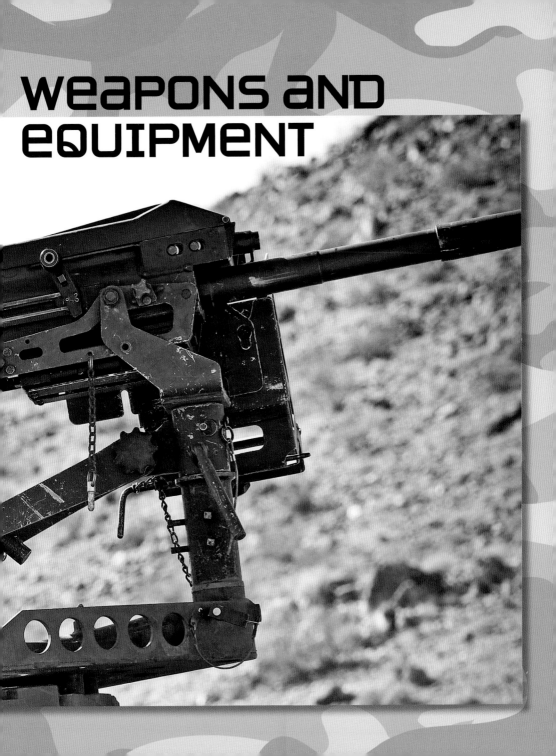

# WEAPONS AND EQUIPMENT

# THE MACHINE GUN

In its various forms the machine gun is one of the standard weapons used by special forces. It is a gun capable of fully automatic fire, and even in its current air-cooled (rather than water-cooled) forms, it is significantly heavier than the assault rifle. Heavy and medium machine guns weigh even more as they have a heavy barrel for sustained fire and a tripod or equivalent mounting to provide stability for the delivery of accurate long-range fire. Another weight factor associated with the machine gun is its need for large (and therefore heavy) quantities of ammunition: even when firing short bursts, rather than delivering sustained fire, the machine gun can use a prodigious number of rounds.

▲ On board a machine of Helicopter Combat Support Squadron Six, a gunner waits to provide suppressing fire with his 7.62-mm (0.3-in) M60 machine gun in support of urban assault and combat search and rescue training at Fort Knox, Kentucky.

▲ A soldier of the U.S. 19th Special Forces Group (Airborne) mans a 7.62-mm (0.3-in) M60 machine gun in the turret of a High-Mobility Multi-Purpose Wheeled Vehicle on the way to Asadabad, Afghanistan.

▶ A 9-mm (0.354-in) MP5K sub-machine gun carried by a boarding team member on one of the ships of the Maritime Interdiction Force (MIF), which was formed during Operation "Desert Shield" to enforce UN trade sanctions against Iraq.

Despite such "debit" factors, however, the machine gun scores very useful points on the "credit" side of the balance sheet, most notably in the delivery of exceptional offensive—as well as defensive—capabilities as compared with the assault rifle. Almost all modern machine guns are of the gas-operated type. Some of the propellant gases driving the bullet down the barrel are tapped off at a point short of the muzzle and ducted back to operate the weapon's unlocking mechanism, extract the spent cartridge, cock the firing mechanism, chamber a fresh round and lock the firing mechanism before the next round is fired. In this way the firing cycle continues automatically as long as the trigger is being pulled and there is ammunition available in the feed system. In the case of the heavy and medium machine gun this is a metal-link belt, and in light machine guns a magazine.

▼ *U.S. Marines of the 26th MEU (Special Operations Command) fire a 7.62-mm (0.3-in) M240G medium machine gun at the Mariam Range in Djibouti.*

▲ *A crewman on a special warfare craft uses a rotary-barrel machine gun for suppressive fire during a practice "hot" extraction from a beach.*

▲ *Pictured in Iraq during "Iraqi Freedom," this U.S. Army sergeant (left) carries his 5.56-mm (0.219-in) M16A2 assault rifle and the Kurdish Peshmerga "special forces" sergeant (right) is armed with a 9-mm (0.345-in) MP5A3 sub-machine gun.*

# MACHINE GUN TYPES

The heavy machine gun has a caliber greater than 7.62 mm (0.3 in), and the classic weapons of this type are the 12.7-mm (0.5-in) U.S. Browning M2 in its many forms, and the Russian (previously Soviet) 12.7-mm (0.5-in) DShKM and more modern NSV. Such weapons generally turn the scales at 55 lb (25 kg) or more excluding their tripods and ammunition, which can be of the armor-piercing type. In special forces applications they are generally mounted in light vehicles that can also carry a useful quantity of ammunition. Thus mounted, the heavy machine gun can deliver up to about 500 rounds per minute out to a range of some 2,000 yd (1,830 m).

On the next rung of the capability ladder is the medium machine gun, otherwise known as the general-purpose machine gun, in calibers of around 7.62 mm (0.3 in). Classic weapons of this type, in 7.62-mm caliber, are the U.S. M240 in its various forms, the Belgian MAG (known to the British as the GPMG), the Russian PK and, in 7.5-mm (0.295-in) caliber, the French AA 52. Many of these weapons can be mounted on a tripod for more accurate long-range fire, but they are generally

▲ This 7.62-mm (0.3-in) M240E6 Machine Gun (Weight Reduction Program) is mounted on an M192 lightweight ground mount for machine guns.

▼ U.S. soldiers in Afghanistan during 2010. The man lying has the 5.56-mm (0.219-in) M249 SAW, and the other man the 5.56-mm M4A1 assault carbine.

operated from a light bipod (often part of the weapon proper) and can fire up to 900 rounds per minute out to a range of 900 yd (820 m) from a bipod. Though possessing neither the weight of fire nor the effective range of heavy machine guns, the medium machine gun is lighter, at some 25 lb (11 kg), and is therefore man-portable.

The smallest-caliber machine guns are characteristically of 5.56-mm (0.219-in) caliber, and are generally designated light machine guns or squad automatic weapons. Good examples of the breed include the FN Minimi from Belgium, the CIS Ultimax 100 from Singapore, the Light Support Weapon from the UK, and the Heckler & Koch HK 23 from Germany. These weapons can be belt- or magazine-fed, and generally weigh around 15 lb (7 kg) with a bipod. Sometimes fitted with a collapsible stock to reduce overall length, such weapons are eminently man-portable and have the advantage of firing the same ammunition as standard assault rifles and carbines. The light machine gun typically fires at up to 1,000 rounds per minute and has an effective bipod-fired range of up to 1,000 yd (915 m).

▲ Bulgarian soldier fires a 12.7-mm (0.5-in) M2 heavy machine gun during a live-fire exercise. The M2 offers exceptional hitting capability at longer ranges.

▲ The PP-19 Bizon sub-machine gun was introduced by the Russians in 1996 and is used primarily for counter-terrorist operations. In common with most sub-machine guns, the PP-19 is offered in several calibers.

▲ Carrying a 12.7-in (0.5-in) M2, the XM153 Common Remotely Operated Weapon Station can be mounted on vehicles for remote aiming and firing capability.

◄ A U.S. Marine fires a 7.62-mm (0.3-in) M240G medium machine gun during live-fire training on the flight deck of an amphibious-warfare dock landing ship.

# OPERATION "FLAVIUS"—THE SAS IN GIBRALTAR (MARCH 6, 1988)

After the Special Air Service's killing of eight Irish Republican Army (IRA) terrorists at Loughall in May 1987, the British rightly anticipated IRA retaliation, but had no idea where this might take place. The IRA selected Gibraltar as being a target that was both militarily soft and indelibly associated with British "imperialism." During November 1987, Daniel McCann and Sean Savage, both known to be members of the IRA, were in the south of Spain under false names, a fact reported by Spanish intelligence. The British could conclude only that the IRA was planning an attack on a member of the large British expatriate population of the Costa del Sol or, more probably, a British Army base in Gibraltar. It was decided that the most likely target was the changing of the guard ceremony outside the governor's residence.

Late in February 1988, MI5 established that several journeys had been made to Gibraltar by an Irish woman traveling under the false identity of Mary Parkin, whom surveillance had seen watching the guard ceremony. On March 1, the woman was back again, and this time she followed the route taken by the bandsmen. The next day, the Joint Intelligence Committee in London decided that a bomb attack was imminent and notified the Joint Operations Centre, which then sent an SAS Special Projects Team to Gibraltar. The resulting "Flavius" operation to seize the terrorist team involved the local Special Branch and police, MI5, and the SAS.

▼ *It was on the edge of the main square of Gibraltar that the IRA terrorists parked the Renault 5 car carrying their bomb.*

▲ *The suspected location of the IRA bomb in Gibraltar meant that its detonation would have resulted in many casualties, most of them innocent civilians.*

▶ *An armed British police officer. Though well trained, such men and women lack the specialized skills required for undercover antiterrorist undertaking.*

The SAS men were instructed to arrest the terrorists, but with the licence to use their own weapons "if those using them had reasonable grounds for believing that an act was being committed or about to be committed, which would endanger life or lives and if there was no other way of preventing that other than with firearms."

On March 4, Savage and McCann arrived by air in Malaga, where they were met by Mairead Farrell. At this time the Spanish police temporarily lost the IRA team, which was then located before it entered Gibraltar on March 6. The IRA team had in fact hired two cars, one to take them to Gibraltar and the other for the bomb: this latter car was later found by the Spanish police in Marbella with 132 lb (60 kg) of Semtex explosive and detonators.

On March 6, the SAS had four men in plain clothes on the streets of Gibraltar, and there were also Gibraltarian armed police and MI5 surveillance officers. The SAS troopers were armed with 9-mm (0.345-in) Browning High-Power automatic pistols. At about 2:30 p.m. the IRA team was identified as having entered Gibraltar, Savage in a car, and McCann and Farrell on foot. At 3:40 p.m. the local police commissioner signed over the power of arrest to the military, effectively giving the SAS control of the situation. On the ground the SAS troopers continued to shadow the three members of the IRA team, which then divided. Farrell and McCann continued toward the border and Savage turned back toward the square. At about

4:00 p.m. the police car also trailing the terrorists was recalled. The driver turned his vehicle round and activated its siren, which was heard by the IRA team.

The next few seconds were confused, but the result was that both McCann and Farrell were shot and killed by Soldiers "A" and "B" who thought that the terrorists were about to detonate the bomb. Savage was confronted by Soldiers "C" and "D" who had followed him. When he heard the shots he spun round, and Soldier "C" shouted at him to halt. Seeing Savage put his right hand down to his jacket pocket, Soldiers "C" and "D" both fired, and kept on firing until he was "no longer a threat to initiate that device." Savage was hit by between 16 and 18 bullets.

# THE GRENADE LAUNCHER

F alling between the machine gun and assault rifle in capability, the grenade launcher has the primary advantages of firing any of a number of different types of rounds, including explosive, and of being capable of indirect fire by dropping its rounds onto an enemy concealed behind cover.

Grenade launchers can be of the single-shot type, generally attached to the barrel of an assault rifle, or of the multi-shot type with dual barrels, or the rotary type. The classic single-shot types are the U.S. M203 and follow-on M320 of 40-mm (1.57-in) caliber. This weighs only 3 lb (1.4 kg), and can fire rounds including dual-role high explosive (offering an excellent capability against light armored and soft-skinned vehicles), high explosive, flare, marker, and buckshot at a rate of up to seven rounds per minute out to a distance of 165 yd (150 m). Almost always mounted on vehicles, belt-fed grenade launchers include the U.S. Mk 19 and German Heckler & Koch Grenade Machine Gun. Both fire 40-mm (1.57-in) grenades, the former out to a range of 1,750 yd (1,600 m) at a rate of 60 rounds per minute, and the latter out to a range of 2,185 yd (2,000 m) at a rate of 340 rounds per minute.

▲ A U.S. Army soldier prepares to drop a round into the tube of a 60-mm (2.4-in) M224 lightweight mortar during live-fire training in Iraq.

▲ The 5.56-mm (0.219-in) M4A1 assault carbine used by U.S. special forces is equipped with the Rail Accessory System/Rail Interface System, 40-mm (1.57-in) M203 grenade launcher, tactical holographic sight, PEQ-2A visible laser/infrared designator, and muzzle-mounted sound suppressor.

◄ Men of the U.S. Army prepare 40-mm (1.57-in) grenades for an automatic grenade launcher during range training within the bi-lateral U.S. and Indian "Exercise Yudh Abhyas" in the Babina area of India during 2009. The Mk 19 launcher can fire about 300 grenades per minute to an effective range of 1,750 yd (1,600 m).

Akin to the grenade launcher in terms of the types of multiple projectiles used and its indirect fire capability, though with a considerably greater range and weight of projectile, is the mortar. Stabilized by a bipod and fired from a baseplate that prevents the weapon from driving itself into the ground, the mortar offers a very useful combination of moderately good portability and great tactical efficiency. The smallest and lightest mortars in current service are of about 50-mm (1.97-in) caliber. These weigh about 14 lb (6.4 kg) and can fire an explosive, illuminating or smoke bomb of about 2 lb (0.9 kg) to a range of 900 yd (825 m).

There are a number of types in the caliber bracket between 50 and 80 mm (1.97–3.15 in), and the largest caliber to be encountered in the hands of special forces is 81 mm (3.19 in). Such weapons are comparatively heavy, at about 80 lb (36 kg), and are therefore carried almost exclusively in vehicles. Mortars of this caliber can fire several types of bomb including a fragmentation type, weighing about 9 lb (4 kg) to a range of 6,000 yd (5,485 m).

▲ *A U.S. soldier fires a training round from the 40-mm (1.57-in) M320 single-shot grenade launcher, which was designed in Germany. This Grenade Launcher Module fires its grenade to an effective range of 165 yd (150 m).*

◀ *Seen in a range in Afghanistan, the 60-mm (2.4-in) M224 Lightweight Company Mortar System fires several types of bomb to an effective range between 75 to 3,815 yd (70 to 3,490 m) at a sustained rate of 20 rounds per minute.*

# assault Rifles

The standard personal weapon of any soldier, including members of the special forces, is the assault rifle. This is now almost invariably of a caliber of 5.56 mm (0.219 in) or less, and the types used by special forces are generally described as carbines, because they are variants of the standard infantry's assault rifle with a measure of range sacrificed to allow for a more compact weapon.

The Special Air Service Regiment's standard carbine is the 5.56-mm (0.219-in) C8SFW, which is a Canadian development of the U.S. Army's M16. The weapon has a 16-in (406-mm) barrel and a 30-round magazine, possesses a rate of fire of up to 950 rounds per minute, and has an effective range of 440 yd (400 m). The C8SFW can be fitted with a 40-mm (1.57-in) grenade launcher, and can also carry a variety of scopes and aiming devices. The C8CQB is a special development with a 10-in (254-mm) barrel and a flash suppressor for the close protection role.

◀ An Australian fires the F89 light machine gun, a version of the Belgian FN Minimi, also in U.S. service as the M249.

▼ U.S. Marines in action with their 5.56-mm (0.219-in) assault rifles during an operation in Helmand province, Afghanistan.

▲ A member of the boarding team assigned to a Spanish frigate provides security as his team approaches a fishing dhow off the Horn of Africa to conduct a search.

▲ This Norwegian soldier is armed with the 5.56-mm (0.219-in) HK416 assault rifle. This German weapon uses 20-, 30-, or even 100-round magazines, and has a cyclic rate of between 700 and 900 rounds per minute.

◄ The modern assault rifle is typified by a U.S. weapon, the M16, developed in a host of variants to fire the standard 5.56-mm (0.219-in) round.

▼ A medical team of the Unidad de Operaciones Especiales (special force of the Spanish marine corps) await a medical evacuation in an exercise. The armed man carries a 5.56-mm (0.219-in) HK G36E assault rifle.

Other modern 5.56-mm (0.219 in) assault rifles used by special forces include the Austrian Steyr Armee Universal Gewehr, French MAS, Israeli Galil SAR, and many members of the U.S. M16 and M4 families, while the Russian AK-74 is of 5.45-mm (0.215-in) caliber. Some special forces prefer large-caliber rifles, perhaps the most popular being the 7.62-mm (0.3-in) FN FAL from Belgium and the Heckler & Koch G3 from Germany, though the latter is also used in its 5.56-mm (0.219 in) HK33 and HK53 forms. There is also a more modern 5.56-mm (0.219-in) G36 from the same source. All of these are semi-automatic weapons firing from 20- or 30-round box magazines below the receiver.

# OPERATION "GOTHIC SERPENT" – U.S. SPECIAL FORCES IN SOMALIA (AUGUST 22–OCTOBER 13, 1993)

Under the supervision of the Joint Special Operations Command, Operation "Gothic Serpent" was a U.S. special forces undertaking in the autumn of 1993, designed to capture the Somali warlord Mohamed Farrah Aidid and two of his lieutenants. A United Nations-led operation—"Restore Hope"—was struggling to restore order in famine-struck Somalia, a country riven by a bitter civil war between a number of warlords. During May 1993, the warring factions agreed to a disarmament conference proposed by Aidid, the most important warlord. The body notionally responsible for running Somalia was the Somali National Alliance, which had been formed in June 1992 and comprised warlords operating under Aidid, who had proclaimed himself president. Many Somalis resented the presence of the U.N. forces and attacked them in the area of the capital, Mogadishu. On June 5, 1993, 24 Pakistani soldiers were ambushed and killed outside the city. On the following day the U.N. Security Council issued Resolution 837 calling for the arrest and trial of those responsible for the ambush, and U.S. warplanes and U.N. troops moved against the stronghold of Aidid.

On August 22, Task Force "Ranger" was deployed to Somalia under the command of Major General William F. Garrison, the JSOC commander. TF "Ranger" comprised one company of the 3rd Battalion, 75th Ranger Regiment, one squadron of the 1st Special Forces Operational Detachment-Delta, 16 helicopters and personnel of the 160th Special Operations Aviation Regiment, U.S. Navy SEALs of the Naval Special Warfare Development Group, and para-rescuemen and combat controllers of the U.S.A.F.'s 24th Special Tactics Squadron.

▼ *A U.S. Marine with an M249 Squad Automatic Weapon (SAW) during the multi-national relief effort Operation "Restore Hope." This weapon is widely used by U.S. special forces.*

▲ Children play on the wreckage of a helicopter in Mogadishu, Somalia. On October 3, 1993, local militiamen shot down two Sikorsky MH-60 Black Hawk helicopters, including this machine, and killed 18 U.S. special forces soldiers.

▼ Master Sergeant Gary Ivan Gordon, who was killed on October 3, 1993 at the age of 33, was posthumously awarded the Medal of Honor.

▶ Sergeant First Class Randall "Randy" David Shughart, who was killed on October 3, 1993, at the age of 35, was the other Delta Force sniper posthumously awarded the Medal of Honor.

During the afternoon of October 3, 1993, TF "Ranger" received information that a pair of leaders of Aidid's clan were in a house in the center of Mogadishu, and accordingly launched a force of 19 aircraft, 12 vehicles, and 160 men to arrest them. The seized men and an injured Ranger were loaded onto ground vehicles, but Somali militia and civilians were now closing on the area. Soon after this, a Sikorsky MH-60 Black Hawk was shot down by a rocket-propelled grenade, both pilots being killed but the other members of the crew surviving the crash landing. Later, another MH-60 was shot down by a rocket-propelled grenade. There was no rescue team available, so the surviving crew remained with their stricken machine. Two Delta Force snipers provided cover from a helicopter, and volunteered repeatedly to try to secure the crash site before receiving permission to make the attempt.

On arriving, the two men tried to secure the site. One of the Delta Force snipers was killed, leaving only the helicopter pilot and the other Delta Force sniper. After killing more than 25 Somali fighters, the second Delta Force sniper was killed, leaving just the pilot, Michael Durant, surviving. Surprised to find him alive, the militia savagely beat him and took him hostage. The remaining Rangers and Delta Force troops meanwhile fought their way to the first crash site, where they found the crew. They were surrounded by militia men, whose commander, Colonel Sharif Hassan Giumale, opted to destroy the Americans with mortar fire, but then called off the planned bombardment after receiving a report of possible civilian hostages. With the aid of rocket and gunfire from helicopters, the Americans were able to drive back several Somali efforts to overrun their position. A ground rescue force of Malaysian, Pakistani, and U.S. forces was now committed, and in the course of heavy fighting broke through the encirclement and rescued the besieged forces.

The battle was the fiercest close combat in which U.S. troops had been involved since the end of the Vietnam War. Two MH-60 helicopters had been shot down and another seriously damaged, and the troop losses totaled 18 Americans and one Malaysian. It has been estimated that the Somalis lost some 1,000 militiamen killed. The Delta Force snipers Randall Shughart and Gary Gordon were posthumously awarded the Medal of Honor. After 11 days in captivity, Durant was released, along with a captured Nigerian soldier, to the custody of the International Committee of the Red Cross.

# THE SNIPER RIFLE

Another rifle in the special forces armory is the sniper rifle. This is generally of 7.62-mm (0.3 in) caliber, with more specialized weapons offered in 12.7-mm (0.5-in) caliber for greater range and the ability to fire an anti-matériel round to immobilize vehicles. The sniper rifle is a remarkable weapon embodying all the finer points of the gunsmith's and ammunition specialist's skills. Although it is very often based on an existing design, a rifle of this type is manufactured to high degrees of precision to ensure that the sniper secures the all-important first-round hit on the target every time. Sniper rifles fall into two general categories. The first has already been mentioned: it is the conversion of an existing standard weapon. The second is notably different, for it comprises specially designed rifles. All sniper rifles require special care and handling, and must be carefully calibrated with the high-quality optical sights without which they are less able to deliver long-range fire of the required accuracy. Current (but obsolescent) sniper rifles include classic 7.62-mm (0.3-in) weapons, such as the Soviet SVD, British L42A1, Israeli Galil Sniper Rifle, Belgian FN Model 30-11 and U.S. M21 and M40. These offer good capability to a range of 875 yd (800 m) or so.

▲ *A U.S. Marine scout sniper adjusts the sight of his rifle during a training exercise aboard the amphibious assault ship* Bonhomme Richard.

▼ *A U.S. Marine scout sniper fires his 7.62-mm (0.3-in) Mk 11 semi-automatic rifle in the first stage of a three-day platoon competition in Djibouti.*

◀ The two men of a U.S. Army sniper team watch for suspicious activity from an observation point during an area reconnaissance mission off Highway 1 in Zabul province, Afghanistan, during 2010.

▼ A sniper of the French Army's 2e Régiment Etranger d'Infanterie (Foreign Legion) in Afghanistan in 2005 with his 7.62-mm (0.3-in) FR F2 bolt-action rifle with its ammunition in a 10-round box magazine.

More effective modern weapons in the same caliber (or 7.5-mm [0.295-in] in the case of the French FR-F1 and updated FR-F2) include the Swiss APR308, U.S. Desert Tactical Arms Hard Hit Stealth Recon Scout, German Heckler & Koch HK417, U.S. M110 Semi-Automatic Sniper System, Swiss SIG-Sauer SSG3000, and Chinese T93.

The standard sniper rifle of the SAS is the L96 in both its standard and updated L115 forms. The most modern version of these weapons, chambered for the 8.58-mm (0.338-in) Lapua Magnum or 7.62-mm (0.3-in) Winchester Magnum rounds, is the L115A3 version of the Accuracy International AWM with a sound suppressor, all-weather day sights with improved magnification and special night sights. The weapon is of the bolt-action type with a five-round magazine, and with the Lapua round is effective to a range of 1,640 yd (1,500 m).

There are an increasing number of larger-caliber sniper rifles chambered for the 12.7-mm (0.5-in) round originally created for the M2 heavy machine gun. A good example, used by the SAS as the L121A1 and also operated by several other special forces, is the Accuracy International AW50, which weighs 33 lb (15 kg) complete with its bipod, and is a bolt-action type firing from a five-round magazine out to an effective range of 1,640 yd (1,500 m) or more.

When firing armor-piercing ammunition, the AW50 can engage many types of soft and hard targets. Vehicles can be disabled with a strategically placed shot to the engine, as can parked aircraft and even light armored vehicles. The AW50 is also an excellent weapon ideal for the counter-sniper role as its bullet can penetrate the enemy marksman's cover.

# SEMI-AUTOMATIC WEAPONS

The two other types of personal weapon used by the members of the world's special forces are the sub-machine gun and pistol, both intended for the short-range role and now almost invariably firing the 9-mm (0.354-in) Parabellum round.

An automatic carbine, designed to fire pistol cartridges, the sub-machine gun combines the automatic fire of the machine gun with the cartridge of a pistol. It is an ideal weapon for close-quarter fighting in which a burst of fire from a short and easily handled weapon is altogether more useful than the single shot from a longer, more unwieldy assault rifle firing an intermediate power round.

There are many types of sub-machine gun, but the weapon preferred by many of the soldiers of the world's special forces is the Heckler & Koch MP5 in any of its many variants of different lengths, with fixed or folding stocks and, on occasion, provision for a suppressor. The MP5A2 with a fixed stock may be taken as exemplifying the breed: it is 26.8 in (680 mm) long with a 225-mm (8.86-in) barrel, weighs 6.55 lb (2.97 kg) loaded, and fires at the rate of 800 rounds per minute from a 15- or 30-round box magazine.

The pistol may be seen as representing merely a last line of personal defense, but it is also an invaluable weapon in urban situations (especially during counter-terrorist operations) and in the close protection role when initial concealment and then rapid drawing and use are all-important. The two types of pistol are the revolver and the semi-automatic weapon. Despite its greater mechanical reliability, the revolver has almost entirely disappeared from military use as the semi-automatic weapon is less bulky and provides a larger magazine capacity than the revolver's six-round chamber.

▲ An explosive ordnance disposal technician of the U.S. Army fires his 9-mm (0.354-in) semi-automatic pistol at a military shooting range in Bahrain.

▲ The 9-mm (0.354-in) Beretta 92 is used by the U.S. forces as the M9, largely for self-protection purposes.

▶ Soldiers of the U.S. Army undertake tactical range training with the 9-mm (0.354-in) M9 pistol, which has a 15-round detachable box magazine and an effective range of 55 yd (50 m).

Typical of the semi-automatic pistols in service with special forces is a Swiss weapon, the SIG-Sauer P226, which is offered in a large number of sub-variants. The P226 is a recoil-operated handgun firing from a mechanically locked breech, and is 7.7 in (196 mm) long and 34 oz (964 g) in weight with a loaded magazine. Enclosed in the grip, the magazine can hold between 15 and 20 rounds. Another well-favored pistol is the Austrian Glock 19, which works on the short recoil system and also fires from a mechanically locked breech. The weapon is classified as compact, with a length of 6.85 in (17.4 cm) and unloaded weight of 21 oz (595 g), and its standard magazine is of 15-round capacity, although the magazines of other Glock pistols, in capacities up to 33 rounds, can also be used. Many pistols can be fitted with a suppressor.

▲　The 9-mm (0.345-in) Heckler & Koch MP5 sub-machine gun is generally fielded with a tactical flashlight below its muzzle for continued viability in conditions of low ambient light.

▲　Special forces personnel carry one of the weapons most favored by such forces, the MP5 sub-machine gun, here in its MP5A3 form. The weapon uses a 15-, 30-, or 32- round detachable box magazine.

◀　Armed with a 9-mm MP5A5E sub-machine gun, a U.S. Navy SEAL gives the thumbs-up after the completion of a training mission. SEALs provided boarding teams for ships of the Maritime Interception Force in their enforcement of U.N. sanctions against Iraq during Operation "Desert Storm" in 1991.

# OPERATION "CHAVIN DE HUANTAR"—THE LIMA EMBASSY SIEGE (APRIL 22, 1997)

The Japanese embassy crisis began on December 17, 1996 in Lima, the Peruvian capital when, led by Néstor Cerpa Cartolini, 14 Túpac Amaru Revolutionary Movement (MRTA) members entered the official residence of the Japanese ambassador, Morihisa Aoki, and took hostage hundreds of international diplomats, Peruvian government and military officials, and Peruvian businessmen attending a party. The revolutionaries' demands included the release of MRTA members from prison, a revision of the government's free market reforms, modification of Japan's foreign assistance program and reform of Peru's cruel and inhumane prisons. Most of the hostages were released as lengthy negotiations started. After being held for 126 days, the remaining 72 Japanese and Peruvian hostages were freed on April 22, 1997 in a Peruvian special forces assault in which one hostage, two commandos, and all the MRTA revolutionaries died.

A team of 142 Peruvian special forces personnel under the command of Lt. Colonel Juan Valer Sandoval was brought together as an extemporized unit for this operation, codenamed "Chavín de Huantar" after a Peruvian archaeological site celebrated for its subterranean passages. Training took place in a replica of the residence built at a military base, and here the assault team rehearsed every aspect of the operation. Light-colored clothing was steadily ferried in to the hostages in order that they could be readily distinguished from the dark-clad insurgents during the assault. Miniature microphones and video cameras were smuggled into the residence in books, bottles of water, and table games, and military

▼ *These are men of the Peruvian Army's "Chavin de Huantar" elite commando group, which was used in the Japanese embassy siege.*

◀▼ *Peruvian actors re-enact for a TV drama the intense last stages of the Peruvian special forces operation to rescue 71 of the final 72 hostages on April 22, 1997. The hostages had been held for 126 days at the Japanese embassy in Lima after being seized, together with many other diplomatic representatives, by a force of 14 guerrillas of the Túpac Amaru Revolutionary Movement (MRTA) on the night of December 17, 1996. The seizure occurred during a reception attended by some 700 guests, including diplomats, politicians, and the Peruvian foreign minister, among others. Most of the hostages were released during the siege.*

officers among the hostages were given the responsibility for placing these devices in secure locations around the house. Eavesdropping on the MRTA members then allowed the planners to monitor and assess the revolutionaries. It was clear that the revolutionaries had made effective security arrangements, and were on a high level of alert during the hours of darkness. However, early every afternoon, eight of the MRTA members, including the four leaders, played indoor football for about one hour.

At 3:23 p.m. on April 22, 1997, the commandos exploded three charges in different ground-floor rooms. The first charge detonated in the center of the room in which the football game was being played, killing two of the men involved in the game and a female onlooker. Through the hole blown through the exterior wall, 30 commandos stormed into the building and hunted the surviving MRTA members in order to stop them pulling back onto the first floor. At the same time 20 commandos launched a direct assault through the front door, guarded by two female revolutionaries, to link with their comrades inside the waiting room and take possession of the main staircase to the first floor. Another group of commandos placed ladders against the rear walls of the building.

In the final prong of this well-coordinated assault, another group of commandos emerged from two tunnels that Peruvian engineers

had secretly dug from the residence's rear gardens to a spot under the building, and rushed up the waiting ladders. Their tasks were to blow out a grenade-proof door on the first floor, through which the hostages were to be led, and to make two openings in the roof so that they could kill any MRTA members on the first floor before they could start to execute the hostages.

The whole operation proceeded according to plan, although one Peruvian hostage, two commandos (including Sandoval), and all 14 MRTA guerrillas died.

# COMBaT KNIVes

In situations where silence is imperative, the preferred weapon of special forces soldiers is the combat knife. The Mk 3 Knife is the standard knife for the U.S. Navy SEALs, and in fact made its first appearance in World War II. The Mk 3 Knife has a stainless steel blade 6.5 in (16.5 cm) long with a saw-tooth back, a black oxide finish and a high impact plastic handle and sheath. The strength and basic durability of the knife are indicated by the fact that its butt can be used as a hammer and its blade as a prybar. The blade holds its edge well.

Manufactured since 2002 in the U.S.A. by Chris Reeves Knives, the Green Beret is a fixed-blade knife with single-row serrations and a stainless steel spearpoint blade, and is offered in 5.5- and 7-in (13.9- and 17.7-cm) blade lengths. A version of this knife with special engraving and a serial number on the blade, known as the Yarborough Knife, is presented to every graduate of the U.S. Army Special Forces Qualification Course.

▼◄ Soldiers of one of the U.S. Army's Ranger units demonstrate an element of knife fighting technique during the African Land Force Summit of 2010.

▲   The combat knife used by the U.S. Marine Corps.

▲   Special forces have considerable discretion in the selection of a tactical knife.

◄   Most modern combat knife techniques find their origins in World War II. Here men of a U.S. Marine Raider battalion in that conflict demonstrate how to disarm a knife-armed enemy.

It is not uncommon for special forces soldiers to buy their own knives from the huge selection of combat and fighting knives available on the commercial market. This allows the soldier to select and use precisely the type of knife he believes suits him best. Spetsnaz soldiers are well trained in the use of the combat knife, and are skilled exponents with the bayonet-knife of the AK series of assault rifles.

▲   The Chris Reeve Knives "Survival Knife" is a custom-made piece that paved the way for the same company's well known One Piece range of fighting knives.

▶   This is the Chris Reeve Knives One Piece Knife Mk IV, introduced in 1983 as the first One Piece production item.

# ROCKET WEAPONS

Although special forces are generally noted for their small-scale, "value-added" operations using comparatively light weapons, there are nonetheless instances when a target of notably high value can be destroyed by small forces with more advanced, yet still comparatively cheap, weapons, such as rockets and light missiles. Notwithstanding the modest number of successes gained by the Taliban in Afghanistan using rocket-propelled grenades against U.S. helicopters flying at low level and therefore with little time or speed for evasive maneuver, the rocket is generally effective only against ground targets, while the light missile can be employed successfully against both ground and air targets.

▲   A Romanian soldier aims an AG-7 (license-made RPG-7) during an exercise in 2010. After the AK-47 series of assault rifles, the RPG-7 is perhaps the most widely used insurgency weapon.

The rocket weapon most commonly associated with light, and by extension special, forces is the rocket-propelled grenade. This is a shoulder-fired antitank weapon, which fires a rocket equipped with an explosive warhead and stabilized in flight by fins. Some RPG types can be reloaded and others are single-use weapons. All are designed primarily for use against armored vehicles, such as armored personnel carriers, and against fixed fortifications.

◀ *Men of an allied unit are instructed how to use a rocket-propelled grenade launcher by a soldier of the Romanian 341st Infantry Battalion during a cross-training event at the Bardia firing range in Iraq during 2008.*

▶ *A soldier holds the launcher unit of a rocket-propelled grenade system with an unfired rocket on the ground in front of him. The RPG-7 and some of its successors are widely used by each side in Afghanistan.*

◀◀ *A Bulgarian soldier scans the battlefield ahead of him with his RPG-7 rocket-propelled grenade launcher during "military operations in urban terrain" training. The launcher is fitted with a "red dot" reflex sight.*

# OPERATION "KHUKRI"—THE INDIANS IN SIERRA LEONE
## (JULY 15-16, 2000)

Operation "Khukri" was a rescue mission undertaken by the Indian Army's Para Commandos special forces unit in the course of the U.N.-mandated international peacekeeping mission in war-torn Sierra Leone, conducted by the U.N. Mission in Sierra Leone (UNAMSIL). Sierra Leonean rebel forces of the Revolutionary United Front (RUF) had surrounded and taken under siege some 223 men of the 5th Battalion, 8th Gorkha Rifles, in the form of the 1st Mechanized Company and 1st Motorized Rifle Company, at Kailahun in the eastern part of Sierra Leone.

"Khukri" was schemed in six phases: the use of U.N. airlift capability for the secret concentration of the ground forces at Kenema and Daru; a ground offensive from Daru and Kenema and a breakout from Kailahun; the simultaneous engagement of key RUF locations by attack helicopters and artillery; the helicopter delivery of selected troops, under attack helicopter cover, at key locations along the road axis to secure them for the passage of the land column; the early link of both columns at Pendembu and their evacuation by air; and the return of all vehicle columns from Pendembu for redeployment at Daru on the completion of the air evacuation. The security of Daru was to be ensured at all times.

▼ *As an elite element of the Indian Army, the "Para Commandos" are among the best equipped of the Indian forces.*

◀◀ Another high-grade element within the Indian Army is the Gorkha Rifles, who are highly motivated and well trained.

◀ Children pass an Indian soldier of a unit serving with the U.N. peacekeeping force in Sierra Leone at a checkpoint in Freetown in May 2000.

The initial phase of "Khukri" started on July 13 as the combat elements of the relief force were airlifted from the UNAMSIL main bases in Freetown and Hastings to Kenema and Daru. This was completed by the evening of the following day. At daybreak on July 15, two helicopter landing sites outside Kailahun were secured by the Gurkhas, and at 6:15 a.m. two Chinook helicopters, guided by men of the SAS's D Squadron who had been monitoring the RUF for some time, touched down 1¼ miles (2 km) to the south of Kailahun, and landed men of the 2nd Parachute Battalion to fight off any RUF soldiers attempting to halt the forthcoming breakout. The Chinooks then continued to Kailahun and at 6:20 a.m. collected 33 sick Gurkhas, 11 military observers, and important stores for air movement back to Freetown.

Once the Chinooks had departed, the two companies at Kailahun began their assault on the town. Mech-1 captured the town square, to be used for forming up, and Mot-1, an RUF checkpoint on the road from Kailahun to Daru. The Gurkha column then moved out. At 7:30 a.m. the 5/8th Gorkha Rifles advanced from Daru, now held by two Nigerian companies. Simultaneously, the Quick-Reaction Company (QRC) was airlifted by six Mi-8 helicopters in two waves to take and hold key bridges. At 07:38 a.m. the column from Kailahun

met 2nd Para and began moving toward Giehun. Mi-35 helicopter gunships arrived overhead at about 09:30 a.m.

At 9:45 a.m. the 18th Grenadiers were airlifted to a point northeast of Giehun to await the arrival of the column from Kailahun. Linking with this by 10:30 a.m. the combined Indian force entered Giehun. An hour later a company from the Kailahun column was airlifted to Daru. By 12:30 p.m. the Daru column of the 5/8th Gorkha Rifles had met the QRC after fighting its way through Bewabu and Kuiva, and prepared to attack Pendembu. This was the headquarters of the RUF's 1st Brigade, and a hard fight seemed likely. An Mi-35 began the engagement by attacking known RUF positions, then Mech-2 moved through the town to occupy its northern part, and Mot-2 started a house-to-house search. There were several firefights, but only the RUF suffered losses. With the town secured, a column was despatched to link with the remainder of the Kailahun column, which was then escorted into Pendembu.

From 8:15 a.m. on July 16, Mi-8 helicopters airlifted the company of the 2nd Para (SF) and most of the 18th Grenadiers to Daru. At much the same time, to the north of Pendembu, an Mi-35 fired on RUF forces moving toward the town. By 10:30 a.m. the Mi-8 helicopters had completed their work, and the 5/8th Gorkha Rifles and the QRC (less two platoons) left Pendembu with Mot-2 in the lead. Mech-2 remained to the north to provide security under cover of a single Mi-35. On the journey to Daru, the column was ambushed at a number of places. Mot-2 was hit outside Bewabu and the 18th Grenadiers outside Kuiva. A vehicle carrying ammunition was hit and destroyed by a rocket-propelled grenade, and a Chetak helicopter evacuated the single casualty. At 5:30 p.m. the column reached Daru to end what had been a very successful joint operation.

# LOCAL DEFENSE

The most ubiquitous rocket-propelled grenade weapons are the Russian series that date from Soviet times. Those currently in service with an antipersonnel warhead are the reloadable RPG-7V2 with thermobaric rockets (i.e. producing a blast wave of longer duration than is produced by condensed explosives), the one-shot RPG-27 with a thermobaric rocket, and the reloadable RPG-29 with a thermobaric rocket; those with antiarmor warheads are the reloadable RPG-16 with a more accurate and longer-ranged rocket, one-shot RPG-18, one-shot RPG-22, one-shot RPG-26, one-shot RPG-27, one-shot RPG-28, reloadable RPG-29, and one-shot RPG-30.

Western counterparts include three U.S. weapons (one-shot M72 Light Antitank Weapon, reloadable Mk 153 Shoulder-launched Multi-purpose Assault Weapon, and one-shot M136 AT4) and a number of European types, including the British LAW80, Italian Folgore, and a widely used Swedish recoilless rifle, the reloadable Carl Gustav. This weapon is 43 in (110 cm) long and weighs 20.5 lb (9.3 kg), and fires an 84-mm (3.31-in) rocket. The type is known in U.S. service, where it is fielded by several special forces, as the M3 Medium Anti-Armor Weapon System. It fires HE (high explosive) dual-purpose, HE antitank, HE illuminating smoke, and flechette rounds.

▲   *A U.S. Marine of a low-altitude air defense battalion fires an FIM-92A Stinger short-range surface-to-air missile during training.*

▶▶   *A U.S. Marine with a field radio indicates the direction of a target aircraft to the operator of an FIM-92 Stinger SAM launcher.*

▼   *A Starstreak SAM launcher is here seen in a more advanced set-up on western Dartmoor, England, during a Royal Marine training exercise.*

These rocket weapons are, of course, unguided. Additional capability is provided over greater ranges by man-portable surface-to-surface (antitank/bunker) and surface-to-air missiles. Antitank missiles are generally too heavy and offer too high a level of capability to be cost-effective for special forces use, but some of the lighter types which have seen service include the French Eryx and U.S. M47 Dragon.

Man-portable SAMs that have been used by special forces include the British Blowpipe and Starstreak, Soviet SA-7 and its successors, and most significantly the U.S. FIM-92 Stinger that was widely used by Afghan resistance fighters against the Soviet invaders in the 1980s.

◀ *Men of the Canadian 129th Anti-Aircraft Defense Battery wait with a Blowpipe surface-to-air missile during training in 1987. The men are wearing nuclear, biological, and chemical (NBC) protective gear.*

# GRENADES

The grenade is a hand-thrown bomb with a delay-action fuse. It can be thrown through an opening or lobbed over an obstacle to land in an enemy's position. There are two basic types of grenade: non-lethal and lethal. The former include smoke, irritant gas, and stun grenades, the last of these developed for the Special Air Service to temporarily neutralize terrorists' combat effectiveness by disorienting them. The flash of light as the "flashbang" detonates momentarily overloads all the light-sensitive cells in the eye, making it impossible for the affected person to see for about five seconds, and its very loud blast adds to the incapacitation by disturbing the fluid in the ear. The U.S. special forces use the basically similar M84 and M141 grenades, and the Israelis have a comparable grenade.

Lethal grenades are filled with thermite to create intense burning, or explosive inside a pre-fragmented casing to cause death or injury by blast and/or high-speed fragments. Examples of the thermite grenade are the U.S. M14, and of the explosive grenade the U.S. M67. This latter weighs 14 oz (397 g) and has a safety clip for ease and safety of handling. The M67 can be thrown about 35 yd (32 m), and has a four- to five-second fuse that ignites explosives packed inside a round body. Steel fragments are provided by the shattered grenade body and produce a fatality radius of 5.5 yd (5 m) and a casualty radius of 16.5 yd (15 m), though some fragments can be hurled out to 275 yd (250 m).

◄ In special forces operations the destruction of rockets, mortars and other ordnance items can often be accomplished with a cache of grenades or explosives, as here in Iraq.

►▲ At Camp Lemonier in Djibouti during 2008, a U.S. Marine assigned to the 3rd Low Altitude Air Defense Battalion prepares to throw a dummy hand grenade and also instructs a trainee before throwing the M67 fragmentation grenade at the firing range. Training also involved the M203 40-mm (1.57 in) grenade launcher and AT-4 antitank/bunker rocket.

▲ At Camp Lemonier in Djibouti a U.S. Marine throws an M67 fragmentation grenade on the live-firing range.

▲ U.S. Marines take cover as the M67 explodes. The grenade's lethal blast radius is 16 ft (5 m), but its fragments fly considerably farther.

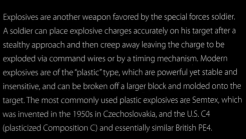

▲ This Iraqi house in New Ubaydi contained a weapons cache and, fearing booby traps, U.S. Marines demolished it with five sticks of C4 explosive.

Explosives are another weapon favored by the special forces soldier. A soldier can place explosive charges accurately on his target after a stealthy approach and then creep away leaving the charge to be exploded via command wires or by a timing mechanism. Modern explosives are of the "plastic" type, which are powerful yet stable and insensitive, and can be broken off a larger block and molded onto the target. The most commonly used plastic explosives are Semtex, which was invented in the 1950s in Czechoslovakia, and the U.S. C4 (plasticized Composition C) and essentially similar British PE4.

# OPERATION "BARRAS"—THE SAS AND SBS IN SIERRA LEONE (SEPTEMBER 10, 2000)

In 2000, a United Nations peacekeeping force in Sierra Leone, then torn by a violent civil war, included a British element. On August 25, soldiers of the Royal Irish Regiment were making a vehicle patrol of the Occra hills, a forested area notorious for its banditry. Here Major Alan Marshall's 11-man patrol was ambushed, surrounded, and forced to surrender. The men were held hostage by a rebel group known as the West Side Boys. Their leader was the 24-year-old Foday Kallay.

On September 3, some nine days after their capture, five of the British soldiers were released in exchange for medical supplies and a satellite phone. Negotiations for the release of the remaining men then stalled and Kallay threatened to kill the hostages. It was at this stage that Tony Blair, the British prime minister, authorized a rescue

mission. The location had been determined by MI6 at Rokel Creek, where the West Side Boys were camped with the hostage British soldiers held in the village of Geberi Bana on the creek's northern bank opposite the rebel camp. The nearby villages of Magbeni and Forodugu were also in rebel hands.

D Squadron of the 22nd SAS, augmented by a number of men of the Special Boat Service, was secretly flown into Sierra Leone to prepare the rescue mission. When it was learned that that there might be hundreds of rebels in Magbeni, the decision was taken to

▼ *British soldiers of the 1st Battalion, The Parachute Regiment, patrol in the areas of the United Nations compound in Freetown, Sierra Leone, May 9, 2000.*

◀ *Helicopters, such as this Boeing Chinook HC.Mk 2 of the Royal Air Force, provide mobility and speed of deployment that cannot be matched by the poorly equipped irregulars of African conflicts, who also have little real understanding of advanced warfare concepts.*

▼ *Specialized vessels, such as the Royal Fleet Auxiliary's logistic landing ship Sir Percivale, provides a safe base and logistic back-up for special forces operating in a low-intensity conflict against poorly trained irregular (often little more than bandit) forces.*

bring in the 1st Battalion, The Parachute Regiment, in the form of the 130 men of A Company boosted by elements of the Support Company and the HQ Company, to attack Magbeni.

Using inflatable raiding craft and under cover of night, Boat Troop personnel, along with marines of the SBS marines, moved upriver to deliver one six-man and one four-man observation teams. These teams moved stealthily into position as close as they could to the rebel positions and sent back vital intelligence on the strength, disposition, and morale of the rebel forces.

The objectives of Operation "Barras" were to rescue the six men of the Royal Irish Regiment along with their liaison officer, capture or kill Kallay, recover or destroy the captured Land Rovers, and suppress and/or drive off the rebels at Magbeni.

At 6:16 a.m. on September 10, the operation started with the lift-off, from Freetown airport, of the helicopter force. This comprised three Boeing Chinook HC.Mk 2 heavy-lift helicopters of the Royal Air Force's No. 7 Squadron (two carrying 70 men of the integrated SAS/SBS fire teams for delivery onto two landing zones, and one carrying paratroopers), two Westland Lynx AH. Mk 7 armed escort and close air support helicopters of the Army Air Corps' No. 657 Squadron, and one Mil Mi-24 "Hind" manned by friendly local forces.

All three Chinook helicopters went into the hover over their LZs at 6:30 a.m., and as the SAS/SBS fire teams fast-roped down to the ground, the Lynx helicopters opened fire on the Magbeni camp with their Minigun multi-barrel machine guns. The first wave of

paratroopers was inserted by the third Chinook, which quickly flew back to base to pick up the second wave.

The speed and deafening power of the British assault, together with the firepower of the Lynx helicopters, was entirely successful. The SAS hostage rescue team was able to find and secure the seven hostages as the combined SAS and SBS fire teams executed their plan, clearing buildings and setting up defensive positions. On the other side of Rokel Creek, the paratroopers were in fierce action with the now thoroughly roused rebels, and a heavy firefight developed.

The hostages were evacuated to the Royal Fleet Auxiliary *Sir Percivale* in Freetown harbor at about 7:00 a.m. Most of the fighting was over by 8:00 a.m., but it was about 2:00 p.m. before it was safe enough to call in the Chinook helicopters to extract the last men of the assault teams. The SAS had lost one man killed and four wounded, while the paratroops had suffered eight wounded, including one man seriously hurt. At least 25 rebels were confirmed killed. The West Side Boys' leader, Kallay, was captured in the raid, and the three Land Rover vehicles were also recovered.

# NIGHT VISION DEVICES

Night vision devices offer their users a distinct advantage over troops lacking such equipment when it comes to nocturnal navigation, target detection and acquisition, and combat. A night vision device is an optical instrument allowing images to be produced in levels of light approaching total darkness. They are most frequently used by the military, and the term is generally applied to the complete unit, which comprises an image intensifier tube, a protective and generally water-resistant housing, and some type of mounting system. Many night vision devices also include "sacrificial" lenses, to protect the primary lenses from possible damage, IR illuminators, and telescopic lenses to magnify the image.

◄ Invaluable tactical advantages are provided to soldiers equipped with night vision equipment. Seen in 2009, this U.S. soldier is wearing the PSQ-20 Enhanced Night Vision Goggles, which was the first helmet-mounted device to combine image intensification and infrared technologies.

▲ The clip-on PVS-29 night sight provides snipers with an enhanced targeting capability offering long-range night sniping possibilities.

▶ U.S. Army, Afghan National Army, and Afghan Border Police personnel establish a perimeter around a helicopter landing zone in the mountains surrounding Shaleh, Afghanistan, during "Operation Enduring Freedom" in 2008.

Night vision devices have developed though five generations since their first appearance in the late 1930s. A good example of the most recent generation is the U.S. PVS-22. Otherwise known as the Universal Night Sight, and designed and made by FLIR Systems, the PVS-22 is a lightweight unit designed for installation on any weapon with a Picatinny rail (or tactical rail) bracket to provide a standardized bore-sighted mounting platform. The PVS-22 can be fitted on any weapon already fitted with a telescopic sight or red dot sight, being mounted ahead of the existing scope to provide it with night vision capability. The PVS-22 can spot a standing man under starlight levels of illumination at a range beyond 545 yd (500 m).

▲ Seen through a night-viewing device that provides notably good definition, men of a U.S. Army unit depart Forward Operating Base Falcon, Iraq, in a Boeing CH-47 Chinook helicopter during 2009.

◀◀ A qualification training instructor tests his night vision equipment before supervising night training with the M240 machine gun.

▶ Seen through a night vision device, students of a Basic Underwater Demolition/SEAL class carry an inflatable boat toward the surf during a first-phase navigation training exercise. The first phase is an eight-week course that trains, prepares and selects SEAL candidates based on physical conditioning, competency in and on the water, mental tenacity, and facility for team work.

# Laser Designators

One of the most important functions of special forces soldiers is to find mobile or concealed high-value targets and then "paint" them with laser light so that the target can be attacked by precision-guided weapons launched from aircraft or land-based weapons systems.

A laser designator is a laser light source, which is used to designate a target, the laser light being reflected by the target and providing the illumination on which laser-guided weapons home. Laser-guided weapons include bombs, missiles or specialized artillery munitions, such as the U.S. Paveway, French BGL, Russian KAB-500L, and several Israeli series of bombs, the AGM-114 Hellfire air-to-surface missile, or the MGM-140 Army Tactical Missile System projectile. When a target is marked by a designator, the beam is invisible and is not continuous but rather a series of coded pulses. These signals are reflected by the target into the sky, where they are detected by the seeker on the

◄ *Calibration tests for support of laser designator and rangefinder test sets. The laser transmitter supports standards and so keeps ordnance on target.*

▼ *The Lightweight Laser Designator Rangefinder locates targets for fire support teams and forward observers.*

laser-guided munition, which then steers itself toward the center of the reflected signal. Unless the crew or occupants of the target have access to laser detection equipment, or physically see or hear the approaching warplane, it is extremely difficult for them to tell whether they are being marked or not. Laser designators work best in clear atmospheric conditions, for cloud, rain, and smoke can degrade or even render impossible effective laser designation.

The standard laser designator used by U.S. and some allied forces is the PED-1 Lightweight Laser Designator Rangefinder (LLDR), permitting them to designate targets for close air support and attack warplanes. Designed and manufactured by Northrop Grumman, the PED-1 employs an eye-safe laser wavelength, recognizes targets, accurately ranges the target, and fixes target locations for laser-guided, GPS-guided, and conventional munitions. In many respects, therefore, the tripod-mounted PED-1 can be regarded as a force multiplication equipment, because it enhances the capabilities of more distant conventional weapons by the provision of accurate range and targeting information.

▲  *Laser designators are vital in ensuring that laser-guided weapons, such as Hellfire (seen here) and Griffin missiles, locate and strike the intended target.*

▼  *Another laser-guided weapon extensively used against insurgent forces in Afghanistan is the Paveway free-fall guided bomb, the green weapon under the wing of this F-16 warplane.*

# U.S. RANGERS AND THE BATTLE OF TORA BORA (DECEMBER 12-17, 2001)

In October 2001, the United States and its allies began military operations in Afghanistan in an effort to destroy the al-Qaeda terrorist movement operating from that country, and also to topple the Taliban fundamentalist regime and install a democratic government. By November 2001, the U.S.A. had come to believe that the al-Qaeda forces and its leader, Osama bin Laden, were based in the Tora Bora complex of caves within the White Mountains of eastern Afghanistan, near the Khyber Pass into northwestern Pakistan. Tora Bora, able to accommodate up to 1,000 persons and believed to contain a very large cache of weapons left over from the *mujahidin* campaign against the Soviets in the 1980s, also included outposts created by the enlargement and strengthening of natural caves achieved with the assistance of the CIA in the early 1980s.

On December 3, a group of 20 U.S. special force soldiers was airlifted into the area by helicopter to support the forthcoming operation, and two days later Afghan militiamen took the ground below the mountain caves and established tank positions from which to shell the defenses of the al-Qaeda fighters, who pulled back with their weapons to fortified positions higher up the mountain. Tribal militiamen opposed to the Taliban regime maintained their advance through this difficult terrain with the aid of air attacks coordinated by U.S. and British special forces. The al-Qaeda forces then negotiated a truce with a local militia commander to give them time to surrender their weapons, though it is now believed that this was a ruse to buy time for senior al-Qaeda leaders, including bin Laden, to escape into the tribal areas of Pakistan.

Combat restarted on December 12, the combination of militiamen, allied special forces and allied air power enabling progress into the cave and bunker positions extending through this mountain region.

▲ *U.S. special forces entered Kandahar airport on December 15, 2001, and here joined U.S. Marines in setting up a base of operations and a detention camp for al-Qaeda prisoners captured in the Tora Bora campaign.*

▶ *Men of the Afghan National Army and U.S. Marines disembark from the rear of a U.S. Army Boeing CH-47 Chinook in Afghanistan's rugged Tora Bora mountains.*

The U.S. contribution was about 50 men of the 1st Special Forces Operational Detachment D (SFOD-D or Delta Force), the 5th Special Forces Group, the 160th Special Operations Air Regiment (Airborne) and the CIA's Special Activities Division (SAD), while the British contributed 13 men, including 12 marines of the Special Boat Squadron, and the Germans an element of the Kommando Spezialkräfte special operations force. As the al-Qaeda and Taliban forces continued to be forced back in the whole region, the main thrust of the U.S. effort became increasingly focused on Tora Bora. Some 2,000 local militiamen, organized and led by U.S. special forces and SAD operatives, were concentrated in the area for a decisive attack even as U.S. and allied warplanes continued to pound the supposed al-Qaeda positions with bombs and other weapons.

By December 17, the allied forces had reduced the last cave complex and either killed or captured the last al-Qaeda and Taliban defenders. The coalition allies had suffered no casualties. Those of the militia forces remain unknown, while of the al-Qaeda and Taliban forces, thought to have numbered between 300 and 1,000, some 200 had been killed. A sweep of the entire Tora Bora complex in the period up to January 2002 then found no major bunkers but merely small outpost positions and some minor training camps.

▲ *Afghan anti-Taliban fighters sit around a Russian T-55 tank while bombs explode during an attack by U.S. Air Force Boeing B-52 Stratofortress bombers on al-Qaeda positions in the Tora Bora area in December 2001.*

▶ *In December 2001, an anti-Taliban fighter looks over abandoned heavy machine gun ammunition in the remains of an al-Qaeda base located deep in the Tora Bora valley of Afghanistan. The base had been comprehensively savaged by U.S. air attack, which the Taliban remain effectively powerless to defeat.*

# GPS Navigation

Operating deep behind the enemy's lines, special forces soldiers often strike at suitable targets themselves, but they may generate even more valuable results by quickly, securely, and accurately relaying tactical and operational data to a higher command echelon. This demands that each team has precise knowledge of its own location so that a target's position can be determined with great accuracy, and a team can relay its information effectively and reliably.

The simplest way in which a special forces team can fix its own location is by means of a Global Positioning System receiver, which can be a small hand-held device that is entirely passive in its operation and, depending on the model, can provide positional accuracy to just a few feet. The GPS receivers used by the military are, of course, ruggedized to enhance their chances of survival under adverse climatic, geographical, and operational conditions, and they must be provided with an adequate number of replacement batteries to ensure continued operability throughout the team's mission.

▲ The latest versions of the PRC-112 survival radio, used largely by aircrew, have a beacon/voice mode as well as an inbuilt GPS that reports the system's position.

▲ U.S. soldiers check their course with their compasses during a foot patrol. Despite the advent of GPS navigational technology, which these soldiers also use, the basic compass remains the most reliable tool for land navigation.

◀ A U.S. Army soldier displays the dismounted combat 21st Century Land Warrior Integrated Fighting System. This includes GPS within the system's computer/radio subsystem. The man is armed with a 5.56-mm (0.219-in) M4 assault carbine.

To relay intelligence information and maintain contact with its higher command echelon, the special forces team needs radio equipment that is reliable, rugged, secure, and light enough to be man-packed, consumes the least possible power to maximize battery life, provides the transmission range required and, if possible, includes an encryption and/or burst transmission capability. Such radio equipment can be wholly terrestrial, although steadily greater use is being made of satellite-bounced communications.

▶   *The PRC-119 Single Channel Ground and Airborne Radio System transceiver is light and readily portable, and provides men, such as this Marine 2nd lieutenant, with the means to send and receive secure voice and data transmissions.*

▼   *U.S. Marines prepare to launch an RQ-14 Dragon Eye Small Unit Remote Scouting System. The air vehicle flies at an altitude of 300 to 500 ft (90 to 150 m) using GPS waypoints to navigate. The air vehicle uses onboard sensors to gather and transmit imagery back to its ground control station.*

# UNDERWATER BREATHING

As one of the primary special forces concerned with underwater operations, the U.S. Navy SEALs use three main types of underwater breathing gear, namely the open-circuit compressed air type (SCUBA), the closed-circuit (100 percent oxygen) type and the closed-circuit (mixed gas) type. Other elements of the U.S. Special Operations Forces possessing an amphibious capability also use these systems.

The SCUBA (self-contained underwater breathing apparatus) comprises tanks of compressed air worn on the diver's back. This is an open-circuit system, and so exhaled air is released into the water. SEAL delivery vehicle team divers may also use the open-circuit breathing system fed from air tanks inside swimmer delivery vehicles. The size and weight of the tanks is something of an impediment to underwater operations, and another adverse feature of the open-circuit system is the telltale column of rising bubbles which is visible to the naked eye and to infrared sensors.

▲  *U.S. Navy divers of Mobile Diving and Salvage Unit Two check their gauges during a training dive to familiarize themselves with the Mk 6 Mod 1 underwater breathing apparatus.*

◄  *A U.S. Navy diver and a SEAL delivery team operator perform SEAL Delivery Vehicle operations with a nuclear-powered missile submarine for material certification. This last allows operators to perform real-world operations anywhere in the world at any time.*

The LAR V Draeger rebreather is a closed-circuit system using 100 percent oxygen. All expelled breath is recycled into the closed circuit, where carbon dioxide is filtered out, and the result is a system that does not leave a trail of expelled bubbles. This makes it ideal for clandestine amphibious operations. With a maximum operating depth of 70 ft (21 m), the LAR V Draeger rebreather cannot be used to the depths that are possible with SCUBA systems, but the unit's relatively small size and front-worn configuration make it eminently suitable for shallow-water operation. The duration of any dive is affected by depth, water temperature, and oxygen consumption rate.

Like the LAR V Draeger, the Mk 15 and Mk 16 Closed-Circuit Mixed Gas Rebreather systems recycle the diver's expelled breath to remove the carbon dioxide but, unlike the Draeger system using pure oxygen, the Mk 15 and Mk 16 dilute the oxygen supply with another gas (typically air, but on occasion a helium/oxygen or other mix) as the diluting element. This mixture maintains a present partial pressure of oxygen level and allows the system to be used at much greater depths than the Draeger unit.

In British service, the divers of the Special Boat Service use either the LAR V Draeger system or, more recently, the Divex Shadow series of rebreather systems, which provide a dive duration of up to six hours. The Shadow is compatible with the Divex Digicom 3000m Diver Through Water Communications system and Divex Stealth Full Face Dual Mode Mask. A more advanced model, which can be used at lower depths, the Shadow Excursion, uses an oxygen/nitrox mix. The Full Face mask that comes with the Shadow can quickly interface with on-board air supplies found on swimmer delivery vehicles.

▲  U.S. Marine Corps training in combatant diving with the LAR V Draeger rebreather.

▲  A Royal Bahamas Defense Force diver conducts a security sweep along the bottom of a Jamaican coastguard vessel's hull during joint diving operations with Mobile Diving and Salvage Unit Two in Jamaican waters in 2011. Counter-terrorist operations are now multi-nation collaborations over much of the world.

◀  Basic Underwater Demolition/SEAL candidates check their underwater breathing apparatuses for proper ventilation and safety before participating in dive training. Combat swimmers use both open-circuit systems that leave a trail of rising bubbles, and closed-circuit rebreather systems, which do not, and therefore are tactically better for the performance of clandestine operations.

# OPERATION "ANACONDA" – SPECIAL FORCES IN THE SHAHI-KOT VALLEY (MARCH 1-8, 2002)

The first major engagement between U.S. and allied forces against al-Qaeda and the Taliban in Afghanistan after the Battle of Tora Bora in December 2001, Operation "Anaconda" was undertaken by U.S. military forces and CIA paramilitary officers, together with other elements of the allied coalition, collaborating with Afghan forces in an effort to eliminate the al-Qaeda and Taliban forces in the Shahi-Kot valley and Arma mountains. In overall terms, in the period between March 2 and 18, some 1,700 air-delivered U.S. troops and 1,000 Afghan militiamen were engaged in combat with a force of between 300 and 1,000 al-Qaeda and Taliban fighters to secure and hold the valley and the mountains above it. The U.S. forces estimated that they killed at least 500 of the al-Qaeda and Taliban fighters, but this is probably a major overestimation of their success.

In late January 2002, the coalition planned an assault in the Shahi-Kot valley: the position was to be attacked by Task Force "Hammer" (Afghan forces with U.S. special forces advisers), while Task Force "Anvil" (other more conventional units) landed in the mountains to the east to prevent escape into Pakistan. Special operations teams of the Advanced Force Operations under the command of Lt. Colonel Peter Blaber were to provide local reconnaissance.

▼ *Part of a U.S. Special Forces Hummer-mounted convoy drives up a mountain pass in Afghanistan. Special Forces were involved in Operation "Anaconda" in eastern Afghanistan to assist hundreds of U.S. and Canadian conventional troops in the mountainous region to search for Taliban and al-Qaeda fighters.*

◄ *Men of the U.S. Marines and the U.S. Army's 10th Mountain Division depart from their Sikorsky H-53 Super Stallion helicopter to begin setting up a forward arming and refueling point for helicopters on March 14, 2002 near the Shahi-Kot valley in eastern Afghanistan.*

▼ *Canadian soldiers of a battalion of Princess Patricia's Light Infantry hold their positions on March 15, 2002 during a combat mission in the Shahi-Kot mountains as part of Operation "Anaconda."*

The operation began on March 2, with the planned movement of TF "Hammer" into the valley, but this was stalled before even entering the valley. At 6:30 a.m. on the same day, helicopters delivered the first wave of TF "Anvil" to the eastern and northern edges of the valley. The men of the 10th Mountain and 101st Airborne Divisions were attacked almost immediately, and pinned down by heavy fire. It was already clear that the opposition strength was greater than estimated.

The Battle of Takur Ghar started on the following day. During the late evening, Blaber was informed by Brigadier General Gregory Trebon, the TF "Anvil" commander, that two SEAL teams (Mako 30 and 31) were to be inserted to establish an observation point at each end of the Shahi-Kot valley. Mako 30 would move to the Takur Ghar peak commanding the southern approach to the valley. For time reasons, the insertion was shifted from 1,425 yd (1,300 m) east of the peak to the peak itself, which air reconnaissance reported free of opposition. The team was delayed by helicopter engine problems, and thus did not approach the peak until shortly after 3:00 a.m. on March 4. As the Boeing MH-47 Chinook prepared to land, it was hit by two rocket-propelled grenades, which caused one engine to fail and one of the SEALs to fall off the lowered rear ramp. Another Chinook later landed Mako 30, which came under immediate fire. A U.S.A.F. combat controller was killed and two SEALs wounded, and Mako 30 was forced off the peak. The team did manage to establish communications with the AFO teams around Takur Ghar.

Communication difficulties now afflicted the progress of the quick-reaction force of 19 Rangers, a tactical air control party, and the three men of a U.S.A.F. special tactics team carried by two Chinooks. At about 6:10 a.m. one Chinook neared the peak and stated to take fire: a Minigunner was killed and a rocket-propelled grenade then hit the helicopter, destroying the starboard engine and forcing the helicopter to crash-land. As the Rangers and special tactics team disembarked, three men were killed. The surviving crew and quick-reaction force took cover on a hillock as the firing intensified. Earlier diverted, the second Chinook arrived with the rest of the quick-reaction force at 6:25 a.m.. With the help of the new arrivals and close air support, the force was finally able to consolidate its position on the peak, but its position remained precarious.

An attack at about 12:00 p.m. mortally wounded an American and, as recovery from the peak was deemed impossible, Mako 30 and the quick-reaction force were ordered to move down the mountain, where they established defenses and tried to keep the wounded warm. Finally, at about 8:00 p.m. the surviving Americans were airlifted out.

# CHAPTER 6

▲ U.S. Marines prepare to jump from an H-53 Sea Stallion helicopter during a parachute training evolution.

# COMBAT SCENARIOS

# HIJACK RESCUE

The conventional solider is trained to operate in what is essentially one primary, though wide-ranging, role. This is not the case with members of the world's special forces. They are more highly trained and tasked with a larger—and somewhat less well defined—number of roles. These may overlap to a degree, inasmuch as a set of skills, techniques and, perhaps most importantly, mental flexibility and strength can be applicable to all, but each role demands specific training that emphasizes the appropriate military tactics in combination with an ability to "think on one's feet." A special forces soldier must be able to analyze an emerging situation rapidly and logically, and adapt flexibly to the situation rather than just reacting along pre-trained lines.

Nowhere is this more important than in the hostage and hijack rescue roles. Sometimes the hostage taker or hijacker may have a criminal motive, such as extorting ransom money, in which case preservation of his own life is a major factor that may persuade him to surrender rather than die. However, hostage takers and hijackers are often driven by ideological factors and such intense beliefs that they may be readier to take the victim's life and be killed themselves so they may be acclaimed as martyrs for a cause.

▲◄ A soldier of the Spanish special forces searches a role player on board a combat stores ship during an exercise devoted to the tactics and implementation to be used during the boarding of a vessel that has refused to halt and be examined.

◄ *A four-man tactical squad of German Panzergrenadier soldiers from the 92nd Mechanized Infantry Training Battalion 92 practice the tactic of forcing an entry into a house.*

The objective of any hostage taker or hijacker must be properly established before any practical rescue plans can be made. Then the nature of the precise tactical scenario must also be taken into consideration. Hostage taking and hijacking can take place almost anywhere, but it is quite likely that the hostage taker and his victim will eventually end up in a building, while the hijacker and his victim will probably be in some sort of vehicle, perhaps an airliner, train, or ship. In either case it is vital that the nature and layout of the building or vehicle should be known accurately and detailed building plans or vehicle specifications obtained.

Even when these are at hand and are used to create a tactical plan in combination with real-time reconnaissance to establish the location of the perpetrator and his victim, the special forces team must always bear in mind that even the best-laid plan can disintegrate on first contact with the enemy. This is why constant training and practicing variations is very important.

◄ *Men of the Spanish special forces collaborate with a U.S. Marine during the mock boarding of a non-compliant vessel as part of a 2004 joint exercise.*

▲ *Men of the Brunei special forces await the start of a visit, board, search, and seizure exercise on board a guided missile destroyer off the coast of Brunei.*

◄ *A maritime interdiction team conducts a visit, board, search, and seizure exercise on board a Chilean frigate during a multi-national 2008 training exercise tailored to the defense of the Panama Canal.*

# HOSTAGE RESCUE

For the British Special Air Service Regiment, the main physical element in its training for hostage rescue operations is the "Killing House." Here hostage rescue teams practice, and then practice again and again, several permutations of any hostage rescue undertaking. This teaches the men how to enter a room and rapidly assess the situation rationally, how to kill the hostage taker before he has a chance to react, and how to quickly lead the hostage to safety.

The Killing House is a two-story building with four rooms on each floor. It is laid out as a conventional building, with furniture, pictures, bathrooms, etc, but has its reconfigurable walls lined with a special rubber coating to absorb bullets rather than allow them to ricochet, extractor fans to clear gun fumes, and video cameras to record the action in the rooms. Each room has at least one metal target. The members of the SAS's counter-terrorism team practice in the Killing House every day with live ammunition.

▲ *U.S. soldiers of the 2nd Squadron, 1st Cavalry Regiment, breach a door during a house-clearing mission in Iraq during 2007.*

◀ *U.S. Navy SEAL trainees scan a room for possible threats as part of a qualification training exercise. Students spend two weeks learning the basics of securing a room from possible threats.*

So successful has the concept of the Killing House proved that it has been adopted by many other special forces including the U.S. Delta force and Israel's special forces. The same basic concept is also applicable to hijack rescue, and for this the teams practice in their own static train and airliner mock-ups.

▲ A U.S. communications specialist assigned to Fleet Combat Camera Group Pacific throws a flashbang grenade into an extemporized but roofless "shoot house" in the course of "Quick Shot 2010." This is a Fleet Combat Camera Group Pacific semi-annual field training exercise designed to provide non-combat personnel with a measure of experience of combat operations.

◄ The men of a Moroccan maritime interdiction operations team receive instruction from U.S. special forces personnel on the basic aspects of close-quarter battle in preparation for a maritime exercise aimed at dealing with illegal immigration, criminal activity, and the illegal trafficking of narcotics and weapons.

# SPETSNAZ AND THE MOSCOW THEATER SIEGE
## (OCTOBER 23-26, 2002)

On October 23, 2002, some 40 to 50 armed Chechens of one of three Muslim separatist (or criminal) movements in Chechnya seized a packed theater in the Dubrovka area of Moscow. With around 850 hostages in their hands, the militants led by Movsar Barayev demanded, on pain of the killing of the hostages, that within seven days the Russians withdraw their forces from Chechnya and end the 2nd Chechen War. Mobile phone conversations between the hostages and family members revealed that the hostage takers had grenades, mines, and improvised explosive devices strapped to their bodies, and had strung large quantities of explosives throughout the building.

The Chechen separatist leadership said it had no information about the attackers, and condemned attacks on civilians. The pro-Russian Muslim leader of Chechnya also condemned the attack. The attackers released some 150 to 200 people, including children, pregnant women, Muslims, some foreigners, and the sick in the hours after they attacked, and two women also managed to escape. The terrorists affirmed that they were prepared to kill ten hostages for every one of their number killed in the event of an attack.

The terrorists freed 39 hostages on October 24, one of them with a message reiterating their earlier demands. Negotiations for the release of non-Russians, conducted by several embassies, Russian journalists, and several public figures, took place on October 24 and 25, and the Chechens said that they would in fact release all foreign hostages to diplomatic representatives of their states. Fifteen Russian citizens, including eight children, were also released. A group of Russian doctors entered the theater with medicines for the hostages and, after leaving reported that the terrorists were neither beating nor threatening the hostages. Later the same day four Azerbaijani hostages were freed.

▲   Men of the Russian special forces soldiers move up equipment near the Moscow theater in which several hundreds of hostages were being held by Chechen rebels in October 2002. These is still debate about the type of gas used in the rescue.

◄   Men of a Russian interior ministry troop detachment take up their positions around the Moscow theater that was seized by a heavily armed Chechen group early on October 24, 2002. The group entered the crowded Moscow theater and took the entire audience hostage.

*▲  Special forces evacuate gassed hostages during the storming of the theater. The operation left many hostages and most of the Chechen militants dead, almost all of them victims of a toxic gas used by the Russian forces in their controversial army assault. There is still argument about the exact casualty figures.*

Before dawn on October 26, men of the "Alpha" and "Vympel" Groups of the Spetsnaz, an element of the FSB (Federal Security Service), aided by the Special Rapid-Response Unit (SOBR) of the interior ministry, stormed the theater, first through a gay club in the building's basement, all wearing masks to protect them from a gas that was being pumped into the theater. Many hostages initially believed that the gas was smoke from a fire, but it soon became evident that an anesthetic had been pumped into the building, and there was panic.

Some of the terrorists had gas masks and started to fire at the Russians surrounding the theater. After 30 minutes, deeming that the gas had taken effect, the Russians assaulted the theater with men entering through the roof, basement, and finally the front door. As terrorists and hostages began to fall unconscious, several of the female terrorists made a dash for the balcony but passed out before they reached the stairs, and were later found shot dead.

After some 90 minutes of intermittent firefights, the special forces blasted open the doors to the main hall and poured into the auditorium. In a fierce firefight, the special forces shot the terrorists, both conscious and unconscious. According to the Russian authorities, fighting between the troops and the still-conscious terrorists lasted between 30 and 60 minutes in other parts of the theater. The government later claimed that all terrorists had been killed, but the fate of 12 of the latter is still not known. At 7:00 a.m. rescuers began carrying the bodies of hostages out of the building and lying them in the foyer and on the pavement outside the theater's main entrance. Medical personnel had been expecting victims of explosions and gunfire, but not of a chemical agent whose nature the authorities refused to divulge. By October 28, of the 646 former hostages still in hospital, 150 were in intensive care and 45 in a critical condition.

At least 33 terrorists and 129 hostages died during or soon after the assault. Some estimates have put the civilian death toll at more than 200, but the Russian authorities have consistently refused to add any details.

# HUMAN TARGETS

Another major special forces mission is the pursuit and capture or killing of high-value human targets. Here the skills of the special forces team, numbering only a few men and with only limited physical support, can exert an influence out of all proportion to its size. They may eliminate a single enemy commander and/or command group heading a sizable military unit or even formation, thereby effectively decapitating it and leaving it more vulnerable to attack by a conventional military unit.

A notable British example of such a mission was Operation "Gaff." On July 18, 1944, a six-man patrol of the Special Air Service was parachuted into German-occupied France to capture or kill Generalfeldmarschall Erwin Rommel, the commander of German Army Group "B." After the location of Rommel's headquarters, a chateau in the village of La Roche-Guyon, had been established, this dedicated team of six specially trained assassins was created under a French SAS officer, Captain Jack William Raymond Lee (aka Raymond Couraud). Lee and his team were parachuted into Orléans. However, on radioing in, they found that Rommel had been severely injured during the previous day when his staff car had been attacked by British fighter-bombers, and he had been replaced by Generalfeldmarschall Günther von Kluge. With its orders cancelled, the SAS team moved toward the advancing front of the U.S. Army, ambushing trains and attacking German units en route, and reached safety on August 12.

▲ *U.S. Navy SEALs undertake immediate action drills to hone their tactical skills as part of the their pre-deployment training in 2010.*

◀ *Perhaps the highest-ranking officer specifically earmarked for assassination in World War II was Generalfeldmarschall Erwin Rommel, who survived two such attempts.*

▶ *A U.S. Navy SEAL fires a 7.62-mm (0.3-in) Mk 11 semi-automatic sniper rifle from an MH-60S Sea Hawk helicopter during a training flight in 2011.*

This episode highlights some of the essential features of such a mission, and also the often ephemeral nature of military intelligence and decision making in the light of rapidly unfolding events. The essential first element of any plan to capture or kill an enemy leader and/or his command group is identification of the right person(s) and the place in which they are likely to be found on any particular day. Only when these facts have been ascertained accurately can the assassination/capture team proceed with realistic planning. After determining the number of men who will be required, they will establish the type of weapons that they will need in the light of the operation planned. Among the options here are short-range killing with a mine or other explosive device, either triggered by the weight or movement of the target vehicle passing over it or by command detonation, slightly longer-range interception with assault weapon and grenades, longer-range killing with sniper fire or missile attack, or stand-off killing with an air-launched missile guided by the "painting" of the target vehicle or building by a laser designator operated by the special forces team.

▲ *U.S. Navy SEALs operating in Afghanistan in support of Operation "Enduring Freedom" in 2005. Despite occasionally heavy losses, the morale of such special forces remains very high.*

With the target located in time and space, the team must then deploy to a safe area within easy reach of the target area without detection and with all its equipment and vehicles. The team must then make its way, again without detection or even arousing the enemy's suspicion of an imminent attack, to the point at which the ambush is to be prepared and then undertaken. With the enemy's leader and/or leadership either killed or captured for interrogation, the special forces team has then to depart rapidly and make for its own army's front line or, more probably, an agreed rendezvous point where it can be extracted by helicopter. The attack on Osama bin Laden's compound in Abbottabad, Pakistan, by U.S. Navy SEAL commandos in May 2011 provides a classic example of just such a search-and-destroy mission.

▲ *The compound in Abbottabad where Osama bin Laden was killed.*

# INTELLIGENCE GATHERING

Reconnaissance and intelligence gathering are also highly important roles undertaken by special forces teams. In many respects these are similar to the task of killing or capturing an enemy leader, inasmuch as they demand undetected delivery of personnel into, and movement through, enemy-controlled territory to reach the designated operational area or specific objective. However, while it is still armed, though largely for defense rather than offense, the team must carry with it the specialized reconnaissance and communications equipment at the heart of its mission, and also larger quantities of consumables (food, water, etc) needed for an operation that is likely to last longer than an assassination or capture mission.

After advancing ahead of its own army's front line, or delivery by helicopter or boat into its initial deployment area, the reconnaissance team must move undetected to the target area, though always remaining conscious of the fact that this may have shifted as the enemy's headquarters or deployment reacts to the nature of the ongoing campaign. With the target area reached, the special forces team must then locate a safe area and establish itself under cover in the base from which it will undertake the key element of its mission, namely the visual or electronic surveillance of its target. As the required information is gathered, it must be transmitted back to base in a timely manner by the "quietest" electronic means possible.

▲ *A sergeant of the U.S. Army's 4th Infantry Regiment provides security during an area reconnaissance mission near Highway 1 in Zabul province, Afghanistan, during 2010. Without proper reconnaissance, most following operations are doomed to early, and often costly, failure.*

◄ *A U.S. Marine of the 1st Light Armored Reconnaissance Battalion provides overwatch security during the passage of a convoy through part of Iraq in 2007. Convoys are notoriously vulnerable to ambush when the appropriate precautions have not been taken.*

►► *U.S. Marines of a deep reconnaissance platoon wait for the word to begin an exercise. Deep reconnaissance requires penetration of the enemy's forward units for an assessment of his rear echelon and materiél support.*

Once the required information has been gained, the special forces team must extract itself from the operational area and regain its own lines, either by surface means or extraction by air. Throughout this whole process, it is very important that the reconnaissance team is not detected, not just for reasons of its own safety and survival, but also to avoid alerting the enemy to what is happening. Any change of enemy plans would render useless the reconnaissance mission and any intelligence derived from it.

▲ *U.S. Marines of the 1st Light Armored Reconnaissance Battalion observe live-fire training operations in the desert of Iraq.*

▲ *Small unmanned aerial vehicles, such as the Boeing Scan Eagle, are runway-independent and provide a long-endurance and autonomous facility for the persistent gathering of intelligence, surveillance, and reconnaissance data.*

# U.S. AND POLISH SPECIAL FORCES SEIZE THE MUKARAYIN DAM (APRIL 2003)

As the U.S.-led coalition of U.N. nations launched the second Iraq War on March 29, 2003, U.S. Navy SEALs undertook their single largest operation. They deployed from U.S. naval vessels as well as the Ras al Qulayah naval base and Ali al Salem air base in Kuwait as part of a mixed force of SEALs, Polish GROM (Grupa Reagowania Operacyjno-Manewrowego, or operational mobile reaction group), and British Royal Marines. Their targets were the al Basrah and Khawr al Amaya oil terminals (both offshore platforms and onshore petroleum pumping locks), as well as the al Faw port and refinery. Each element of the assault forces was delivered by helicopter or boat to the perimeter of the target area. The first attacks were those on the pumping locks for each offshore terminal. At the al Basrah

*◀ Men of the Polish GROM unit take part in a special forces operation at sea.*

pumping lock the team's landing zone was covered in concertina wire the presence of which had not been detected, so the helicopters carrying the assault team had to hover just above the wire as the Royal Marines and then the SEALs jumped out, only to become entangled and taken under fire by the defenders. The landing at the Khawr pumping lock encountered the same sort of difficulty, but at both places the attackers managed to regroup and then successfully assault the pumping locks, in the process capturing the main buildings and several occupied bunkers.

The attacks on the offshore platforms were carried out from the water by SEALs in rigid-hull inflatables against al Basrah and GROM personnel in small assault transport craft against Khawr. Two days earlier the Iraqis had replaced the al Basrah garrison with higher-quality Republican Guards. Given this late Iraqi change and the possibility that the Republican Guards might blow up the platforms

*▶ U.S. sailors walk along part of the Khawr al Amaya oil platform just off the coast of Iraq. Such installations were vitally important to the success of the coalition undertaking.*

▲ The Sikorsky MH-53 "Pave Low" helicopter is a vital asset for special forces operations.

◀ The Fairchild Republic A-10 Thunderbolt II is a very capable close air support warplane.

ground was impassable to the low-powered DPVs with rear-wheel drive. Even so, the SEALs began to advance on foot against a defense believed to total 300 well-entrenched troops supported by armored vehicles, the Americans relying on air power for assistance if required. This close air support proved wholly effective, and the SEALs seized the whole facility before dawn on March 21, when they were replaced by No. 42 Commando of the Royal Marines after killing several hundred Iraqis and capturing 100 men. All of the Iraqi armored vehicles were destroyed.

From the start, coalition military planners had been worried that retreating Iraqi forces would destroy the Mukarayin dam. Lying on the Euphrates River some 56 miles (90 km) northeast of Baghdad, the Iraqi capital, this was a hydro-electric installation whose destruction would flood large areas and thus slow the advance of the coalition forces.

▲ A U.S. Marine on security watch on the deck of the ABOT (Al Basrah oil terminal), another key target early in the campaign.

as the attack started, the SEALs elected to kill the defenders before seizing the installation. In fact, as soon as the attack started, the Republican Guards began to surrender. The Poles met the same type of response at Khawr, so both installations were taken without a fight.

The attack on the Iraqi refinery and port on the al Faw peninsula was made by a SEAL force in DPVs (desert patrol vehicles), and at the same time a larger force (U.S. Marines of the 1st Marine Expeditionary Force's 5th Regimental Combat Team) tackled the Iraqi positions farther north in the Rumaila oil fields. There were concerns that the terrain might be unsuitable for DPVs, but the attack was committed with the assault teams landing straight from their transport helicopters in their DPVs. Then it was discovered that the earlier fears had been well founded: the peninsula's oil-soaked

A mixed SEAL and GROM force of about 40 men was tasked to seize and hold the dam in April. The force was delivered, after a flight of several hours, by Sikorsky MH-53 "Pave Low" helicopters of the U.S.A.F. The SEALs used DPVs to establish blocking positions to provide warning of any counter-attack and to drive off bands of Iranian bandits. As on the al Faw peninsula, the SEALs found the DPVs to be ineffective. For the attack on the dam, the coalition decided on a foot assault, and after they had fast-roped from their helicopters the SEAL and GROM teams immediately stormed the dam. There were only a small number of Iraqi troops in the immediate area, and they immediately surrendered. The only coalition casualty was a GROM solder who broke an ankle during the insertion.

# Sabotage and Demolition

Another task with similarities to the assassination or capture of an enemy leader, or the garnering of intelligence by a reconnaissance patrol is the sabotage and demolition role, at least in its basic tactical method of reaching and then operating in enemy-controlled territory.

The value of this type of operation, in which a small force can create an effect out of all proportion to its size, came to be appreciated in World War II through undertakings such as Operation "Harling." This was a mission conducted by members of the Special Operations Executive on November 25, 1942 to destroy the Gorgopotamos viaduct across a river on the Greek rail line linking Athens with Thessaloniki. The Allied strength available for the operation was 150: 12 SOE operatives to blow the viaduct and 138 Greek resistance fighters to provide cover and neutralize the garrison. Two teams of eight resistance fighters were to cut the rail and telephone lines in

◄ A demolition crew of the 6th Marine Division watches its charges explode and destroy a Japanese cave bunker in Okinawa in May 1945.

▼ Navy explosive ordnance disposal technicians detonate four 16-lb (7.25-kg) blocks of C4 explosive on the Natural Fire Live Fire range in Kenya during 2006.

each direction and also cover the approaches to the viaduct while other resistance fighters attacked the garrison. The three demolition teams waited upriver until the garrison had been subdued, and then laid the charges. The first explosion heavily damaged the central pier of the bridge and brought down two spans, and the second achieved similar results on another pier and span. The entire attacking force, which had suffered only four wounded, then broke off and fell back to its safe assembly area.

The primary targets for sabotage and demolition attacks, now as then, are chokepoints in the enemy's logistic network, such as bridges, tunnels, marshalling yards, and canal locks. The destruction of these assets can prevent or slow the movement of reinforcements and/or supplies to an extent that can delay an enemy attack or weaken his ability to fight off an assault. Targets of comparable importance are electricity pylons, power-generating stations, communications nexuses, and associated equipment.

▲  *Soldiers of the Philippine Army attach blasting caps to detonation cord for the controlled demolition of live ordnance near Zamboanga City, Philippines.*

▼  *A U.S. Navy explosive ordnance disposal technician measures time fuse for demolition skills practice on a live-fire range in Kenya during 2006.*

# MOBILITY CAPABILITIES

An important element in all special forces undertakings is a high degree of mobility over all types of terrain while leaving the minimum "footprint" for detection by the enemy. Some aspects of mobility depend on the personal capabilities of individual soldiers, such as endurance in marching, while others are acquired skills, such as parachuting, abseiling (rappelling), fast-roping, skiing, snow-shoeing, canoeing, and underwater movement using breathing equipment. All of these are taught or honed by special forces training and practice.

These skills are also enhanced by the capabilities offered by support elements, such as the Special Air Service Regiment's mobility troop, whose men are all experts in the use of vehicles and heavy support weapons. Thus, the men of the mobility troop support SAS operations by enabling them to move through an operational area and also by providing the offensive/defense punch of weapons that are too heavy to be man-carried or fitted onto light vehicles, so making them in part independent of other conventional forces.

▲  This underwater shot of a U.S. special forces combat diver reveals his automatic rifle and DPV (Diver Propulsion Vehicle) movement aid.

▼  In the Gulf of Oman during 2004, members of a U.S. boarding team make a fast-rope descent into a rigid-hull inflatable boat.

SAS soldiers allocated to the mobility troop are specially trained to a very high standard in a number of vital technical disciplines, including maintenance and repair of vehicles; basic mobility, such as getting heavily laden vehicles over all kinds of terrain; navigation to ensure that SAS operations, often undertaken in featureless terrain, remain on course through the use of electronic navigation aids, such as Global Positioning System receivers, allied to older methods, such as map reading and stellar navigation; and effective logistical control so that extended missions behind enemy lines without resupply do not suffer from any lack of fuel, ammunition, and other stores pre-loaded onto the vehicles before departure.

The soldiers of the mobility troop are also skilled in the use of heavy support weapons, and as a result an SAS fighting column, typically of eight vehicles, can attack and, when demanded, defend with the effective firepower of a larger and notionally more powerful tactical unit. It is the responsibility of the mobility troop's men to bring to bear on the enemy the heavier weapons, such as mortars, antitank missiles, heavy machine guns, and grenade launchers, as the more lightly armed elements move forward on foot or in their lighter vehicles. The men are trained to fire their heavy weapons from their carrying vehicles or from the ground once they have been dismounted.

▲ *A U.S. Marine starts to control the parachute lines and canopy by which a supply of water and food has been dropped to his team by a C-130 transport aircraft in Afghanistan during 2008.*

▲ *In Iraq during 2003, U.S. Marines move to support fellow Marines in a "Humvee" (High-Mobility Multi-Purpose Wheeled Vehicle) equipped with a 12.7-mm (0.5-in) heavy machine gun. The Humvee is the "maid of all work" light transport for the U.S. forces, and has a very good record for reliability.*

▶ *The Sikorsky HH-60 "Pave Hawk" helicopter is a combat search and rescue (CSAR) variant of the Sikorsky S-70 family. The HH-60's primary function is the conduct of day and/or night CSAR operations to a considerable radius into hostile territory for the location and recovery of downed aircrew or other isolated personnel during war.*

# RUSSIAN SPECIAL FORCES– THE BESLAN SCHOOL HOSTAGE CRISIS (September 1-3, 2004)

The Beslan school hostage crisis started on September 1, 2004, when a group of armed men and women (mostly Ingush and Chechen Muslim militants) seized more than 1,100 people (including 777 children) at School Number One in Beslan, a town in the North Ossetian autonomous republic of the Russian Federation. The operation was carried out by the Riyadus-Salikhin group on the orders of its leader, Shamil Basayev, a Chechen separatist warlord.

The terrorists drove their hostages into the gymnasium, seized all cellphones and ordered everyone to speak in Russian. When a father repeated the rules in Ossetic, the local language, a terrorist shot him. When another father refused to kneel when ordered, he was also shot and allowed to bleed to death. The terrorists then gathered a group of between 15 and 20 male teachers, school employees and fathers, and systematically killed them.

The Russians soon established a cordon of police, internal ministry troops, and Russian Army personnel round the school, and called in Spetsnaz special forces (including the "Alpha" and "Vympel" groups) of the Federal Security Service, and of the OMON (special-purpose police unit) of the interior ministry.

The terrorists rigged the gym and the rest of the building with improvised explosive devices and installed tripwires, and also threatened to kill 50 hostages for every one of their own number killed or wounded. To prevent being gassed in the fashion

▼ *A Russian special police soldier (left) carries an injured colleague as two soldiers and two women take cover behind the armored personnel carrier during the rescue operation of Beslan's school, North Ossetia.*

◀  Russian special forces soldiers carry an injured colleague during the rescue operation of Beslan's school, North Ossetia, September 3, 2004.

▼  An Orthodox Christian cross and flowers in the gym of School Number 1 in Beslan commemorate those killed during the hostage crisis.

which had overwhelmed their compatriots in the Moscow theater crisis of 2002, they broke the windows. The Russian government announced that it would not use force to rescue the hostages, and negotiations took place on the first and second days, even as the Federal Security Service planned the assault that might be needed to resolve the crisis.

During the afternoon of the second day the terrorists allowed Ruslan Aushev, ex-president of Ingushetia, to enter the school and agreed to release 11 nursing women and all 15 baby children to him. The women's older children were to be kept, and when one mother refused to leave, Aushev carried out her child.

At about 1:00 p.m. on the third day, the terrorists agreed to allow four paramedics in two ambulances to remove 20 bodies from the school grounds. Only three minutes later as the paramedics were nearing the scene, there was an explosion in the gym and the terrorists opened fire, killing two of the paramedics. Less than half a minute later there was another explosion and at 1:05 p.m. fire seen on the roof of the gym. Soon burning rafters and roofing fell onto the hostages, and eventually the whole roof collapsed, apparently killing some 160 persons. There have been many widely conflicting accounts about the cause of the two explosions.

Part of the gym's exterior wall was demolished by the blast, and some hostages managed to escape. Local militiamen opened fire and the terrorists responded, several people being killed in the

crossfire. In these circumstances the Russian authorities felt that they had no alternative but to storm the building, and a chaotic battle broke out as the special forces entered the school. Many local civilians also joined the fighting using their own weapons. The terrorists moved many hostages from the burning gym to other parts of the school, in particular the cafeteria, where they were forced to stand at windows. Many of them were shot by the troops outside. It is estimated that up to 110 hostages died after being moved to the cafeteria.

Two hours after the start of the assault, Russian troops had control of most of the school. A group of some 13 militants had broken out of the school, and several were thought to have entered a nearby two-story building that was then destroyed by tanks and flamethrowers at about 9:00 p.m. Another group of terrorists escaped over the railway into the town with helicopters in pursuit.

The exact casualty list has never been revealed, but there were at least 385 dead (334 hostages, including 186 children) and about 783 wounded.

# MOBILITY VEHICLES

Some of the vehicles available to the mobility troop are the Land Rover 110 Desert Patrol Vehicle 4x4 vehicle, generally known as the "Pink Panther" or "Pinky" (so named for the camouflage found to be best suited to desert operations), carrying machine guns and other weapons; the Supacat HMT 400 4x4 vehicle that is replacing the Land Rover; the Supercat HMT 6x6 enlarged version of the Supacat HMT 400, successor to the Unimog U1100 as a "mothership;" Australian Bushmaster IMV (Infantry Mobility Vehicle) 4x4 fully enclosed carrier with better capabilities against mines and improvised explosive devices; U.S. Light Strike Vehicle three-man scout and attack vehicle based on the dune buggy concept (for lack of size and payload suitable only for short-range work); and German Unimog U1100 or more modern French ACMAT VLRA.

▲ Seen here in Dutch service during 2008, the Thales Australia Bushmaster was designed by the Irish company Timoney, and is a 4x4 protected mobility vehicle carrying nine men and its driver.

◄ The Land Rover "Pink Panther," so called from its sandy pink paint, is a 4x4 desert patrol vehicle used by the British Army. Though obsolescent, it is reliable and rugged.

*◄ Seen here in British service, the Ridgeback is a mine-protected multi-role medium vehicle designed and built in the U.S.A. by Force Protection in 4x4 and 6x6 variants.*

These last are cut-down 4x4 cross-country army trucks that operate as "motherships" with extra equipment, spare parts and supplies of fuel, water, and ammunition for the other vehicles of the fighting column. Intended for a support rather than an offensive role, the U1100 and ACMAT VLRA trucks are generally fitted with heavy or medium machine guns, or Mk 19 grenade launchers, with which to defend themselves. For greater security, support vehicles, such as the U1100 and ACMAT VLRA, usually travel in the middle of the fighting column.

Fighting columns are accompanied by motorcycle outriders to scout ahead of the column and provide early warning of possible attacks on its flanks and rear. The scouting aspect has the dual tasks of searching for the enemy and finding the appropriate route. Moreover, while the column is operating in conditions of electronic silence, the outriders are available to deliver messages between the wheeled vehicles.

*► The U.S. Desert Patrol Vehicle is in essence a "dune buggy" outfitted with a comprehensive communications suite and able to carry several types of weapon. The vehicle was designed for harsh desert terrain.*

*◄ The U.S. Mine-Resistant Ambush-Protected All-Terrain Vehicle is built by Oshkosh Defense. The vehicle carries five men, and is a rugged 4x4 machine that can be armed with several types of weapon (7.62-mm/ 0.3-in machine gun, 40-mm/1.57-in grenade launcher and TOW antitank missile launcher). The maximum speed is 65 mph (105 kph), and the range 320 miles (515 km).*

# BY SNOW AND WATER

Not all operations take place on terrain passable by wheeled vehicles, however, and for Arctic conditions of snow and ice the mobility troop works with the mountain troop in the operation of the appropriate vehicle types, including snowmobiles and tracked vehicles, such as the Hägglunds Bv 206D designed and built in Sweden. This achieves the low ground pressure required for movement across snow and ice through the use of rubber tracks, which are wide and extend over the full length of the vehicle, and the light weight of its body. The vehicle's two parts are articulated, allowing it to keep contact with the ground over broken terrain and pressure-ridged ice, and fully heated. The Bv 206D can travel over loose snow without sinking into it. Its light weight and the waterproof fiberglass body also combine to make the Bv 206D fully amphibious, with waterborne propulsion by the tracks.

Another approach to some targets is by water. Small teams can be delivered under the surface by swimming or delivery vehicle, but larger numbers can best be transported by air-cushion craft or assault vehicles, such as the LVTP7 (now AAV7).

▲　Long-range patrols or insertions in Arctic conditions can be made by fast one-man snowmobiles (foreground) or, for larger parties, by larger and slower tracked snowcats with enclosed and heated accommodation (background).

▲   AAV7 amphibious assault vehicles (AAV) arrive
on the Philippine shore during an exercise. The 29-ton
armored AAV7 can operate on water right through
into desert, carries 25 men and a three-man crew,
and is armed with a 25-mm (1-in) cannon or 40-mm
(1.57-in) grenade launcher as well as a 7.62-mm (0.3-in)
machine gun.

▶   U.S. Marines return from the beach at Salinas,
Peru, in an AAV7 amphibious assault vehicle during
an amphibious exercise to enhance partnerships
between the marine forces of the United States and
several Central and South American nations. The
AAV7 has a maximum land speed of 45 mph (72 kph)
and range of 300 miles (480 km).

◀◀   Minnesota national guardsmen on skis are
towed by a Bv 206 tracked vehicle while on cold-
weather training near Værnes in northern Norway
during 2008. The Bv 206 articulated vehicle can carry
17 persons (six and 11 in the front and rear sections,
respectively) or 4,940 lb (2,240 kg) of cargo.

# SPECIAL BOAT SERVICE KILLING OF TALIBAN LEADERS (2007-2008)

British special forces have been notably active in Iraq and Afghanistan since the first involvement of U.S.-led U.N. and later NATO coalition forces. The Special Air Service initially concentrated its primary efforts in Iraq, and the Special Boat Service in Afghanistan, especially in the south. Here, in May 2007, the service's C Squadron, assisted by the United States's Task Force "Orange," a highly secret electronic surveillance unit, attacked the leadership of the Taliban movement, which the coalition was determined to destroy.

▼ *Afghan journalists take photographs of the body of the Taliban's most important military commander, Mullah Dadullah, in Kandahar on May 13, 2007.*

Mullah Dadullah (Dadullah Akhund) fought with the *mujahidin* against the Soviet occupation of Afghanistan during the 1980s, and lost one of his legs. A close associate of Mullah Omar, the spiritual leader of the Taliban and head of the Supreme Council of Afghanistan in 1996–2001, Dadullah eventually rose to become the senior military commander in the Taliban. He was thus a high-value target, and an operation to locate and neutralize him was launched. In March 2007, a controversial prisoner exchange took place in which the government in Kabul agreed to release two senior Taliban leaders in exchange for an Italian reporter, Daniele Mastrogiacomo, and his two Afghan assistants, who were being held by the Taliban.

▼ *The senior Taliban leader Abdul Matin speaks with the media on March 7, 2002. Matin launched attacks on coalition and Afghan government targets, but was killed in an ambush by SBS operatives on February 18, 2008.*

▲ *A British soldier of the Royal Artillery on duty at a security outpost on May 15, 2007 in the southern part of Helmand province. NATO troops operating in the south and in the province of Helmand were preparing for a new offensive after the SBS and U.S.-trained Afghans had killed the Taliban's top military commander, Mullah Dadullah, during the preceding weekend.*

The undertaking was severely criticized for pandering to an insurgent movement, but it was in fact a superb example of military deception, for Task Force "Orange" was able to follow the movements of the released Taliban commanders, possibly through the implantation of trackers in their bodies, but more probably through the interception of satellite phone conversations between the released Taliban leaders and Dadullah. Task Force "Orange" was very confident that it would be able to locate Dadullah. This proved to be the case, and by May 2007 Task Force "Orange" had pinpointed Dadullah's location as Bahram Chah, in the south of Helmand province close to the border with Pakistan. Thus, some 50 special forces operatives of the SBS's C Squadron were tasked to raid Dadullah's stronghold.

A reconnaissance team approached the area in a Supacat 6x6 all-terrain vehicle. It concluded that there was no guarantee that an air attack on the mud-built compound would result in Dadullah's death. The alternative was for the rest of C Squadron to move in on foot and kill him. The majority of C Squadron and a detachment of Afghan government troops embarked on two Boeing CH-47 Chinook heavy-lift transport helicopters of the Royal Air Force and were landed on May 12 in the assault area, where they came under fire from the Taliban defenders. Once landed, though, the SBS operatives delivered an infantry attack on the compound, with one

group providing fire support as another advanced, and then exchanging roles to maintain the progress. There were only about 20 Taliban defenders, but these hard-line fighters fought with great determination using assault rifles, machine guns, and rocket-propelled grenades. After a four-hour action, C Squadron cleared the compound, in the process suffering only four men wounded. Dadullah was killed in the attack, shot twice in the torso and once in the head, either by the SBS or U.S.-trained Afghan soldiers.

Another senior Taliban leader in Afghanistan was Mullah Abdul Matin, who in 2007 became the governor of the Musa Qala district, which had fallen into Taliban hands after the breakdown of a truce between the insurgents and the NATO coalition. From this area Matin launched ambushes and suicide attacks on coalition and Afghan government targets in the northern part of Helmand province. In December 2007, Matin only just evaded capture during Operation "Mar Kardad," a joint coalition and Afghan offensive to retake Musa Qala. Then, on February 18, 2008, Matin and Mullah Karim Agha, one of his senior subordinates, were riding through the desert on motorcycles when they were ambushed and killed near Gereshk in Helmand province by SBS operatives who were landed in their path by helicopter. In the firefight that followed, both Taliban leaders and all their bodyguards were killed.

# SPECIAL FORCES MEDICINE

Given the fact that they operate, sometimes for extended periods, out of contact with other troops, the world's special forces have had to develop a unique form of military medicine specifically tailored to the support of special operations and the tasks of the special forces in the field. The nature of this support can include humanitarian assistance both within and without the military missions (the former making a "hearts and minds" contribution to the mission, and the latter a "first response" contribution when the special forces are deployed in a humanitarian disaster), casualty care in the field, preventative care in garrison situations, medical care of highly trained personnel operating under extreme stress in hostile psychological and physical environments, and provision of and/or support of civilian and public health care in developing nations, again within the overall context of a "hearts and minds" context.

▼   The "medic" of a special forces team treats a U.S. Army soldier for shrapnel wounds caused by the explosion of a rocket-propelled grenade during the course of an engagement with Taliban fighters in Helmand province, Afghanistan, in 2007.

▲   A U.S. Army hospital corpsman assigned to a combat team cleans the facial wounds of a fellow soldier after an improvised explosive device had been detonated under a patrol in Afghanistan during 2010.

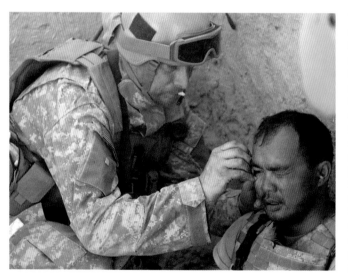

The core principles and methods of special forces medicine are essentially the same as those of conventional military medicine, but the manner in which those principles and methods are applied can be entirely different as a result of the unique mission requirements, the environmental extremes, and, frequently, the non-availability of resources in the field. Here the special forces medical specialist is as much concerned with preventative measures, to check the onset of problems, as with the treatment of ailments. Within this context the special forces medical specialist is trained in the medical practices that are known to work for the population in which his team will be deployed, and how to deal with insect and other bites, and the problems that can arise from the ingestion of contaminated water or foodstuffs.

► *Men of the Sri Lankan navy's Special Boat Squadron listen to a riot control class taught by U.S. Marines during a humanitarian assistance and disaster relief demonstration. This instructed the SBS personnel in aspects of riot control, as well as how and when to implement them safely and correctly.*

◄ *A U.S. combat medic examines and prepares to treat a boy's infected wound during a dismounted patrol to a village in the Deh Chopan district of Afghanistan's Zabul province in 2009.*

▼ *During 2011 in Belize, U.S. hospitalmen of the Security Cooperation Task Force, Ground Combat Element, working alongside the Belize Defense Force, demonstrate the treatment of a sucking chest wound in a jungle warfare and survival exercise.*

# CHAPTER 7

▲ Soldiers of the Italian Army load Bv-206 Armored Snow Cats into a CH-47 helicopter.

# TRANSPORT

# PARACHUTE DROPS

One of the main methods whereby special forces soldiers are delivered into operational areas is by parachute. The classic methods are termed HALO (high-altitude/low-opening) and HAHO (high-altitude/high-opening), also known as military free-fall.

In the HALO technique, which is used for the delivery of equipment and supplies as well as men, the soldier opens his parachute at a low altitude after free-falling for some time, while in the HAHO technique, used only for the delivery of men, the soldier opens his parachute at a high altitude just a short time after exiting the aircraft. In standard HALO and HAHO drops, the soldiers generally leave the aircraft at an altitude of between 25,000 and 35,000 ft (7,600 and 10,000 m).

◀ A member of the Combat Control Team, from the U.S. 1st Special Operations Wing, gathers the canopy of his parachute after touching down safely in a HALO (High Altitude Low Opening) jump.

When making a HALO jump, the parachutist exits the aircraft, free-falls for a time at terminal velocity, and opens his parachute at a low altitude. The combination of high downward speed and minimal forward air-speed serves to prevent radar detection, thereby making possible a stealthy insertion. The HAHO technique is used to drop personnel at a high altitude when aircraft are unable to overfly the drop zone (DZ). The personnel then "fly" their parachutes to the landing zone. HAHO jumps are used for the covert insertion of special forces soldiers in circumstances where the undercover nature of an operation could be compromised by the noise of parachutes opening at low altitude. In a typical HAHO jump, the parachutist leaves the aircraft and deploys his parachute some ten to 15 seconds after the jump and at a typical altitude of 27,000 ft (8,200 m). The soldier then uses his compass or GPS device for guidance while "flying" for 30 miles (48 km) or more. During this time the soldier uses waypoints and terrain features to fly to his drop zone, and makes course corrections to compensate for changes in wind speed and direction. When a team is deployed, it forms up in a stack while airborne, and normally it is the soldier at the bottom of the stack who sets the course and serves as guide for the other team members.

▲ *U.S. para-rescuemen from the 38th Rescue Squadron and 58th Rescue Squadron jump from a HC-130P/N Hercules in a high altitude low opening free-fall drop from 13,000 ft (3,960 m) in support of Operation "Enduring Freedom."*

High-altitude parachute drops can encounter problems as a result of the ambient air's low oxygen pressure, which can result in the parachutist experiencing hypoxia. Moreover, rapid ascent in an unpressurized aircraft can lead to decompression sickness ("the bends") if all the nitrogen has not been flushed from the jumper's bloodstream. For a HALO jump there should be a 30- to 45-minute pre-breathing period before the jump when the soldier breathes 100 percent oxygen in order to flush nitrogen from his blood. The HALO jumper also uses an oxygen bottle during the jump to prevent hypoxia, which can cause the paratrooper to lose consciousness and so fail to open his parachute. A jumper suffering from decompression sickness may die or become permanently disabled from nitrogen bubbles in the bloodstream. Another risk is posed by the low temperature at higher altitudes. At 35,000 ft (10,670 m) the soldier faces a temperature of -50°F (-46°C) and can suffer frostbite. HALO jumpers generally wear polypropylene-knit undergarments and other warm clothing to prevent this.

▲ *Three Special Warfare Combatant-craft crewmen of the U.S. Special Boat Team 22 link up during a free-fall parachute drop near Key West, Florida, nicely epitomizing the "triphibian" nature of the U.S. Navy's special forces.*

◄◄ *A U.S. special forces HALO jumper pulls his rip cord while two instructors observe and critique his jump. The jumper is about 4,000 ft (1,220 m) above the surface at Yuma Proving Grounds, Arizona.*

In a typical HALO drop, the soldier's equipment (other than his parachute) generally includes an altimeter, automatic activation device set to deploy the parachute at a given height above the ground, knife, helmet, gloves, military free-fall boots, emergency oxygen, and combat pack. Carrying combat and survival equipment, the pack can weigh anything between 50 lb (22.5 kg) and more than 100 lb (45 kg).

# HeLICOPTeR TRANSPORT

The helicopter is much used for the delivery and extraction of special forces as these aircraft can land almost anywhere and require no runway. The techniques used to land special forces from a helicopter include a conventional landing, after which the soldiers disembark via the rear ramp of a heavy-lift machine or the side door of a medium-lift machine, or any of three aerial methods. Of the latter, the parachute drop from the rear ramp of the heavy-lift helicopter in forward motion is not much used, but more common are rappelling or fast-roping from the ramp or door of a helicopter hovering above the ground. Rappelling is abseiling with the rope looped through a carabiner attached to the soldier's harness. For a faster, but more dangerous, descent, fast-roping involves gripping a thicker rope with gloved hands and booted feet and sliding down it.

Tactical heliborne insertion of special forces is undertaken close to the target when a runway is not available. Rappelling is more often used in urban warfare scenarios, and is increasingly being replaced by fast-roping. Examples include insertion into urban environments, boarding of vessels at sea and insertion of forces to seize and secure a landing zone in enemy territory.

▲  An MH-47 Chinook, assigned to the U.S. Army's 160th Special Operations Aviation Regiment, departs from an amphibious assault ship's flight deck. Note the capacious fuselage and the inflight-refueling probe for long-range operations.

▼  The MH-47 Chinook helicopter has advanced avionics suiting it to long-distance flights at low altitude for special operations missions with a substantial payload.

▲ *U.S. and Iraqi soldiers are collected by a UH-60 Black Hawk helicopter after a three-day air assault mission in Iraq during 2007.*

The most important heavy-lift helicopter used by Western forces is the twin-rotor Boeing Chinook, which includes several special forces support variants in its many guises. The current variant is the MH-47E developed during the late 1980s for service from 1994. Offering capability for rappel or fast-roping delivery, the MH-47E can lift a maximum of 44 troops, and its typical mission of 5 hours 30 minutes is designed to deliver 36 troops under adverse day/night conditions over a radius of 345 miles (555 km) in temperate operating conditions, or 30 troops over the same radius under "hot and high" operating conditions. The MH-47E has the lengthened fuselage of the CH-47D International Chinook with the forward wheels moved closer to the nose to allow the use of longer side pannier tanks that increase fuel capacity to 2,243 gal (8,490 liters) in conjunction with two floor tanks, an inflight-refueling capability, via the retractable probe on the starboard side of the forward fuselage, and an advanced electronic suite.

The helicopter is armed with two 12.7-mm (0.5-in) Browning M2 machine guns mounted in the port forward and starboard aft windows for the suppression of defensive fire, and can also carry defensive FIM-92 Stinger short-range air-to-air missiless aimed via the FLIR system. The more recent MH-47G is an upgraded development of the MH-47E for the U.S. special forces, and while similar to the MH-47E, it features more sophisticated avionics, including a digital CAAS (Common Avionics Architecture System), which has a common "glass" flight deck of the type also used by other helicopters, such as the Sikorsky MH-60K/L, Sikorsky CH-53E/K, and Bell ARH-70A.

▲ *The MH-53 "Pave Low" helicopter can fly long ranges at low levels in adverse weather with 37 troops and a six-man crew.*

▶ *In Iraq during 2006, U.S. soldiers disembark from a CH-47 Chinook. The large rear ramp/door facilitates speedy loading and unloading.*

# OPERATION "THALATHINE" – THE FRENCH RESPONSE TO THE SEIZURE OF *LE PONANT*
## (APRIL 11, 2008)

*Le Ponant* is a three-masted French luxury yacht operated on a commercial basis to provide cruises for up to 67 passengers in 32 cabins. While sailing though the Gulf of Aden on April 4, 2008 with a crew of 30 (22 French, six Filipino, one Cameroonian, and one Ukrainian) on passage from the Seychelles Islands to the Mediterranean, the yacht was seized by a group of six Somali pirates armed with Kalashnikov assault rifles. The pirates, from the village of Garaad-Ade, had earlier seized a Yemeni trawler, which had a crew of 27, and used this as their mother vessel for further attacks.

The crew of the yacht were not alarmed as the trawler closed on them, and were alerted only when three armed men put off from the Yemeni vessel in a speedboat. The yacht's crew planned to fight off the attack with powerful hoses, but when the Somalis opened fire with their rifles, they decided to surrender. The three men in the speedboat were then joined by six men in another boat, and so nine pirates boarded the yacht, which then headed for Garaad-Ade with the pirates' boats in tow. Here up to 30 of the 90 villagers took turns in guarding the yacht and its crew. The pirates demanded a ransom

(believed to be in the order of US$2 million) from the owners for the release of the yacht and her crew.

Antipiracy forces, including the French naval sloop *Commandant Bouan* and a Sikorsky CH-124 Sea King helicopter from the Canadian destroyer *Charlottetown*, had kept a watch on the yacht after its seizure, having been alerted secretly by the yacht's skipper. After the ransom had been paid, the yacht was released and most of her crew members taken on board *Commandant Bouan*.

After the hostage release, French naval helicopters tracked the pirates as they moved to the village of Jariban. During this period the French had alerted the Groupe d'Intervention de la Gendarmerie

▲ *A Canadian Sikorsky CH-124 Sea King helicopter was one of the assets used by the antipiracy forces to provide surveillance.*

◄ *The French luxury yacht Le Ponant. Somali pirates boarded and seized the yacht off the coast of Somalia and took hostage its entire crew on April 4, 2008.*

◀ *With her helicopters and provision for landing troops by air, the French helicopter carrier Jeanne d'Arc was a key element of the rescue effort.*

Nationale (National Gendarmerie Intervention Group, or GIGN) for an intervention codenamed Operation "Thalathine." Operating from the frigate *Jean Bart* and helicopter cruiser *Jeanne d'Arc*, elements of the GIGN supported by Commandos Marines (naval commandos) moved in when the pirates attempted to flee into the desert. A sniper disabled their getaway vehicle with a shot to its engine, and three commandos were landed from a Eurocopter France Gazelle helicopter to capture the six men. Local officials claimed that three people died in the raid, with a further eight wounded, but France strongly denied this. The commandos also recovered some US$200,000 of the ransom, suggesting that the pirate operation was larger than it had seemed, and that perhaps more senior pirates had escaped with the bulk of the ransom money.

The six captured pirates were later flown to France for trial.

▲ *Another major French asset for the hostage-rescue operation was the French antiaircraft frigate Jean Bart, which offered a high level of surveillance and secure communications capabilities.*

▲ *A reconstruction of the release of the crew of the luxury sailing vessel Le Ponant, which was held hostage, together with her crew, by Somali pirates in April 2008. There were no passengers on board the yacht.*

◀ *A member of the French National Gendarmerie Intervention Group (GIGN) with the clothing and helmet typical of the world's special forces, and also a sub-machine gun. This latter is fitted with a suppressor and an advanced optical sight.*

# SWIMMER DELIVERY

In situations where coastal conditions and/or the enemy's defenses make it impossible for a submarine to deploy underwater special forces at a sufficiently close range to their target, the special forces are carried over the final leg of their underwater journey by a swimmer delivery vehicle (SDV). This is a midget submersible designed to transport combat swimmers over long distances. The SDV carries its two-man crew (pilot and co-pilot) and a combat swimmer team and its equipment; the pilot and co-pilot often form part of the swimmer team. For longer-range missions, the SDV can carry an onboard compressed air supply to extend the range of a swimmer's own air tank or rebreather equipment.

◄▼ In the Atlantic Ocean during 2005, members of a SEAL Delivery Vehicle team prepare to launch their SDV from a dry-deck shelter on the back of a submarine during a training exercise. The SDV has a two-man crew and can transport a complete combat swimmer team.

The two types of SDV are the "wet" type on which the combat swimmers ride on the outside, exposed to the water, and the "dry" type in which the swimmers travel in an interior compartment without being exposed to the water. Examples of "wet" SDVs include the U.S. SEAL Delivery Vehicle and the Russian Protei-5, and of the "dry"

▲ *Underwater shot of U.S. special operations combat divers under way courtesy of their diver propulsion vehicles.*

▼ *A U.S. combat diver, brought to shore by a diver propulsion vehicle, prepares to land with his personal weapon at the ready.*

type the U.S. Advanced SEAL Delivery System that was canceled in 2006, and STIDD Systems' Multi-Role Combatant Craft (MRCC).

SDVs are used in maritime missions, such as infiltrating combat swimmers into an enemy port or planting limpet mines on the hulls of target vessels. They are also used to land a combat swimmer team covertly on a hostile shore in order to conduct missions on land. After completing their mission, the team may return to the SDV to be extracted and returned to the mother ship or, more probably, submarine.

The SEAL Delivery Vehicle is powered by lithium-ion batteries, has a range of 42 miles (67 km), and is equipped with propulsion, navigation, communication, and life-support equipment. The Mk 8 Mod 1 SDV can deliver six fully equipped SEALs to the mission area, then loiter in the area, and finally retrieve the SEALs.

Another option, known to be used by the British Special Boat Service, is the diver propulsion vehicle. This is a one- or two-man unit driven by an electrically powered propeller, and the crew either hold onto, or clip themselves onto, the unit.

# INFLaTaBLe CRaFT

Another method by which special forces can be delivered and extracted by water is through the use of canoes or inflatable raiding craft. In the current age of high-technology warfare it may seem anachronistic that special forces, such as the Special Boat Service, still make use of the canoe in a form that has remained little changed since World War II. It has to be borne in mind, however, that non-metallic canoes still offer an effective and stealthy way to transport small teams of men around an enemy's coasts and along his waterways. The idea actually dates back to 1906 when German Johannes Klepper first started manufacturing folding boats.

◀ U.S. Marines depart from an amphibious dock landing ship during a ship-to-shore combat rubber raid craft offload exercise.

▼ Men of the French special forces in training, here in a heavily camouflaged two-man paddled canoe.

The current Klepper canoe can be broken down into two sections, each of which can be carried or concealed by one of the canoe's two crew. The canoe's carrying capacity can accommodate the crew and a general-purpose machine gun or mortar, and the boat can also be provided with antitank rockets to deal with enemy surface craft. The Klepper canoe is also versatile in the way it can be deployed: it can be launched from other boats and surfaced submarines, carried to the surface by divers, or paradropped from a Lockheed Hercules transport aircraft or Boeing Chinook helicopter.

Another option for naval coastal forces is the inflatable rubber raiding craft, which is small enough to be paradropped or deployed from submarines. The craft are provided with compressed air cylinders so that they can be inflated rapidly, and a rigid deck can be installed in some types. Inflatable craft are usually powered by outboard diesel engines, but paddles are also carried, not just in case of engine failure but also to allow a quieter approach to shore.

▲ *U.S. Marines of an amphibious reconnaissance platoon are photographed at high speed in the course of combat rubber raiding craft training from a forward-deployed amphibious assault ship in the Pacific Ocean.*

▼ *Soldiers of the Japanese Ground Self-Defense Force prepare to bring their combat rubber reconnaissance craft into the docking well of an amphibious transport dock ship.*

# SEALS AND THE HIJACKING OF *MAERSK ALABAMA*
## (APRIL 8-9, 2009)

On April 8, 2009, four Somali pirates boarded the 17,375-ton U.S.-registered container ship *Maersk Alabama* about 280 miles (450 km) southeast of the Somalia port of Eyl as the ship was heading for Mombasa, Kenya, with a full load of cargo, some of which was relief supplies for Somalia, Uganda, and Kenya. The ship's engineers succeeded in sinking the pirates' speedboat shortly after the boarding by continuously swinging the container ship's rudder and thereby swamping the boat. As the pirates boarded the ship, most of the crew locked themselves in the engine room while the captain and two other crew members remained on the bridge. The engineers took control of the ship, rendering the bridge controls useless and thus denying the pirates the capability to control the ship. The crew later overpowered one of the pirates and freed one of the hostages.

The pirates decided to leave the ship in one of the ship's lifeboats, and took Captain Richard Phillips with them as a hostage. The crew tried to arrange an exchange of their captured pirate for Phillips. The captured pirate was released, but the pirates then refused to free Phillips. After exhausting the fuel of the ship's small man-overboard boat, the pirates transferred into the ship's covered lifeboat (with food, water, and other basic supplies for ten days), taking Phillips with them.

On the same day as the ship had been hijacked, two U.S. warships (destroyer *Bainbridge* and the frigate *Halyburton*) had been sent into the Gulf of Aden, where they were later joined by the amphibious assault ship *Boxer*. They approached the *Maersk Alabama*'s position early on the following day. *Maersk Alabama* then left the area, carrying an escort of 18 armed marines, for Mombasa, with the chief mate in temporary command. On April 11, the ship reached Mombasa, where it was secured as a crime scene.

Two days earlier, on April 9, an impasse developed between U.S.S. *Bainbridge* and the pirates in the lifeboat where Phillips was held captive. As the requisite authorization had been given by President Barack Obama, *Bainbridge*'s captain ordered a small-scale operation to secure the safe recovery of Phillips, whose life was deemed to be in immediate danger, because members of the U.S. Navy SEAL team

▲   *The men of the U.S. Navy's SEAL teams are highly trained in a multitude of tasks, including ship-boarding and hostage rescue.*

◀   *The U.S.-registered* Maersk Alabama *is owned by the Danish Maersk Line, the world's largest container ship operator.*

▼ *The U.S. guided-missile destroyer Bainbridge tows the lifeboat of the* Maersk Alabama *to the U.S. amphibious assault ship Boxer to be processed for evidence after the successful rescue of Captain Richard Phillips.*

▲ *A team from the U.S. amphibious assault ship Boxer boards the lifeboat from the* Maersk Alabama *(left) after the rescue of Captain Richard Phillips. Phillips had been held captive by Somali pirates in the lifeboat in the Indian Ocean for five days after a failed hijacking attempt off the Somali coast.*

embarked on *Bainbridge* indicated that the pirates were pointing an AK-47 assault rifle at their hostage. SEAL snipers on the destroyer's stern opened fire, killing three pirates in the lifeboat. A fourth pirate, who had been injured during the hijacking of *Maersk Alabama*, and was currently on board *Bainbridge* in an effort to negotiate a ransom, then surrendered and was arrested. Taken back to the U.S.A., he was later placed on trial and pleaded guilty, being sentenced to a term of more than 33 years in prison.

▶ *On November 19, 2009, Captain Richard Phillips, former captain of the container ship* Maersk Alabama, *publicly thanks sailors assigned to the U.S. guided-missile destroyer Bainbridge for his dramatic rescue at sea in an operation during which three of the pirates were killed by Mk 11 Mod 0 (Stoner SR-25) sniper rifles.*

# RIGID CRAFT

The delivery of special forces units across the surface of the water can also be effected by rigid inflatables (rigid lower hull and inflatable upper hull) or rigid raiding craft, although both of these types are powered by large outboard engines and are therefore noisy in operation.

The British Special Boat Service uses VT Halmatic rigid inflatables in 22- and 28-ft (6.7- and 8.5-m) lengths. Delivered in both sizes, the Pacific type is diesel-powered and has a range of 345 miles (555 km) and a maximum speed of 35 kt (65 kph) for the smaller type and more than 51 kt (95 kph) for the larger type. The Pacific craft can be outfitted with communications and navigation gear, boarding equipment, and mountings for 7.62-mm (0.3-in) medium or 12.7-mm (0.5-in) heavy machine guns. The Arctic series, in the same two lengths, comprise the Arctic 22 and Arctic 28. The smaller type is used as a boarding vessel and also for shore insertions, and with its petrol outboard engines has a maximum speed of 45 kt (83 kph) and can carry six men (coxswain and five others) over a distance of 174 miles (280 km). Like the Arctic 28, the Arctic 22 has a sturdy lower hull made of glassfiber-reinforced plastics (GRP) material.

▲ *Special Warfare Combatant-craft crewmen of a Special Boat Team navigate their rigid-hull inflatable boats under helicopter escort. Such craft offer greater speed and better sea-keeping than inflatable craft.*

◄ *U.S. Navy Special Warfare Combatant-craft crewmen of a Special Boat Team attach their rigid-hull inflatable boat to a CH-47 Chinook helicopter during an external air transport system training exercise.*

The Arctic 28 is used primarily for the maritime counter-terrorism and ship-boarding duties with up to ten men positioned on saddle seats. The Arctic 28 is powered by two 200/250-hp (149/186-kW) outboard motors that deliver a maximum speed of more than 52 kt (93 kph) and a range of 230 miles (370 km). The flexibility of the design is reflected in the fact that weapons, ship-boarding equipment (such as boarding poles and ladders), and navigation and communications gear can be mounted and/or installed to suit the type exactly to its operational requirement. The sturdy GRP hull means that the Arctic 28 can be dropped onto the surface of the sea by helicopter or paradropped from a Hercules aircraft.

The standard light assault craft of the Royal Marines and SBS is the Rigid Raider. It comes in various lengths—17, 21 ft 4 in, and 26 ft 3 in (5.2, 6.5, and 8 m)—and has a sturdy GRP hull, making it well suited to the beach assault role. Some Rigid Raiders are powered by single or twin outboard engines, while the latest Mk 3 has an inboard diesel engine.

It is thought that the SBS uses two types of high-speed intercept craft. One is the VSV (Very Slender Vessel), a wave-piercing design with stealth characteristics, and the other the FB MIL-50P. The MIL-50, produced by the Italian company Fabio Buzzi Design, is powered by three 1,000-hp (746-kW) engines giving a maximum speed of 70 kt (130 kph). These high-speed intercept craft are well suited for the fast insertion and extraction of SBS teams, as well as intercepting fast-moving drug runners or terrorist vessels.

It is believed that the SBS has used the VSV since 1999. This type is designed to pierce the waves rather than ride over them, giving them greater range and speed and making for a smoother ride. Wave-piercing boats can also operate in rougher seas than more traditional vessels. The VSV provides the SBS with long-range insertion and extraction capability, as well as the ability to chase down drug runners.

▲ *A Special Operations Craft Riverine craft during live-fire training. The craft was designed specifically for the clandestine insertion and extraction of U.S. Navy SEALs and other special operations forces along shallow waterways and open water.*

▲ *Special Warfare Combatant-craft crewmen of Special Boat Team 22 operate a Special Operations Craft Riverine during the filming of a notably realistic scene to be used in a motion picture.*

The type can mount two 12.7-mm (0.5-in) machine guns, and carries advanced communication and navigation equipment.

The SBS apparently uses the VT Halmatic VSV 16, which is 52.5 ft (16 m) long but only 10 ft (3.1 m) wide, and is powered by two 750-hp (559-kW) engines, which give a speed of more than 60 kt (111 kph). The angling of the VSV 16's design also offers a low radar profile and reduced wake generation. In combination with radar-absorbent materials and paint, this makes the boat very stealthy.

◄ *A Special Warfare Combatant-craft crewman reloads a 12.7-mm (0.5-in) M2HB heavy machine gun while conducting live-fire immediate action training drills.*

# aIR-CUSHION veHICLeS

The air-cushion vehicle, or hovercraft, is propelled by one or more propellers that are powered by engines that also direct air downward under the vehicle to create a cushion of slow-moving high-pressure air, which is contained within a circumferential "skirt." This offers unique transport capabilities as a hovercraft can travel over almost every type of comparatively flat surface. The air cushion allows it to travel from a ship lying off the shore across a beach or marshy area before touching down to unload its payload. The air-cushion vehicle is therefore an attractive option for amphibious forces including, to a limited extent, special forces. However, the disadvantage of air-cushion vehicles is that they cannot be stealthy in electro-magnetic terms, and are also very noisy in operation.

The most numerous class of military air-cushion craft is the U.S. Navy's LCAC (Landing Craft Air Cushion), which is used to support U.S. Marine Corps assault landing operations and, to a very much more limited extent, U.S. special forces operations from amphibious warfare vessels with a docking well. The LCAC entered service in 1986, and is a very blocky vehicle being 87 ft 11 in (26.4 m) long and 47 ft (14.3 m) wide.

▲   *Somewhere in the Pacific ocean during 2011, a man of the U.S. Navy guides a Landing Craft Air Cushion as it approaches the amphibious transport dock ship* New Orleans *during a training exercise.*

▼   *A Landing Craft Air Cushion moves up onto the beach during a series of amphibious operations involving U.S. Navy and Marine Corps personnel.*

The LCAC uses gas turbine power for lift and propulsion, the latter by a pair of well-shielded propellers over the vehicle's rear. The payload is 60 tons standard or 75 tons overload, and the vehicle's maximum speed is more than 70 kt (130 kph) reducing to 40 kt (74 kph) or more with maximum payload. Its range is 345 miles (555 km) at 35 kt (65 kph) with payload decreasing to 230 miles (370 km) at 40 kt (74 kph) with payload. The LCAC is also used by the Japanese navy.

The Soviet (now Russian) equivalent is the altogether larger "Zubr" class vehicle also used by Greece, Russia, and Ukraine. With a crew of 31 and power provided by five 11,836-shp (8825-kW) Kuznetsov NK-12MV gas turbines (two for lift and three for propulsion), the vehicle is 187 ft (57 m) long and 84 ft (25.6 m) wide, and its payload can include three battle tanks, or a larger number of light vehicles, or up to 500 men. The performance includes a maximum speed of 63 kt (117 kph) and a range of 300 miles (480 km) at a cruising speed of 55 kt (102 kph). A smaller air cushion vehicle used by the Russians is the "Czilin" class able to carry six fully armed men.

▲   *The Landing Craft Air Cushion is capable of moving sizable loads swiftly.*

▼   *A Landing Craft Air Cushion arrives to offload vehicles supporting a mock embassy evacuation scheduled biennially by the U.S. Pacific Fleet. As well as the U.S.A., the participants include Australia, Canada, Chile, Japan, the Netherlands, Peru, Singapore, South Korea, and the U.K.*

The Chinese navy has the "Jingsah II" class broadly equivalent to the LCAC. With a length of 72 ft (22 m), this has four gas turbines (two for propulsion and two for lift) for a maximum speed of 55 kt (102 kph) and a payload of 15 tons.

# OPERATION "MOSHTARAK" AND THE SAS IN AFGHANISTAN (2010)

Operation "Moshtarak" was a two-phase undertaking by the U.S.-led International Security Assistance Force in Afghanistan (February 13–25 and February 26–December 7, 2010) to wrest control of the "poppy-growing belt" of Helmand province in southern Afghanistan from the Taliban and its supporters. Involving more than 15,000 allied troops, largely in the Nad Ali and Lashkar Gah districts, "Moshtarak" combated a Taliban strength said by the allies to total between 400 and 1,000 men, but by the Taliban itself as 2,000 men. The operation cost the allies more than 61 dead, and the Taliban more than 120 dead and 56 captured in the first phase alone.

"Moshtarak" proper was preceded by a little known and still heavily classified undertaking in which the Allies sought effectively to decapitate the Taliban in this theater by killing or capturing much of its leadership. A leading role was played in this task by the

so-called Task Force 42, whose size was revealed by Prime Minister Gordon Brown to be slightly fewer than 500 men of the British special forces. Historically, the core element of the British special forces in Afghanistan was the Special Boat Service supplemented by a detachment from the Special Reconnaissance Regiment, men of the Special Forces Support Group, reservists of the 21st and 23rd SAS, supported by assorted communications, intelligence, and aviation assets. With the U.K.'s withdrawal of its last combat forces from Iraq in 2009, the special forces in Afghanistan were bolstered by the arrival of the regulars of two squadrons of the 22nd SAS.

▼ *U.S. soldiers of Alpha Company, 1st Battalion, 17th Infantry engage insurgent forces in a small-arms firefight (assault rifles, grenade launcher, and medium machine gun) in the course of Operation "Moshtarak" in Badula Qulp, Helmand province, Afghanistan.*

An unknown number of the various elements of the British special forces were allocated to TF 42, a unit closely associated with two comparable U.S. units, TFs 121 and 373. These three task forces are believed to have carried out a series of so-called "capture/kill" operations on the basis of the "Joint Prioritized Effects List" (JPEL), which is a classified "hit list" of Taliban leaders. It is believed that U.S. special operations forces were assigned high-level targets while the British special forces concentrated on medium-level targets.

From January 2010 the Allied forces had launched a number of smaller undertakings, so-called "shaping operations" to ready the way for the start of the main assault on February 13. One of these "shaping operations" comprised a series of nocturnal raids by four-man SAS and U.S. Navy SEAL teams to locate, pin, and destroy key Taliban personnel. The leadership of the Allied coalition reported that these efforts led to the deaths of some 50 Taliban leaders in the area, although the effects of this decimation of the local Taliban leadership in even the shorter term remained a matter of debate.

▲ *A 2nd lieutenant of the U.S. Army engages insurgents during Operation "Moshtarak" in Badula Qulp, Afghanistan (left). A lance corporal of the U.S. Marine Corps carefully crosses a stream while on a patrol in Marjah in Helmand province, Afghanistan (right).*

◄ *Soldiers of the Afghan National Army relax after a patrol in Marjah, Helmand province, Afghanistan. Together with U.S. Marines of the 3rd Battalion, 6th Marines, the ANA soldiers had been conducting Operation "Moshtarak" to eliminate the Taliban presence in Marjah and intimidate its citizens.*

# PATROL VEHICLES

With patrol and reconnaissance a major part of their tactical responsibilities, it is not surprising that special forces make extensive use of specialized patrol vehicles, which emphasize light weight, high speed, and high mobility as their primary attributes. The fact that the most extensive commitment of special forces is currently in desert and semi-desert conditions, in places such as Iraq and Afghanistan, has resulted in a crop of vehicles optimized for such conditions. These range from off-road motorcycles and quadbikes to more fully optimized lightweight four-wheeled vehicles of the 2x4 and 4x4 types.

One of the most extensively used is the U.S. Desert Patrol Vehicle (DPV). The DPV is a variant of the FAV, which was developed during the 1980s as part of the U.S. Army's High Technology Light Division (9th Division). The FAV was one of the equipment items that resulted and, in 1982, Chenowth Racing Products delivered 120 FAVs to the 9th Division. Along with light off-road motorcycles, the FAV was intended to provide the division with an exceptionally mobile component. The FAVs were later replaced by examples of the more standard Humvee, which offered neither the speed nor the mobility of the two-man FAV,

▲ Men of one of the U.S. Navy's SEAL teams, part of the U.S. special forces, in a Fast Attack Vehicle in 2001.

◀ In Kuwait during 2002, U.S. Navy SEALs operate Desert Patrol Vehicles in preparation for a mission. Each DPV carries advanced communication and weapon systems, and is optimized for desert terrain.

which was transferred to the special forces. It was redesignated the DPV and was first used in combat during the Gulf War in 1991. The first U.S. forces to enter Kuwait City were U.S. Navy SEALs in DPVs. The DPV is a product of Chenowth Racing Products, and its 200-hp (149-kW) Volkswagen air-cooled engine provides rapid acceleration as well as a maximum speed of 80 mph (130 kph). The standard 21-gal (79.5-liter) fuel tank offers a range of about 210 miles (340 km), while the addition of an optional fuel bladder can extend the range to more than 1,000 miles (1,610 km). The maximum payload is 1,500 lb (680 kg).

The DPV's basic weapon fit comprises one 12.7-mm (0.5-in) Browning M2 heavy machine gun, two 7.62-mm (0.3-in) M60 medium machine guns, and two M136 AT4 antiarmor weapons; the driver's M60 or gunner's M2 is replaced by a 40-mm (1.57-in) Mk 19 grenade launcher. Other light machine guns, such as the 7.62-mm (0.3-in) M240 and 5.56-mm (0.22-in) M249 SAW, can also be mounted.

The Light Strike Vehicle (LSV) is an improved version of the DPV. Several Light Strike Vehicles exist, including a version by Chenowth, the British Longline LSV, and the Singaporean Spider Light Strike Vehicle. U.S. special forces adopted the LSV for its small size and high mobility, and it is used for fast raiding operations, scouting missions, special forces support, and other elements of low-intensity warfare. The LSV is not armored, even against small arms fire. The driver and two passengers sit side-by-side in the front, and the gunner in an elevated rear seat in front of engine. The gunner's seat can be turned through 180° so that he can operate the 7.62-mm (0.3-in) machine gun. The LSV can be air transported internally by the Boeing CH-47 and Sikorsky CH-53 transport helicopters. The new Advanced LSV has a more conventional appearance and differs from the original versions in several ways, including better performance and improved armament.

▲ *A Fast Attack Vehicle prototype undergoes testing in 1982 at a test driving range. The FAV is equipped with an M60 machine gun in front of the passenger's seat and a Mk 19 Mod 3 40-mm (1.57-in) automatic grenade launcher on the roll cage.*

▲ *In the U.K. during 1989, a Wessex Saker light strike vehicle is put through its paces. The vehicle was produced for use by the Special Air Service and was also used during antipoaching patrols guarding endangered species of wildlife.*

◄ *In Singapore, the Malaysian southern state of Johore's Crown Prince Ibrahim Ismail Iskandar (right) rides in a Light Strike Vehicle during a visit to the Singapore commando headquarters on April 13, 2007.*

# HEAVY VEHICLES

For their ability to move men, equipment, and supplies in enemy territory, the world's special forces rely on heavier vehicles with 4x4 and, increasingly, 6x6 drive. Typical of the older type of vehicle still in extensive service is the British Land Rover, which is operated by the Special Air Service Regiment in a number of forms. Its rugged nature, reliability, maneuverability, and ease of maintenance make the Land Rover ideal for special forces operations that require long range and the ability to carry a useful armament. Weapon mounting facilities have increased from the fixed variety to power-assisted mounts with adjustable swivel seats, which are capable of carrying weapons ranging from single 7.62-mm (0.3-in) medium machine guns to 30-mm (1.2-in) cannon. The vehicle usually has a three-man crew, with space for water, rations, radio and navigation equipment, and enough fuel to give an operational range of 400 miles (645 km). There is a medium machine gun mounting in front of the commander's seat, next to the driver, and two medium machine guns or one larger-caliber gun can be mounted on the back of the vehicle. A camouflage netting roll is strapped to the front end of the hood and the side, allowing the vehicle to be rapidly covered. All vehicles are fitted with a special belly plate beneath the cab for protection against mine attack. Sand channels and spare wheels are mounted on the side and back

of the vehicle. Land Rovers can be carried inside the Lockheed Hercules transport aircraft or slung beneath a medium-lift helicopter.

The Remote Area Patrol Vehicle variant is 14.5 ft (4.43 m) long and 5.9 ft (1.79 m) wide, and with the 134-hp (100-kW) V-8 gasoline engine has a maximum speed of 75 mph (120 kph).

▲ British paratroopers on patrol in their Land Rover outside Camp Bastion, Afghanistan. Though only poorly protected, the Land Rover is very reliable and rugged.

◄ Men of the Royal Air Force Regiment halt on a road in their Land Rover while conducting a combat mission near Kandahar airfield, Afghanistan, during 2010.

◀ Men of the U.S. special forces, on foot and in up-armored HMMWVs ('Humvees'). These personnel are from the 7th Special Forces Group and are operating in the Iraqi village of Makarim during 2008.

▼ "Humvees" of the new Iraqi Army during a routine patrol in 2008. The crews watch for signs of insurgent activity, and also for improvised explosive devices under or beside the road.

The U.S. counterpart of the Land Rover, though somewhat more modern and considerably more versatile, is the "Humvee," or more formally the High Mobility Multi-purpose Wheeled Vehicle (HMMWV). It entered service in 1984 and has since been built in very large numbers for U.S. service in a host of tasks with armored and unarmored bodies, and also for export. The variant for the U.S. special forces is the Ground Mobility Vehicle (GMV). This has been developed in several variants, tailored to different special forces, including the GMV-S for the special forces, GMV-R for the 75th Ranger Regiment, GMV-N for the U.S. Navy SEALs, GMV-T, GMV-SD, and GMV-ST for the U.S. Air Force Special Operations Command, and GMV-M for the U.S. Marines Special Operations Command.

The particular features of the GMV are heavier suspension, more rugged tires, greater ground clearance, more powerful engine, an open bed for improved storage/access, a winch for towing other vehicles, GPS navigation system, and a set of mounts onto which various weapons can be fitted. These include belt-fed heavy and medium machine guns, 5.56-mm (0.219-in) M249 SAW light machine guns, and Mk 17 and Mk 47 40-mm (1.57-in) grenade launchers. The GMV can also be fitted with smoke grenade launchers. The GMV has an open, rather than enclosed, rear; this flat bed is used to store fuel, ammunition, rations, and other supplies. It can be covered to keep out dust and sand.

# OPERATION "NEPTUNE'S SPEAR" AND THE KILLING OF OSAMA BIN LADEN (MAY 2, 2011)

After U.S. intelligence had fixed the "permanent" residence of Osama bin Laden, head of the al-Qaeda organization, as a compound in the Pakistani town of Abbottabad, President Barack Obama authorized a special forces mission to kill the U.S.A.'s "number one" enemy. The CIA briefed Vice Admiral William H. McRaven, commanding the Joint Special Operations Command (JSOC), in January 2011, and McRaven assigned a captain of the Naval Special Warfare Development Group, and a group of six other JSOC personnel, to work with a CIA team in planning the attack. It was decided not to involve the Pakistanis, or even inform them, as the U.S.A. had no confidence in the Pakistanis' ability to maintain operational security.

The raid on May 2 was carried out by about 24 SEALs of Red Squadron of the JSOC's Naval Special Warfare Development Group temporarily transferred, for legal reasons, to the CIA. The SEALs were divided into two teams, and were supported by about 55 other personnel, including a translator, the handler of a dog to track any fugitives and warn of any Pakistani approach, helicopter crew, tactical signals operatives, intelligence collectors, and navigators using classified imaging equipment.

The SEALs entered Pakistan by air after staging through Jalalabad, in eastern Afghanistan, in modified Sikorsky MH-70 Black Hawk helicopters. The raid was undertaken at a time of little moonlight so the helicopters could overfly Pakistan with little chance of visual detection, and the flight from Jalalabad to Abbottabad took some 90 minutes. The mission plan called for the first helicopter to hover above the southern part of the compound as the embarked SEALs

▶ *Operation Neptune's Spear logo depicts all agencies and commands that participated in the operation.*

◀ *Men of a U.S. Navy SEAL team practice the important fast-roping technique from a Sikorsky H-60 Seahawk helicopter and then rapid deployment to create an initial defensive perimeter.*

▼  *A Pakistani policeman moves a vendor from the compound in which Osama bin Laden was killed by SEALs in Abbottabad, Pakistan.*

▲  *President Barack Obama, Vice President Joe Biden and members of the national security team receive an update on "Neptune Spear" in one of the conference rooms of the Situation Room of the White House on May 1, 2011.*

fast-roped to the ground. The second helicopter was to fly to the compound's northeastern corner to land the translator, the dog and its handler, and four SEALs to secure the perimeter before moving to hover over the house as the team leader and six SEALs fast-roped onto the roof. The team in the courtyard was to enter the house from the ground floor.

The first helicopter's tail rotor grazed a wall and the machine crash-landed. No one on board was seriously injured, so the second helicopter landed outside the compound and deployed its men, who scaled the walls. The SEALs then used explosives to blow their way through walls and doors as they entered the buildings. The SEALs entered the main building on the second and third floors where bin Laden lived with his family.

The SEALs found bin Laden on the second or third floor of the main building. After spotting the approaching SEALs, bin Laden moved into a bedroom as a SEAL fired at him but missed. Inside this room, two of bin Laden's wives shielded him. One of them shouted at the

SEALs and made as if to charge, and after shooting her in the leg one of the SEALs seized both women and bundled them out of the way. A second SEAL then shot bin Laden in the chest and, as the al-Qaeda leader fell backward, shot him again in the head. In addition to bin Laden, four other persons were killed—one of bin Laden's adult sons, his courier and the courier's brother, and the latter's wife. Bin Laden's 12-year-old daughter was struck in her foot or ankle by a piece of flying debris, and the wife of one of the dead men was also injured.

It had been planned that the whole operation should last 30 minutes, and in fact the time the SEALS spent on the ground was 38 minutes, with the task of finding and killing bin Laden being completed in the first 15 minutes. The helicopter which had crash-landed could not be used to extract the team, and was destroyed to safeguard its classified equipment, including an apparent stealth capability. The assault team called in another helicopter and the Americans departed to Bagram air base with bin Laden's body.

# APPENDIX

▲ *Iraqi Special Operations Forces (ISOF) set a perimeter after fast-roping insertion training with members of U.S. special forces.*

# THE WORLD'S
# SPECIAL FORCES

# THE WORLD'S SPECIAL FORCES

## AFGHANISTAN
Afghan National Army Commando Brigades and
  Special Forces

## ALBANIA
Albanian Joint Forces Command "Black Tigers"
  and Special Forces Battalion
Albanian Navy Naval Commandos

## ALGERIA
National Army Groupe d'Intervention Spécial

## ARGENTINA
**Argentine Air Force:**
Grupo de Operaciones Especiales (Special
  Operations Group)
**Argentine Army:**
Agrupación de Fuerzas de Operaciones Especiales
  (Special Operations Forces Group)
Regimiento de Asalto Aéreo 601 (601st Air
  Assault Regiment)
Compañía de Comandos 601 (601st
  Commando Company)
Compañía de Comandos 602 (602nd
  Commando Company)
Tropas de Operaciones Especiales de Montaña
  (Special Operations Mountain Troops)
Compañía de Cazadores de Montaña 6 (6th
  Mountain Hunters Company)
Compañía de Cazadores de Montaña 8 (8th
  Mountain Hunters Company)
**Argentine Marine Corps:**
Agrupación de Comandos Anfibios
  (Amphibious Commandos Group)
**Argentine National Gendarmerie:**
Grupo Alacrán (Scorpion Group)
Grupo Monte (Hill Group)
**Argentine Naval Prefecture:**
Grupo Albatros (Albatross Group)
**Argentine Navy:**
Agrupación de Buzos Tácticos (Tactical Divers
  Group)

## ARMENIA
**Armenian Army:**
Army Commandos

## AUSTRALIA
**Australian Defence Force Special Operations
  Command:**
1st Commando Regiment
2nd Commando Regiment
Australian Special Air Service Regiment
Incident Response Regiment

What is now the Australian Special Air Service
Regiment (SASR) came into being on July 25, 1957
as the 1st Special Air Service Company, which in
1960 became part of the Royal Australian Regiment
and was given the responsibility for commando
and special forces operations in the Australian
Army. The unit was expanded to three saber
squadrons and on August 20, 1964 became the
Australian SASR. The SASR is based conceptually on
the British SAS, but also on World War II Australian
special reconnaissance and commando units. The
SASR's squadrons are rotated through the two roles
performed by the SASR. One squadron undertakes
the counter-terrorism role, and the other two the
surveillance and reconnaissance roles. On operations,
each squadron is supported by a troop of the 152nd
Signal Squadron. In the reconnaissance role, the
SASR operates in small patrols tasked with infiltration
of enemy-held territory to gather intelligence on
troop movements. In this role the SASR generally
seeks to avoid directly engaging enemy units,
though its men can summon air and other support
to destroy enemy units whenever possible. Such
reconnaissance patrols can be inserted by air, land,
or sea (including by submarine), and have showed
their ability to undertake lengthy operations in
jungle and desert terrain. In the counter-terrorism
and special recovery roles, the SASR specializes in
tasks such as direct action and hostage rescue,
including the boarding of ships while they are
under way. The SASR provides the Tactical Assault
Group (West) and the 2nd Commando Regiment
the Tactical Assault Group (East).

The SASR first saw combat in 1965 during the
Indonesian Confrontation, working with its British
and New Zealand counterparts to prevent
Indonesian infiltration into North Borneo. The SASR
was next involved in the Vietnam War as part of the
1st Australian Task Force from April 1966. In Vietnam
the SASR undertook reconnaissance throughout
the 1st ATF's area of responsibility. In this conflict
the SASR worked closely with the New Zealand SAS,
a New Zealand troop being attached to each
Australian squadron. After the bombing of the
Sydney Hilton hotel in February 1978 the SASR
became the Australian military counter-terrorist
response force and, as well as offering the capability
for response to terrorist attacks in Australian cities,
the SASR counter-terrorism unit was also required
to be capable of boarding ships and oil platforms.
In more recent years the SASR has been committed
to peacekeeping operations (Zimbabwe, Somalia,
Cambodia, and Rwanda), and has also been heavily
involved in operations in Iraq and Afghanistan.

## AUSTRIA
**Austrian Army:**
Jagdkommando

## AZERBAIJAN
**Azerbaijani Navy:**
641st Special Warfare Naval Unit

## THE BAHAMAS
**Royal Bahamas Defence Force:**
Commando Squadron
Special Operations Unit

## BANGLADESH
**Bangladesh Army:**
1st Para Commando Battalion
ASOCOM (Army Special Operation Command)
Counter-Terrorism and Intelligence Bureau
PGR (Presidential Guard Regiment)
SOTRACOM (Special Operation Training Command)
SSF (Special Security Force)
**Bangladesh Navy:**
SWADS (Special Warfare Diving and Salvage)
ODD 71
**Bangladesh Police:**
RAB-12 (12th Rapid Action Battalion)

## BELARUS
**Armed Forces of Belarus:**
5th Separate Spetznaz Brigade

## BELGIUM
**Belgian Land Component:**
Immediate Reaction Cell
Special Forces Group

## BHUTAN
**Royal Bhutan Army:**
Royal Bodyguard

## BRAZIL
**Brazilian Air Force:**
Para-SAR
**Brazilian Army:**
1º Batalhão de Forças Especiais
Brazilian Special Operations Brigade
**Brazilian Navy:**
COMANF (Comandos Anfibios)
GRUMEC (Grupamento de Mergulhadores de
  Combate)

## BULGARIA
63rd Maritime Special Reconnaissance Force "Black
  Sea Sharks"

68th Special Forces Brigade
SOBT (Special Unit for Combating Terrorism)

## CAMBODIA
**Royal Cambodian Army:**
911th Para-Commando Battalion

## CANADA
**Canadian Special Operations Forces
   Command:**
427th Special Operations Aviation Squadron
Canadian Joint Incident Response Unit
Canadian Special Operations Regiment
Joint Task Force 2
Task Force Arrowhead

## CHILE
**Chilean Air Force:**
Grupo de Fuerzas Especiales (Special Forces
   Group)
Agrupación Antisecuestros Aéreos (Air
   Counter-Terrorism Group)
Comandos de Aviación (Aviation
   Commandos)
Paracaidistas de Busqueda, Salvamento y
   Rescate (Parachute Search, Rescue, and
   Recovery)
**Chilean Army:**
Brigada de Operaciones Especiales "Lautaro"
   1º Batallón de Paracaidistas "Pelantaru"
      (1st Parachute Battalion "Pelantaru")

1º Compañía de Comandos "Iquique"
   (1st Commando Company "Iquique")
10º Compañía de Comandos
   (10th Commando Company)
13º Compañía de Comandos "Escorpión"
   (13th Commando Company
   "Escorpión")
Grupo Especial de Montaña (Special
   Mountain Group)
**Chilean Navy:**
Buzos Tácticos de la Armada (Tactical Divers
   of the Navy)
Comando de Fuerzas Especiales (Special
   Forces Command)
Equipo de Intervención Rápida (Rapid
   Intervention Team)
Grupo de Abordaje y Registro de la Armada (GARA)
   (Naval Boarding and Search Group)

## CHINA
**People's Armed Police:**
Immediate Action Unit
Snow Leopard Commando Unit
Special Police Unit
**People's Liberation Army Ground Force:**
People's Liberation Army Special Operations
   Forces

The People's Liberation Army (PLA) Special
Operations Forces was created to provide a
capability for rapid-reaction combat in a limited

▲ *Australian Special Operations Task Group (SOTG)
soldiers and Afghan police patrol among the isolated
village communities in the the mountains of Uruzgan,
Afghanistan, in 2009.*

regional war, commando operations, counter-
terrorism actions, and intelligence gathering.
Although the size of the Special Operations Forces
remains classified, it is estimated to number
between 7,000 and 14,000 troops. The PLA first
became interested in the modern form of special
warfare in the mid-1980s when it was shifting
conceptually from its traditional "people's war"
thinking to the ability to "fight a local war under
hi-technology conditions." Chinese military
theoreticians postulated that the next war would
be a short-lived but fast conflict on the periphery of
the Chinese sphere of interest rather than a total
war on Chinese territories, and thus that
conventional massed infantry-heavy ground forces
would be at a disadvantage.

On December 23, 2008, the Special Operations
Forces made their first publicly known mission by
deploying on board three Chinese warships tasked
with the escort and protection of merchant
shipping in waters infested with Somali pirates. This
task was undertaken in co-operation with other
nations as part of a U.N. mandate.

The Guangzhou Military Region Special Forces
Unit was created in 1988 as the PLA's first specialized
reconnaissance group, and in 2000 was expanded

into the first PLA special operations unit capable of air, sea, and land operations. The Chengdu Military Region Special Forces Unit ("Falcon") was created in 1992 and specializes in target locating and indicating, airborne insertion, sabotage and offensive strike, and emergency evacuation. Created early in the 1990s, the Beijing Military Region Special Forces Unit is equipped with an assortment of high-technology equipment, including unmanned aerial reconnaissance vehicles, individual explosion devices, and hand-held laser dazzling weapons.

Other Chinese special forces elements are the Shenyang Military Region Special Forces Unit, Nanjing Military Region Special Forces Unit ("Flying Dragon"), Nanjing Military Region Special Forces Unit ("Oscar"), Lanzhou Military Region Special Forces Unit, Hong Kong Special Operations Company ("Five-Minute Response Unit") and Macau Quick-Reaction Platoon.

## COLOMBIA
**Colombian Air Force:**
ACOEA (Agrupación de Comandos Especiales Aéreos)
**Colombian National Army:**
AFEAU (Agrupación de Fuerzas Especiales Antiterroristas Urbanas)
AFEAUR (Agrupación de Fuerzas Especiales Antiterroristas Urbanas y Rurales)
Brigada Contra el Narcotráfico
Brigada de Fuerzas Especiales
Fuerza de Despliegue Rápido (FUDRA)
GAULA (Grupo de Acción Unificada por la Libertad Personal)
**Colombian National Navy:**
AFEAUR (Agrupación de Fuerzas Especiales Antiterroristas Urbanas)
BFEIM (Batallón de Fuerzas Especiales de Infantería de Marina)
GAULA (Grupos Autónomos y Unificados por la Libertad y la Antiextorsión)

## COSTA RICA
**Military of Costa Rica:**
UEI (Unidad Especial de Intervención)

## CÔTE D'IVOIRE
**National Armed Forces of Côte d'Ivoire:**
Rapid Intervention Battalion

## CROATIA
**Croat Army:**
VOB (Military Intelligence Battalion)
BSD (Special Operations Battalion)
**Croat Military Police:**
SPN VP (Special Military Police Company)

## CUBA
**Cuban Revolutionary Navy:**
Desembarco de Granma

Formacion de Missiones Especial Naval
**Cuban Revolutionary Army:**
Tropas Especiales Avispas Negras

## CYPRUS
**Cypriot National Guard:**
Special Forces Command
**Cypriot Navy:**
Underwater Demolition Command

## CZECH REPUBLIC
**Armed Forces of the Czech Republic:**
102. Průzkumný Prapor (102nd Reconnaissance Battalion)
601st Special Forces Group

## DENMARK
**Danish Home Guard:**
SSR (Special Support & Reconnaissance Company)
**Royal Danish Army:**
Jægerkorpset
Protection Team
**Royal Danish Navy:**
Frømandskorpset
Slædepatruljen Sirius

## ECUADOR
**Ecuadorian Army:**
9th Special Forces Brigade PATRIA
GEO (Grupo Especial de Operaciones)
Jungle Warfare Special Operations Iwia Battalion No. 60
Ratas de Río (or Fusileros Fluviales)

## EGYPT
**Egyptian Army:**
Army Rangers
Unit 777 (or Task Force 777)
**Egyptian Navy:**
Egyptian Navy SEALs

## EL SALVADOR
**Salvadoran Army:**
Comando Especial Anti-Terrorista

## ESTONIA
**Estonian Army:**
Estonian Special Operations Force

## FINLAND
**Finnish Army:**
Utti Jaeger Regiment (Erikoisjääkärit [Special Jaegers] and Laskuvarjojääkärit [Airborne Jaegers])
**Finnish Border Guard:**
South-East Finland Border Guard District (Erikoisrajajääkärit [Special Border Jaegers])
**Finnish Navy:**
Gulf of Finland Naval Military Command

(Raivaajasukeltajat [EOD Divers] and Taistelusukeltajat [Combat Divers])

## FRANCE
Most French special forces are attached to the COS [Commandement des Opérations Spéciales]
**Primary:**
Bureau des Forces Spéciales (reassembling)
FKSOD (Commando Parachutiste de l'Air no. 10, Escadrille Spécialisée Hélicoptères 1/67 Pyrénées becoming Escadron de Hélicoptères 1/67 Pyrénées, and Escadron de Transport 3/61 Poitou)
Brigade des Forces Spéciales Terre (1er Régiment de Parachutistes d'Infanterie de Marine, 4e Régiment d'Hélicoptères des Forces Spéciales and 13e Régiment de Dragons Parachutistes)
Commandos-Marine (Commando Jaubert [Escouade de Contre-Terrorisme et de Libération d'Otages], Commando Kieffer, Commando de Montfort, Commando de Penfentenyo, Commando Trépel [Escouade de Contre-Terrorisme et de Libération d'Otages] and Commando Hubert)
**Secondary:**
17e Régiment du Génie Parachutiste
Groupement des Commandos Parachutistes (Chuteurs Opérationnels)
Escadron Parachutiste d'Intervention de la Gendarmerie Nationale
Groupe de Sécurité de la Présidence de la République
Groupe d'Intervention de la Gendarmerie Nationale

The Brigade des Forces Spéciales Terre has two ground elements (1er Régiment de Parachutistes d'Infanterie de Marine and 13e Régiment de Dragons Parachutistes) and one air element (4e Régiment d'Hélicoptères des Forces Spéciales). The origins of the 1er RPIMa can be found in World War II, in which the regiment was formed in the U.K. as the 1ère Compagnie d'Infanterie de l'Air before being redesignated as the 1ère Compagnie de Chasseurs Parachutistes. The unit had about 50 paratroopers when it was transferred to the Special Air Service in the North African campaign, and then also served in Crete, France, Belgium, the Netherlands, and Germany. In its current form, the regiment is the successor to the two Free French Special Air Service (SAS) units, namely 3 SAS (3e RCP) and 4 SAS (2e RCP). After World War II, 3 and 4 SAS were transferred to the French Army on October 1, 1945. The regiment fought in the Indo-China War, and was re-formed after returning to serve as the training depot for the colonial parachute force during the Algerian War. It remained in this role until 1974 when it became a Special Forces regiment.

As a result of early history with the Special Air Service, much of the 1er RPIMa's core is derived from that of the SAS. Each company specializes in a particular operational aspect, such as maritime, air operations/pathfinder, mobility, etc. Thus, the 1ére Compagnie has pathfinders, divers, and snipers, 2e Compagnie has mountain and jungle specialists, 3e Compagnie specializes in mobility and desert operations, and 4e Compagnie concentrates on urban warfare, counter-terrorism, and the bodyguard role. There is also a command and logistics company.

The 13e RDP is an airborne special forces unit with the primary task of airborne reconnaissance. It was after World War II that the 13e RDP underwent a change of role into a long-range reconnaissance unit. During the Cold War, the regiment's primary task was the provision of intelligence to the 1ère Arme, while that of each company of the 1er RPIMa was the provision of intelligence for a corps. Since the end of the Cold War, the 1er RPIMa has become a direct-action unit while the 13e RDP specializes in reconnaissance for the planning of special operations in a fashion similar to the U.S. Army's Long Range Surveillance Detachment or Long Range Surveillance Company, and the British Army's Special Reconnaissance Regiment.

The 13e RDP took part in the First Gulf War. It was also involved in the Kosovo campaign, in which its task, together with other French units, was the exploitation of advanced tactics and equipment to force the Serb Army into engagements with the Kosovo Liberation Army and other Allied forces in the open, where it was destroyed by Allied bombing. The 13e RDP also undertakes reconnaissance in hostile terrain, and operates in other special forces tasks.

The brigade's third element is the 4e RHFS, which provides air support for the two other regiments with one squadron of transport helicopters and another of armed helicopters.

## GEORGIA

**Georgian Armed Forces:**

Special Forces Brigade
Internal Forces (SOD, KUD, SIAG, and CTC)

## GERMANY

**German Army:**

Fernspählehrkompanie 200
Kommando Spezialkräfte
Special Operations Force Air Rotary Wing

**German Navy:**

Kampfschwimmer

The Fernspählehrkompanie 200 (FSLK200) numbers some 220 men. It is a notably specialized German Army unit optimized for long-range intelligence-gathering missions. Until the creation of the Kommando Spezialkräfte (Special Forces Command) late in 1996, the German Army had

▲ *Men of the Danish forces run with full combat load during endurance training.*

three Fernspählehr companies, of which one was attached to each corps. The companies undertook a task not practiced by the German Army in World War II, so the basic concept for the three companies was derived from Finland's long-range patrol teams of World War II. These undertook reconnaissance, sabotage, and prisoner capture missions as far as 185 miles (300 km) behind the Soviet front line, surviving for days on supplies they carried with them or weeks when they were supplied by parachute drops. Other elements of the new companies' operational methods were derived from the special skills of German Gebirgsjäger (mountain infantry) and Fallschirmjäger (parachute infantry) units in World War II, and of the foreign special forces the Germans had faced during the war.

The first Fernspählehr company was initially designated as the Lehrgruppe R (Training Group R), but was soon redesignated as the Fernspählehrkompanie 200. When the Kommando Spezialkräfte came into existence, it drew its personnel mainly from the Fernspähkompanie 100 and Fernspähkompanie 300, which were disbanded.

The third syllable (lehr) in Fernspählehrkompanie 200 signifies training and demonstration for the German special forces, and as such the company trains other troops as well as undertaking field

evaluation and demonstration of new tactics and equipment. It still has an offensive role, however. The Fernspählehrkompanie 200 is controlled by the German Army's Division Spezielle Operationen (Special Operations Division) and is also an element of the new Heeresaufklärungstruppe (army reconnaissance troops) whereas, up to 2007, the Fernspähtruppen (long-range reconnaissance troops) had been independent.

The FSLK200 comprises four scout/reconnaissance platoons, a special-purposes scout/reconnaissance platoon (covering the technical aspects of intelligence gathering as well as analysis of gathered data), a special applications maintenance group, a special applications support group, two medical squads, and a military intelligence platoon.

As with all parts of the German armed forces, the FSLK200 requires parliamentary approval for any involvement outside Germany. However, this approval can be obtained retrospectively if the situation requires immediate action. Details about the FSLK200's operations are scarce, but it is known that Fernspäher carried out missions in Bosnia and Herzegovina, during the Kosovo War, and later during Operation "Enduring Freedom" in Afghanistan. Fernspäher soldiers were also sent to the Democratic Republic of the Congo in 2006 as part of a European Union mission.

### GReece
**Hellenic Air Force:**
31 MEE (31st Special Operations Squadron)
**Hellenic Army:**
1st Raider/Paratrooper Brigade, including ETA (Special Paratrooper Detachment) and "Z" MAK (Zeta Amphibious Raider Squadron)
**Hellenic Navy:**
DYK (Underwater Demolition Command)

### Guatemala
**Guatemalan Army:**
Kaibiles

### HUNGARY
**Hungarian Defense Forces:**
34th "László Bercsényi" Special Operations Battalion

### INDIA
**Indian Air Force:**
Garud Commando Force
**Indian Army:**
Ghatak Force
Para-Commandos
**Indian Navy:**
MARCOS (Marine Commandos)
**Indian para-military forces:**
COBRA (Commando Battalion for Resolute Action)
National Security Guards
Special Protection Group

▲ *German forces demonstrate fast-roping from a Bell UH-1 Iroquois helicopter.*

**Research and Analysis Wing:**
Special Frontier Force
Special Group

The Para-Commandos of the Indian Army were established in 1966, and are currently the largest and most significant element of the Indian special forces. The Para-Commandos are an element of the Indian Army's Parachute Regiment, from which they select most of their personnel.

In the course of the Indo-Pakistani War of 1965, an extemporized commando unit, the Meghdoot Force of volunteers from infantry units, was created by Major Megh Singh of the Brigade of the Guards. The unit proved very capable, and the Indian government then authorized a properly established commando unit, at first to be part of the Brigade of the Guards but then, in recognition of the need for a parachute capability, within the Parachute Regiment. Thus, the 9th Battalion (Commando) was created on July 1, 1966 with the members of the Meghdoot Force as its core. In June 1967, the unit was divided to create a second commando unit (the 10th Battalion). The 9th and 10th Battalions were to operate in the northern mountains and western desert, respectively. The battalions were redesignated as the 9th and 10th Para (Commando) Battalions in 1969.

In 1978, the 1st Battalion, The Parachute Regiment, was for trials purposes converted into a third commando battalion, then remaining in its revised form as a reserve element, and in 1995 a fourth commando battalion came into existence when the 21st Maratha Light Infantry was selected for similar conversion for service in eastern India as the 21st Battalion (Special Forces), The Parachute Regiment. Reflecting the changing requirements of the Indian Army from the last years of the 20th century, placing greater emphasis on special forces, the 2nd, 3rd, and 4th Battalions, The Parachute Regiment, were also converted to the Para-Commando role, so increasing the strength of the special forces to seven battalions. The Parachute Regiment presently incorporates seven special forces, three parachute, two territorial army, and one counter-insurgency battalions in its fold.

The role of the Para-Commandos includes intelligence collection; special reconnaissance; subversion and sabotage of key enemy infrastructure items and communications through deep penetration and surgical strikes behind the lines; covert and overt direct-action special operations within the Indian Army's counter-terrorist and counter-insurgency remits; and hostage rescue both inside and outside India.

The Para-Commandos have been involved in the 1971 Indo-Pakistan War, 1984 Operation "Bluestar" to remove Sikh militants from the Golden Temple in Punjab, 1987 Operation "Pawan" peacekeeping effort in Sri Lanka, 1988 Operation "Cactus" to liberate the Maldives from a take-over by mercenaries, 1995 to liberate six tourists taken hostage by Kashmiri militants, 1999 Kargil War with Pakistan, 2000 Operation "Khukri" peacekeeping in Sierra Leone, and continuing counter-insurgency in Jammu and Kashmir and also in the eastern states of India.

## INDONESIA
**Indonesian Air Force:**
Korps Paskhas
Den Bravo-90 Paskhas
**Indonesian Army:**
Kopassus
SAT-81 GULTOR
**Indonesian Navy:**
Denjaka
Kesatuan Gurita
KOPASKA (Komando Pasukan Katak)
Taifib

## IRAN
**Iranian Army:**
Takavar
**Revolutionary Guards:**
Quds Force

## IRAQ
**Iraqi Army:**
ISOF (Iraqi Special Operations Forces)

## IRELAND
**Irish Army:**
Fianoglach
**Irish Naval Service:**
Naval Service Diving Section

## ISRAEL
**Israeli Air Force:**
Shaldag Unit
Unit 669
**Israeli Army:**
Duvdevan Unit
Egoz Reconnaissance Unit
Sayeret Golani
Sayeret Maglan
Sayeret Matkal
Sayeret Yahalom
**Israeli Navy:**
Shayetet 13

## ITALY
**Carabinieri:**
GIS (Gruppo di Intervento Speciale)
**Italian Air Force:**
17° Stormo Incursori
**Italian Army:**
4th Alpini Parachutist (Ranger) Regiment "Monte Cervino"
9th Parachute Assault Regiment "Col Moschin"
26th Special Operations Helicopter Unit "Giove"
185th Reconnaissance Target Acquisition Regiment "Folgore"
**Italian Navy:**
COMSUBIN (Comando Subacquei e Incursori)

## JAPAN
**Japan Coast Guard:**
Special Security Team
**Japan Ground Self-Defense Force:**
Special Forces Group
**Japan Maritime Self-Defense Force:**
Special Boarding Unit

## JORDAN
69th Special Reconnaissance Regiment
Unit 71 Special Forces Division
Unit 101 Special Forces Division
Royal Special Forces

## LATVIA
**Latvian Army:**
Special Tasks Unit

## LEBANON
**Lebanese Army:**
Lebanese Commando Regiment
**Lebanese Navy:**
Lebanese Navy SEAL Regiment

## LITHUANIA
**Lithuanian Special Operations Force:**
ARAS (Anti-terrorism force squad)
CDS (Combat divers service)
Special Operations Element
VGJB (Vytautas Great Jaeger Battalions)
YPT (Special Purpose Service)

## MALAYSIA
**Malaysian Army:**
Grup Gerak Khas
11th Rejimen Gerak Khas
21st Commandos
22nd Commandos
**Royal Malaysian Navy:**
PASKAL (Naval Special Forces)
**Royal Johor Military Force:**
JMF Elite Forces
**Royal Malaysian Air Force:**
PASKAU (Special Air Service)

## MALDIVES
**Maldives National Defence Force:**
Special Forces

## MALTA
**Armed Forces of Malta:**
C (Special Duties) Company
Rapid Deployment Team

## MEXICO
**Mexican Army:**
Grupo Aeromóvil de Fuerzas Especiales
Grupo Aeromóvil de Fuerzas Especiales del Alto Mando
Grupo Anfibio de Fuerzas Especiales
**Mexican Navy:**
Fuerzas Especiales

## NEPAL
**Nepalese Army:**
Shree Singha Nath Battalion (Commandos)
Shree Bhairavnath Battalion (Para Commandos)
Shree Mahabir Battalion (Rangers)
Shree Yuddha Bhairav Battalion (Special Forces)

## NETHERLANDS
**Netherlands Marine Corps:**
MARSOF (Maritime Special Operations Forces)
**Royal Marechaussee (Netherlands gendarmerie corps):**
BSB (Brigade Speciale Beveiligingsopdrachten)

**Royal Netherlands Army:**

KCT (Korps Commandotroepen)

The Maritime Special Operations Forces (MARSOF) is the new special forces disposition of the Dutch Marine Corps created by amalgamating the Mountain Leader Reconnaissance Platoon, the Unit Interventie Mariniers, and the combat divers platoon. MARSOF training takes about 40 weeks and turns the selected marines into specialized long-range reconnaissance and special forces operatives and maritime counter-terrorism specialists, with emphasis on maritime special operations. Any marine wanting to specialize in the mountain leader and combat diver roles can apply for these specializations after completing MARSOF training. In overall terms, the MARSOF is based on the British Special Boat Service.

The Korps Commandotroepen (KCT) are the special forces of the Royal Netherlands Army, and are optimized for deployment to any point in the world under any and all circumstances to undertake any of the entire gamut of special forces missions, including counter-terrorism. The KCT's origins can be found in World War II when, with the designation No 2 (Dutch) Troop, the first Dutch commandos were trained in the U.K. as part of No 10 (Inter-Allied) Commando. The unit was created on March 22, 1942 with the object of undertaking special operations. The unit was disbanded in October 1945, but its members continued fighting

in the Dutch East Indies, while others staffed the Stormschool (1945–50) in the Netherlands. In the East Indies between 1942 and 1945 the Korps Insulinde had fought a guerrilla war in Sumatra against the occupying Japanese and, after the defeat of Japan, searched for and recovered Dutch prisoners of war. In November 1945, the unit was disbanded, and its members joined the Depot Speciale Troepen and former members of No 2 (Dutch) Troop to form the Regiment Speciale Troepen, which fought Indonesian nationalists between 1945 and 1950. After Indonesia's independence had been recognized by the Dutch in 1949, the RST returned to the Netherlands. On July 1, 1950, on parliamentary recommendation, the RST merged with the Stormschool in Roosendaal to form the present Korps Commandotroepen.

After the end of the Cold War in 1989, the changed nature of world relations was reflected in the modification of many elements of the world's armed forces, including the KCT, to reflect altered priorities, such as  the emergence of a greater degree of irregular warfare in third-world countries, and of politically and/or religiously motivated terrorism. This latter demanded specialized counter-terrorism units with the capacity to operate both at home and in other countries. Thus, the KCT's Commando Waarnemer-verkenner (commando force reconnaissance) task gave way to that of the Commando Speciale Operaties (commando special operations).

Within this change, the KCT switched from a mix of regular and conscript soldiers to become a professional unit in 1995. Since that time the KCT has matured, both organizationally and tactically, into a versatile special forces unit. Deployments to Bosnia, Kosovo, Macedonia, Iraq, and, most recently, Afghanistan provided many new insights and knowledge. Successful counter-terrorist operations in Côte d'Ivoire and the Middle East, in 2004 and 2006, have confirmed KCT's capabilities.

## NEW ZEALAND

**New Zealand Army:**

New Zealand Special Air Service

The New Zealand Special Air Service came into being as a result of the February 1955 decision of the New Zealand government that a squadron based on the British Special Air Service should be created within the New Zealand Army as a contribution to the Far East Strategic Reserve and the British counter-insurgency effort in Malaya. It was also decided to recruit largely from the general public around a cadre of regular army personnel. More than 800 men applied, and of these 182 (including 138 civilians, many of them with earlier military experience) were chosen. Training began in

▼  *Two Commando soldiers of the Malaysian Grup Gerak Khas (Special Forces Group) use a jet ski during a training demonstration.*

June 1955. Later in the same year the 133-man NZSAS Squadron was attached to the British SAS in Malaya, and spent 18 of the 24 months it was in Malaya operating in the jungle against Communist insurgents. It also collected local villagers and trained them to protect their own settlements. Soon after that the New Zealand SAS Squadron was replaced by an infantry battalion and disbanded. The New Zealand SAS was also involved in the mid 1960s in operations against Indonesian insurgents in Borneo alongside their British and Australian counterparts.

In the Vietnam War, the New Zealand SAS's 4 Troop was attached to the Australian SASR. Here New Zealand SAS was named 1st Ranger Squadron, NZSAS, and its primary tasks were ambush of Communist forces and reconnaissance missions. The New Zealand SAS was operational in Vietnam from November 1968 to February 1971. Some 24 men of the New Zealand SAS were deployed to Kuwait in February 1998 under Operation "Griffin" during a period of international tension with Iraq. They were tasked with rescuing downed airmen in hostile territory in the event of a U.S.-led aerial campaign, and a smaller force replaced the original deployment in May 1998 for a further two-month tour. There were no missions into Iraq during the deployment, though the whole undertaking was nonetheless of value as it allowed the practice of mobile desert warfare skills and re-established contact with the U.S. forces, which had been limited since the U.S.A. suspended its ANZUS relations with New Zealand in 1986. In 1999–2000, men of the New Zealand SAS were part of the Australian-led peacekeeping force on Timor. From a time late in 2001, the New Zealand SAS began operations in Afghanistan. Three six-month rotations of between 40 and 65 soldiers from the New Zealand SAS served in Afghanistan during Operation "Enduring Freedom" before the unit was withdrawn in November 2005. During this time the New Zealanders at first undertook foot patrols (with insertion and extraction by helicopter), but in May 2002 the focus changed to mobility patrols using borrowed Humvees, and later motorcycles and New Zealand Army Pinzgauer vehicles. These patrols often lasted some 20 to 30 days and covered anything between 620 and 1,240 miles (1,000 and 2,000 km).

## NIGERIA
**Nigerian Navy:**
NNSBS (Nigerian Navy Special Boat Service)

## NORTH KOREA
**Korean People's Army:**
Special Operation Forces

## NORWAY
**Ministry of Defense:**
FSK (Forsvarets Spesialkommando)
HJK (Hærens Jegerkommando)
KJK (Kystjegerkommandoen)
MJK (Marinejegerkommandoen)

## OMAN
Sultan's Special Force

## PAKISTAN
**Inter-Services Intelligence:**
Joint Intelligence Miscellaneous Wing
**Pakistan Air Force:**
SSW (Special Service Wing)
**Pakistan Army:**
SSG (Special Service Group)
**Pakistan Navy:**
SSGN (Special Service Group Navy)
**Para-military:**
PAR (Pakistan Army Rangers)

The Special Service Group is the primary special forces element of the Pakistan Army, of which it is an independent division. The SSG is tasked with 14 special missions, namely asymmetric warfare, antipiracy, special operations, counter-proliferation, unconventional warfare, foreign internal defense, special reconnaissance, underwater demolition, direct action, hostage rescue, counter-terrorism, hydrographic reconnaissance, amphibious reconnaissance, and personnel recovery. The SSG is thought to have a strength in the order of 7,000 men in nine or ten 700-man battalions (each of four companies) to make possible the creation of three special forces brigades.

The SSG was created by the 1956 amalgamation of the 17/10th Baluch (19 Baluch) and 312 Garrison Company. Based in Cherat and Attock, the SSG was trained along the pattern of the U.S. special forces. At first the SSG had six companies, each of which included desert, mountain, ranger, and underwater warfare specialists. In August 1965, the SSG was increased in size and its name was changed from 19 Baluch (SSG) to Special Service Group. Chinese training, tactics, weapons, and equipment were also introduced at a later stage in conformity with Pakistan's greater alignment with China.

First used on the Afghan border to repel Afghan incursions into Pakistan, the SSG first saw major combat in the 1965 Indo-Pakistan War. Some 120 men were dropped near three Indian air bases to destroy Indian combat aircraft and put the bases out of action, but the operation was badly planned and executed, and ended in disaster, most of the men being taken prisoner. By 1971, the SSG had three battalions, of which one was based in East Pakistan (now Bangladesh). The SSG performed more capably in the 1971 Indo-Pakistan War.

During the Soviet war in Afghanistan in the 1980s, men of the SSG, disguised as Afghans, provided support to the mujahidin fighting the Soviets. The SSG was also active on the eastern border with India and also fought in Siachen. In the Kargil conflict the SSG infiltrated relatively deep into Indian territory undetected as sheep herders.

In 1980, the SSG's Musa Company, first established in 1970 as a combat diver unit, became an antiterrorist unit, and its training received considerable aid from the British SAS. In September 1986, Pan Am Flight 73 was hijacked by four Palestinian terrorists while refueling in Karachi. As negotiations stalled and the terrorists started to kill passengers, the SSG stormed the airliner, killing one hijacker and capturing the other. The SSG has also been involved in other counter-terrorist operations. More recently the SSG has been active in antiterrorist operations along Pakistan's border with Afghanistan and in combating Islamic extremists in Pakistani cities.

## PANAMA
**Panamanian Public Forces:**
Institutional Protection Service

## PERU
**Peruvian Army:**
1ra Brigada de Fuerzas Especiales
3ra Brigada de Fuerzas Especiales
26th Special Forces Group "Quevedo"
Special Forces Group "Puma"
**Peruvian Navy:**
Fuerza de Operaciones Especiales

## PHILIPPINES
**Armed Forces of the Philippines:**
Presidential Security Group
**Philippine Air Force:**
710th Special Operations Wing
**Philippine Army:**
1st Scout Ranger Regiment
Special Forces Regiment
Light Reaction Battalion
**Philippine Coast Guard:**
Special Operations Group
**Philippine Marine Corps:**
Philippine Marine Corps Force Reconnaissance
Battalion
**Philippine Navy:**
Naval Special Warfare Group

## POLAND
Dowództwo Wojsk Specjalnych (GROM, FORMOZA, COMMANDO, AGAT, and NIL)
Wojska Specjalne Rzeczypospolitej Polskiej (Special Forces of the Republic of Poland):

## PORTUGAL

**Portuguese Army:**
Comandos
Companhia de Precursores Aeroterrestres
   (Pathfinders Company)
Operações Especiais (Rangers)
**Portuguese Navy:**
DAE (Destacamento de Acções Especiais)

## ROMANIA

**Romanian Army:**
528th Reconnaissance Battalion
DIR (Detaşamentul de Intervenţie Rapidă)
Regimentul 1 Operaţii Speciale (The Eagles)

## RUSSIA

**Russian Armed Forces:**
45th Detached Reconnaissance Regiment
Russian commando frogmen
Spetsnaz GRU

The Spetsnaz GRU are generally accepted as being the best trained and most experienced units of the Armed Forces of the Russian Federation. They are a special unit under the control of the GRU (Glavnoye Razvedyvatel'noye Upravleniy), or foreign military intelligence directorate of the General Staff of the Armed Forces of the Russian Federation. The Spetsnaz are also used for counter-terrorism, and for operations of several types deep behind the enemy lines.

During World War II, reconnaissance and diversionary forces were formed under the supervision of the Second Department of the General Staff and subordinated to army group commanders. When the structure of the Red Army was reviewed after World War II, one of the results was the complete reorganization of the GRU between 1947 and 1950. The first independent special-purpose reconnaissance companies were created in 1949 to work with tank and combined armies. In 1957, the first Spetsnaz battalions were formed, five of them specifically tasked with the destruction of enemy short-range nuclear weapons systems. The first Spetsnaz brigades were created in 1962, apparently for operations as far as 465 miles (750 km) into the enemy's rear for the destruction of longer-ranged U.S. battlefield nuclear weapons systems. Two "study regiments" were established to train specialists and NCOs, the first in 1968 at Pechora near Pskov, and the second in 1970 at Chirchiq near Tashkent.

Current Spetsnaz-GRU units (together with their locations and command parent), have an overall strength of about 12,000 men. They comprise the 2nd Detached Special Operations Brigade (Promezhitsy in Pskov Oblast with about 960 men and controlled by the Leningrad Military District), 3rd Guards Detached Special Operations Brigade

(Roshinskiy in Samara Oblast and controlled by the Volga-Ural Military District), 10th (Mountain) Detached Special Operations Brigade (Molkino near Krasnodar Krai and controlled by the North Caucasus Military District), 12th Detached Special Operations Brigade (Asbest-5 in Sverdlovsk Oblast and controlled by the Volga-Ural Military District but being moved to Chaikovskyy near Perm), 14th Detached Special Operations Brigade (Ussuriysk near Primorsky Krai and controlled by the Far Eastern Military District), 16th Detached Special Operations Brigade (Chuchkovo and controlled by the Moscow Military District), 22nd Guards Detached Special Operations Brigade (Kovalevka in Rostov Oblast and controlled by the North Caucasus Military District), 24th Detached Special Operations Brigade (Kyakhta and controlled by the Siberian Military District), 67th Detached Special Operations Brigade (Berdsk in Novosibirsk Oblast and controlled by the Siberian Military District), and 216th Detached Special Operations Battalion (Moscow and controlled by the Moscow Military District).

Spetsnaz-GRU units have fought in Soviet War in Afghanistan (1979–89), 1st and 2nd Chechen Wars (1994–96 and 1999–present), and South Ossetia War (2008).

## SAUDI ARABIA

**Saudi Armed Forces:**
1st Special Brigade
64th Brigade
85th Battalion
88th Battalion
99th Battalion

## SERBIA

**Serb Armed Forces:**
Serb Military Police Battalion "Cobras"
Serb Army Special Brigade (Counter-Terrorist
   Battalion "Falcons," 63rd Parachute Battalion and
   72nd Reconnaissance-Commando Battalion)

## SINGAPORE

**Republic of Singapore Army:**
Singapore Armed Forces Commando Formation
Singapore Special Operations Force
**Republic of Singapore Navy:**
Naval Diving Unit

The Singapore Special Operations Force is a special forces unit in the Singapore Armed Forces Commando Formation, and specializes in direct action, counter-terrorism, hostage rescue, and special reconnaissance.

On September 27, 1972, a flight engineer aboard Olympic Airways Flight 472 accidentally activated a hijack alarm of a Boeing Model 707 airliner outward bound from Sydney, Australia, to Singapore.

A member of the Australian Civil Aviation Safety Authority warned Paya Lebar Airport "to be ready for a possible hijacking." After it landed, the airliner was immediately surrounded by police before the authorities could confirm the false alarm. This incident was of benefit to Singapore inasmuch as it highlighted the lack of forces trained and equipped to deal with a hijack or hostage situation. This led to the creation of the SOF in 1985 as a dedicated unit to tackle such possible future contingencies.

The first of these was Operation "Thunderbolt," the 1991 rescue of Singapore Airlines' Flight 117 at Singapore's Changi Airport. The Airbus A310 was hijacked by Pakistani militants on March 26, 1991 while flying from Kuala Lumpur to Singapore. SOF commandos stormed the Airbus on March 27: the operation was completed in 30 seconds, and 123 passengers and crew were freed with no injuries to hostages or SOF commandos; all four hijackers were killed.

## SLOVAKIA

**Slovak Army:**
5th Special Forces Regiment

## SLOVENIA

**Slovene Armed Forces:**
Enota za Specialno Delovanje (Special Operations
   Unit)
Light Divers Platoon
Posebna Enota za Specialno Taktiko (Specialized
   Unit for Special Tactics)

## SOUTH AFRICA

**South African National Defence Force:**
Special Forces Brigade ("Recces")

The Special Forces Brigade ("Recces") is the South African National Defence Force's only special forces unit, and has its origins in the period before the end of white-only rule in South Africa. On October 1, 1972, No. 1 Reconnaissance Commando was created as the first South African special forces unit, and specialized in airborne operations. Two other special forces units were later established as No. 4 Reconnaissance Commando specializing in seaborne operations, and No 5 Reconnaissance Commando. These South African special forces played a significant role in the country's 30-year border war in Namibia and Angola.

On January 1, 1981, in a reorganization of the special forces, the reconnaissance commandos and other special forces became an independent force controlled directly by the South African Defence Force rather than the South African Army. As part of the reorganization, the reconnaissance commandos became regiments. Later in the same decade, a special forces headquarters and a special forces stores depot were added to the organization.

In 1991, the special forces underwent another organizational change, with the special forces headquarters replaced by a Directorate Reconnaissance reporting directly to the Chief of the Army. Further change followed in 1993, when the Directorate Reconnaissance became No 45 Parachute Brigade, No 1 Reconnaissance Regiment became the 452nd Parachute Battalion, No 4 Reconnaissance Regiment became the 453rd Parachute Battalion and No 5 Reconnaissance Regiment became the 451st Parachute Battalion.

As a result of the changes that took place in South Africa after the nation's first fully democratic elections, the organization of the special forces reached its more current form in 1996. What is now the Special Forces Brigade comprises Nos 4 and 5 Special Forces Regiments as well as No 1 Maintenance Unit, which provides logistic support. It should be noted, however, that the combat strength of the brigade is less than that of a regular infantry battalion. No 1 Special Forces Regiment was disbanded in 1996. No 4 Special Forces Regiment specializes in maritime-related activities, and No 5 Special Forces Regiment specializes in overland techniques, especially long-range infiltration. The brigade is not a part of the South African Army, but is controlled directly by the Joint Operations Division of the South African National Defence Forces.

## SOUTH KOREA

**Republic of Korea Air Force:**
Combat Control Team
Office of Special Investigation
Special Air Rescue Team ("Red Berets")
**Republic of Korea Army:**
Defense Intelligence Command
(Headquarters of Intelligence Detachment)
Joint Security Area Security Battalion
Special Warfare Command (707th Special Mission Battalion ["White Tigers"])
**Republic of Korea Capital Defense Command:**
Military Police Special Guard Team
33rd Rangers
35th Commandos
**Republic of Korea Marine Corps:**
1st Special Reconnaissance Battalion ("Sharkmen")
**Republic of Korea Navy:**
Naval Special Warfare Flotilla (Special Missions Group), Ship Salvage Unit, Naval Special Warfare Brigade and Underwater Demolition Unit)

## SPAIN

**Guardia Civil:**
Unidad Especial de Intervención
**Spanish Air Force:**
Escuadrón de Zapadores Paracaidistas
**Spanish Army:**
Mando de Operaciones Especiales

▲ *Members of the Slovak Republic 5th Special Forces Regiment conduct a security exercise.*

**Spanish Marine Corps:**
Unidad Especial de Buceadores de Combate
Unidad de Operaciones Especiales

## SRI LANKA

**Sri Lanka Air Force:**
SLAF Regiment Special Force
**Sri Lanka Army:**
Commando Regiment
Special Forces Regiment (Long-Range Reconnaissance Patrol)
**Sri Lanka Navy:**
Rapid Action Boat Squadron
Special Boat Squadron

## SWEDEN

**Swedish Armed Forces:**
Fallskärmsjägarskolan (Parachute Ranger School, and home of the SIG and SSG)
Kustjägarna (Coastal Rangers)
Särskilda Inhämtningsgruppen (Special Reconnaissance Group)
Särskilda Skyddsgruppen (Special Protection Group)

## SWITZERLAND

**Swiss Army:**
Army Reconnaissance Detachment
20th, 30th, and 40th Grenadier Battalions

# SYRIA

**Syrian Army:**
14th Special Forces Division

# TAIWAN

**Republic of China Air Force:**
Paratrooper Special Tactics Unit
**Republic of China Army:**
101st Amphibious Reconnaissance Battalion
Special Operation Command
**Republic of China Marine Corps:**
Amphibious Reconnaissance and Patrol Unit
**Republic of China Navy:**
Navy SEALs
Underwater Demolition Units

# THAILAND

**Royal Thai Air Force:**
Royal Thai Air Force Commando Company
Royal Thai Air Force Pararescue
**Royal Thai Army:**
Special Forces
**Royal Thai Marine Corps:**
Marine Reconnaissance Battalion
**Royal Thai Navy:**
Royal Thai Navy SEALs

# TURKEY

**Turkish Air Force:**
MAK (Combat Search and Rescue)
AKİP (commandos)
**Turkish Gendarmerie:**
Jandarma Özel Asayiş Komutanlığı (gendarmerie commandos)
Jandarma Özel Harekat (gendarmerie special operations)
**Turkish General Staff:**
Özel Kuvvetler ("Maroon Berets")
**Turkish Navy:**
Su Altı Savunma (underwater defense)
Su Altı Taarruz (underwater attack)

# UNITED KINGDOM

**British Army:**
18 (UKSF) Signal Regiment
Special Air Service
Special Reconnaissance Regiment
**Joint Service:**
Special Forces Support Group
**Royal Air Force/Army Air Corps:**
Joint Special Forces Aviation Wing
**Royal Navy:**
Special Boat Service

The current Special Air Service is a British Army unit created on May 31,1950. The SAS is important in British special forces thinking, and has also served as a model for many others of the world's special forces, many of which have been trained with SAS support. Together with the Special Boat Service, Special Reconnaissance Regiment, and Special Forces Support Group, the SAS is a key component of the U.K. Special Forces controlled by the Director Special Forces. The SAS presently comprises 22 Special Air Service Regiment of the Regular Army, and 21 and 23 Special Air Service Regiments of the Territorial Army. It is tasked with the undertaking of special operations in time of war, and largely with counter-terrorism operations in time of peace.

The SAS was created in the British Army in World War II, and was formed in July 1941 as "L" Detachment, Special Air Service Brigade, to operate behind the Axis lines in North Africa. "L" Detachment initially comprised five officers and 60 other ranks. Its first foray took place in November 1941 as a parachute drop in support of the Operation "Crusader"offensive, but this was a complete failure as 22 men were killed or captured. The second foray was successful. After being transported by the Long Range Desert Group, the SAS attacked the Italian airfields in Libya, destroying 60 aircraft without loss. In September 1942 it was renamed 1st SAS, consisting at that time of four British squadrons, one Free French, one Greek, and the Folboat Section, the last with folding canoes. In January 1943, the 1st SAS's commander, Lt. Colonel David Stirling, was captured in Tunisia and Lt. Colonel "Paddy" Mayne replaced him. In April 1943, the 1st SAS was reorganized into the Special Raiding Squadron under Mayne's command, and the Special Boat Squadron was commanded by Major the Earl Jellicoe. The Special Raiding Squadron fought in Sicily and Italy along with the 2nd SAS, which had been formed in North Africa in 1943 in part by the renaming of the Small Scale Raiding Force. The Special Boat Squadron fought in the Aegean Islands and Dodecanese until the end of the war. In 1944, the SAS Brigade was formed from the British 1st and 2nd SAS, French 3rd and 4th SAS, and Belgian 5th SAS, and took part in parachute reconnaissance and harassment raids behind the German lines in France and then similar operations in support of the Allied advance through Belgium, the Netherlands, and eventually western Germany.

At the end of the war the British government ordered the SAS's disbandment on October 8, 1945, but as early as the next year it became clear that there was an operational requirement for a deep-penetration special forces unit, and a Territorial Army unit, the Artists Rifles, assumed the task as the 21st Battalion, SAS Regiment (Artists Rifles) (V) on January 1, 1947. In 1950, a 21 SAS squadron was raised to fight in the Korean War. After three months of training in England, it was informed that the squadron would no longer be required in Korea and so it instead volunteered to fight in the Malayan Emergency. Upon arrival in Malaya, it came under the command of Lt. Colonel

J. M. Calvert, who had commanded the SAS Brigade in the later stages of World War II and was now creating the Malayan Scouts (SAS). Calvert had already formed one squadron of 100 volunteers in the Far East. This became A Squadron, and the 21 SAS squadron became B Squadron. Following a Calvert's recruitment visit to Rhodesia, C Squadron was formed from 1,000 Rhodesian volunteers. The Rhodesians returned home after three years' service and were replaced by a New Zealand squadron. By this time, the need for a regular SAS regiment had been recognized, and 22 SAS Regiment came into being in 1952. In 1959, the third regiment, 23 SAS Regiment, was formed in the Territorial Army by renaming the Reserve Reconnaissance Unit, which had succeeded MI9 and whose men were skilled in escape and evasion.

Since serving in Malaya, men of 22 SAS Regiment have taken part in covert reconnaissance and surveillance by patrols and some larger-scale raiding missions in Borneo, Oman, the Aden Emergency, Northern Ireland, and Gambia. The regiment's Special Projects team assisted the West German GSG 9 counter-terrorism group in its airliner rescue operation at Mogadishu. The SAS counter-terrorist wing gained worldwide fame for its hostage rescue operation during the Iranian embassy siege in London. In the Falklands War, D and G Squadrons were deployed and participated in the raid on Pebble Island. Operation "Flavius" was a controversial operation in Gibraltar against the Provisional Irish Republican Army (PIRA). The SAS provided forward air control for NATO aircraft attacking Serb positions, and hunted war criminals in Bosnia. The Gulf War, in which A, B, and D Squadrons were deployed, was the largest SAS undertaking since World War II. In Sierra Leone it was involved in the Operation "Barras" operation to rescue men of the Royal Irish Regiment being held hostage by local militia forces. In the Iraq War, it was part of Task Forces "Black" and "Knight." In 2006, the SAS was involved in the rescue of three peace activists who had been held hostage in Iraq for 118 days. Operations against the Taliban in Afghanistan have involved men of the 21 and 23 SAS Regiments.

The 22 SAS Regiment has four operational squadrons, namely A, B, D, and G. Each of these comprises some 60 or more men commanded by a major and divided into four troops and a small headquarters section. Troops usually consist of 16 men divided into four four-man patrols, each man possessing a particular skill (signals, demolition, medic, or linguist) in addition to basic skills learned during the course of his training. The four troops specialize in different areas. The men of the Boat Troop are specialists in maritime and riverine skills using scuba diving, kayaks and rigid-hulled inflatable boats, and often train with the Special Boat Service. The men of the Air Troop are experts in free-fall

parachuting using high-altitude low-opening (HALO) and high-altitude high-opening (HAHO) techniques. The men of the Mobility Troop are specialists in the use of vehicles and are experts in desert warfare. The men of the Mountain Troop are specialists in Arctic combat and survival using specialist equipment, such as skis, snowshoes, and mountain climbing techniques. In 1980, R Squadron was formed, and this has since become L Detachment. Its men are all ex-regular SAS regiment soldiers who have a commitment to reserve service.

Established in 1975, the Special Projects team is the SAS's anti-hijacking and counter–terrorism team, and is trained in close-quarter battle and sniping techniques for use in hostage rescue tasks in buildings or on public transport under the aegis of the SAS Counter-Revolutionary Warfare Wing. Once the wing had been established, each squadron has been rotated on a continual basis through counter–terrorist training, including hostage rescue, siege breaking, and live firing exercises. Squadrons have their training refreshed every 16 months. The CRW Wing's first deployment was during the Balcombe Street siege in London: the Metropolitan Police had trapped a Provisional IRA unit, which surrendered when it heard that the SAS was being committed against it. The first documented action abroad by the CRW Wing was its aid to the West German GSG 9 at Mogadishu. Under the command of a major general, the U.K. Special Forces, which at first comprised the three

SAS regiments and the SBS, but was later bolstered by the addition of the Special Forces Support Group and the Special Reconnaissance Regiment. The U.S. special forces are supported by 18 (UKSF) Signal Regiment and the Joint Special Forces Aviation Wing.

The Special Reconnaissance Regiment was created on April 6, 2005 to satisfy the demand for a special reconnaissance capability, and undertakes a broad spectrum of classified activities related to covert surveillance and reconnaissance. The SRR draws its personnel from existing units and can recruit volunteers from serving male and female members of all the British armed forces. The SRR was raised at the Royal Military Academy Sandhurst round a core provided by 14 Intelligence Company for surveillance operations, mainly but not wholly associated with counter-terrorism activities. Its formation was designed to relieve the SAS and SBS of that role, and is believed to total between 100 and 300 personnel.

The Special Boat Service is the special forces unit of the Royal Navy, and like the SAS its origins can be found in World War II, when it was established in 1940 as the Special Boat Section, becoming the Special Boat Squadron after the war and the Special Boat Service in the 1980s. The SBS's personnel are mainly Royal Marines, and its remit is akin to that of the SAS though with greater emphasis on amphibious operations. The SBS has four squadrons: C and X Squadrons specialize in general operations;

▲ *American and British soldiers take a tactical pause during a combat patrol in the Sangin District area of Helmand province, Afghanistan, in 2007.*

S Squadron in the use of mini-submarines and small boats; and M Squadron in maritime counter-terrorism. The SBS also operates on land, and has recently seen service in the deserts of Iraq and the mountains of Afghanistan. The SBS's primary tasks include intelligence gathering, counter-terrorism operations (surveillance or offensive action), sabotage and the disruption of enemy infrastructure, capture of specific individuals, close protection of senior politicians and military personnel, and reconnaissance and combat action in enemy territory.

The Special Boat Section was created in July 1940 by a commando officer, Captain Roger Courtney. The initial 12-man unit was the Folboat Troop, which became No 1 Special Boat Section early in 1941. The unit was attached to "Layforce"and moved to the Middle East, where later it worked with the 1st Submarine Flotilla based at Alexandria and carried out beach reconnaissance of Rhodes, evacuated troops left behind on Crete and made a number of small-scale raids. Courtney returned to the U.K. in December 1941 and established No 2 SBS, while No 1 SBS became attached to the SAS as its Folboat Section. In September 1942, No 1 SBS undertook Operation "Anglo." This was a raid on two airfields on Rhodes, and only two men returned though the small force destroyed three aircraft, a fuel dump and numerous buildings. After this No 1 SBS was absorbed into the SAS as a result of its losses.

In April 1943, the 1st SAS was divided, 250 men of the SAS and the Small Scale Raiding Force forming the Special Boat Squadron under Major the Earl Jellicoe. The SBS moved to Haifa and trained with the Greek Sacred Regiment for operations in the Aegean. The SBS operated in the Dodecanese and Cyclades island groups, and was also involved in the battles for Leros and Kos. In August 1944, the SBS and Long Range Desert Group combined for operations in the Adriatic, on the Peloponnese, in Albania, and, finally, Istria.

Throughout the war, the No 2 SBS did not use the Special Boat Squadron name but instead retained the name Special Boat Section and operated in the Mediterranean as far east as Crete before transferring to Ceylon to work with the Special Operations Executive's Force 136 and Special Operations Australia. Part of No 2 SBS was committed to the South-East Asia Command's Small Operations Group, operating on the Chindwin and Irrawaddy rivers, and in the Arakan coastal region, during the Burma campaign. In 1946, all elements of the SBS were disbanded, and the title passed to the Royal Marines. As part of the School of Combined Operations, its first operations were in Palestine, but then the SBS fought in the Korean War with operations along the North Korean coast, as well as undertakings behind Communist lines to attack lines of communication and gather intelligence. It was during the Korean War that the SBS first started operating from submarines. In 1961, the SBS undertook reconnaissance missions during the Indonesian Confrontation. It was in 1972 that the SBS first came to major public attention when a combined SAS and SBS team parachuted into the Atlantic Ocean after a bomb threat on board the liner *Queen Elizabeth 2*.

In 1977, the Special Boat Service became the Special Boat Squadron and in 1982, after the Argentine invasion of the Falkland Islands, deployed to South Georgia. In 1987, the name Special Boat Service was readopted for what was now part of the U.K. Special Forces alongside the SAS and 14 Intelligence Company. In the 1st Gulf War the SBS liberated the British embassy in Kuwait, abseiling from helicopters hovering above the embassy, and carried out diversionary raids along the Kuwaiti coast. In September 1999, the SBS was involved in peacekeeping operations in East Timor. In September 2000, the SBS played a part in the Operation "Barras" hostage rescue in Sierra Leone, and in November 2001 the SBS was committed in the invasion of Afghanistan and was involved in the Battle of Tora Bora. Since that time the SBS has

undertaken many operations in Afghanistan. When it became the Special Boat Service once again in 1987, the SBS was revised along SAS lines, with 16-man troops instead of the traditional sections. The SBS has some 200 to 250 men. The SBS currently possesses four active squadrons (C, M, S, and X) and the SBS Reserve, which provides individual reservists to serve with the regular SBS rather than forming independent teams.

## UNITED STATES OF AMERICA

**U.S. Special Operations Command:**
Joint Task Force Sword
Joint Task Force 487

**Joint Special Operations Command:**
1st Special Forces Operational Detachment-Delta
U.S. Naval Special Warfare Development Group
724th Special Tactics Group
Aviation Tactics and Evaluation Group
Flight Concepts Division
66th Air Operations Squadron
Technical Application Programs Office
Targeting and Analysis Center
Joint Communications Unit
JSOC Intelligence Brigade
Intelligence Support Activity
19th Intelligence Squadron
JSOC Special Operations Logistics Support Element

**U.S. Marine Corps Special Operations Command:**
Marine Special Operations Regiment
Marine Special Operations Support Group
Marine Special Operations Intelligence Battalion

**U.S. Air Force Special Operations Command:**
Air Force Special Operations Weather Technician
Tactical Air Control Party
U.S. Air Force Combat Controllers
U.S. Air Force Pararescue
U.S. Air Force Office of Special Investigations
Strategic Irregular Tactics Team

**U.S. Army Special Operations Command:**
75th Ranger Regiment
Special Forces ("Green Berets")
4th Military Information Support Group (Airborne)
95th Civil Affairs Brigade (Airborne)
U.S. Army Special Operations Aviation Command
160th Special Operations Aviation Regiment
(Airborne) ("Night Stalkers")

**U.S. Naval Special Warfare Command:**
U.S. Navy SEALs
U.S. Navy Special Warfare Combatant-craft Crewmen
U.S. Navy Explosive Ordnance Disposal

Established in 1980 in the aftermath of Operation "Eagle Claw," the failed attempt to recover U.S. citizens being held hostage in the U.S. embassy in Tehran, the Joint Special Operations Command is part of the U.S. Special Operations Command, and is tasked to consider special operations requirements and techniques with a view to interoperability and

equipment standardization, plan and conduct special operations exercises and training, and develop Joint Special Operations tactics. The JSOC also controls the special mission units (SMU) of the U.S. Special Operations Command. The only three publicly revealed SMUs are the U.S. Army's 1st Special Forces Operational Detachment-Delta, the U.S. Navy's Naval Special Warfare Development Group, and the U.S. Air Force's 24th Special Tactics Squadron. Units of the U.S. Army's 75th Ranger Regiment and 160th Special Operations Aviation Regiment are controlled by the JSOC when deployed as part of JSOC Task Forces, such as Task Force 121 and Task Force 145.

The 1st SFOD-D is often known as Delta, The Unit or Delta Force, and is the army counterpart of the U.S. Navy's Naval Special Warfare Development Group (DEVGRU): these two SMUs are the primary U.S. providers of counter-terrorism, direct action and national intervention operations. The 1st SFOD-D can also undertake a host of covert missions, including hostage rescue and raids. The 1st SFOD-D was established as a counter-terrorist unit in the wake of several terrorist incidents in the 1970s. Colonel Charles Beckwith, a member of the U.S. Army Special Forces, had served as an exchange officer with the British 22 SAS Regiment and, on returning to the U.S.A., wrote a report highlighting the U.S. Army's limitation in not possessing a unit comparable with the SAS. The U.S. Army Special Forces at that time concentrated on unconventional warfare, but Beckwith urged the creation of highly capable and wholly autonomous small teams with a broad array of special skills for direct action and counter-terrorist missions. The Pentagon ordered Beckwith to create such a capability, and Beckwith estimated that it would take two years to bring his new unit up to operational status. Meanwhile, the 5th Special Forces Group created Blue Light, a small counter-terrorist contingent, which operated until the 1st SFOD-D became fully operational in the early 1980s.

On November 4, 1979, shortly after the creation of the 1st SFOD-D, 53 U.S. citizens were seized and held in the U.S. embassy in Tehran, Iran. The unit was assigned to Operation "Eagle Claw" and ordered to enter Iran secretly and recover the hostages on the night of April 24–25, 1980. The operation was aborted after flying problems and accidents. After this failure the U.S. government created several new units. The 160th Special Operations Aviation Regiment (Airborne) came into existence as the 1st SFOD-D's infiltration and extraction unit; the U.S. Navy's SEAL Team Six was created for maritime incidents; and the JSOC was created to control and oversee joint training between the counter-terrorist assets of the various branches of the U.S. military.

Since that time the 1st SFOD-D has been committed to a number of operations, including those in Central America (fighting the Salvadoran revolutionary group Farabundo Marti National Liberation Front and assisting the Central Intelligence Agency-funded Contras in Nicaraguan operations), Operation "Urgent Fury" (rescue of political prisoners during the liberation of Grenada in December 1983), Aeropostal Flight 252 (support for Venezuelan special forces recovering a hijacked airliner on July 31, 1984), the *Achille Lauro* hijack (standby with SEAL Team 6 should a recovery operation be needed in October 1985), Operation "Round Bottle" (unexecuted plan for the recovery of western hostages in Beirut), Operation "Just Cause" (invasion of Panama in January 1990), Operations "Desert Shield/Desert Storm" (support for invasion of Iraq in February 1991), Operation "Gothic Serpent" (cooperation with U.S. Army Rangers in Mogadishu in October 1993), Operation "Uphold Democracy" (invasion of Haiti in 1994), Operation "Allied Force" (operations in former Yugoslavia in 1995–98), Operation "Enduring Freedom" (war against the Taliban in Afghanistan in 2001) and Operation "Iraqi Freedom" (invasion of Iraq in 2003).

The 1st SFOD-D has a strength estimated at between 800 and 1,000 men, who are divided into a number of operational groups: Detachment D (headquarters), Detachment E (communications, intelligence and administrative support), Detachment F (operational arm, i.e. the teams of operators), Medical Detachment, Operational Support Troop ("Funny Platoon" in-house intelligence element), Aviation Squadron (12 Boeing AH-6 attack and MH-6 transport helicopters), Operational Research Section and Training Wing. The structure of the 1st SFOD-D is similar to that of the 22 SAS Regiment, and comprises the A, B, and C Squadrons, which are operational elements each based on the SAS Saber squadrons with 75 to 85 operators. Each saber squadron comprises one Recce/Sniper Troop and two Direct Action/Assault Troops, which can operate either in teams or in groups as small as four to six men.

The United States Naval Special Warfare Development Group is often known just as DEVGRU and informally as SEAL Team Six, its former name. DEVGRU is supported administratively by the Naval Special Warfare Command but commanded operationally by the JSOC. Like those of the 1st SFOD-D, the origins of ST6 can be found in the failure of Operation "Eagle Claw." During the planning phase of this undertaking, Lieutenant Commander Richard Marcinko had been one of the two naval representatives on the Joint Chiefs of Staff task force, known as the TAT (Terrorist Action Team), and after the failure was ordered to draft the plan for a U.S. Navy specialized full-time counter-terrorist team. Marcinko then became the first commander of the unit, which he named SEAL

Team Six. At the time there were only two SEAL teams, and Marcinko seems to have called his unit SEAL Team Six to confuse Soviet intelligence. SEAL Team Six became the U.S. Navy's most significant counter-terrorist unit.

SEAL Team Six was formally created in October 1980, and drawing its personnel primarily from other U.S. Navy special force elements became operational in only six months after a high-pressure training program. The existing SEAL teams, including the 12 platoons of SEAL Team One on the western seaboard, had already begun counter-terrorism training, establishing a specialized two-platoon group, known as MOB Six (Mobility Six). SEAL Team Six started with 75 men, and received significant funding to obtain the best possible weapons and equipment.

In 1987, a new unit was established as the Naval Special Warfare Development Group (DEVGRU) after SEAL Team Six had been disestablished, and the essentially similar DEVGRU is often called SEAL Team Six. DEVGRU is divided into Red Squadron (Assault), Blue Squadron (Assault), Gold Squadron (Premier Squadron), and a later Silver Squadron (Assault). There is also a Gray Squadron (Boat Crews) and a Black Squadron (Reconnaissance and Surveillance Squadron). Each squadron is divided into three troops, and the troops are also divided into smaller teams.

In 2010, the DEVGRU name was changed, although the new name was not revealed, and at the same time the 1st SFOD-D became ACE (Army Compartmental Elements).

Another component of the SOCOM is the U.S. Marine Corps Special Operations Command (MARSOC), which undertakes the direct action, special reconnaissance, and foreign internal defense roles as its primary task, and the counter-terrorism, information operations and unconventional warfare roles as its secondary task. The MARSOC came into formal existence on February 24, 2006. The involvement of the USMC in SOCOM was controversial and, for since the creation of the SOCOM in 1986 the USMC had felt that its Force Reconnaissance units should be kept within the USMC core structure and that any detachment of an elite USMC special force from the USMC would not be beneficial. A re-evaluation following the September 11, 2001 attacks and the start of the "War on Terrorism" called for closer integration of U.S. special forces, and the creation of the MARSOC was a major step in this direction.

MARSOC followed in the steps of MCSOCOM Detachment One (DET1), a small USMC detachment designed to validate USMC integration into SOCOM. It comprised mostly Force Reconnaissance Marines of the 1st and 2nd Force Reconnaissance Companies together with specially selected support men, and operated with U.S. Navy SEALs

under Naval Special Warfare Group One. DET1 undertook many special operations in Iraq alongside other special forces, and SOCOM's assessment of DET1's deployment revealed good results. DET1 was disbanded in 2006 after MARSOC's creation. The finalization of MARSOC's structure was begun in 2007 to make it more compatible with other Joint Special Operations Task Force elements.

The MARSOC has about 2,500 Marines and sailors, and its basic unit is the 14-man Marine Special Operations Team. The MARSOC has three subordinate elements, namely the Marine Special Operations Regiment, Marine Special Operations Support Group, and Marine Special Operations Intelligence Battalion, all supported by the Marine Special Operations School. The MSOR comprises a headquarters company and the 1st, 2nd, and 3rd Marine Special Operations Battalions. These latter are tasked with direct action, special reconnaissance, counter-terrorism, and information operations. They are also trained to carry out peacetime foreign internal defense and unconventional warfare. Each MSOB comprises four Marine Special Operations Companies, each of four Marine Special Operations Teams (MSOT). Each MSOT can operate on its own, but can also operate as a component of a larger unit.

The 400-man Marine Special Operations Support Group has the MARSOC's administrative, intelligence, and support assets. The Marine Special Operations Intelligence Battalion provides intelligence support.

### VENEZUELA
Special Operations Brigade "Generalísimo Francisco de Miranda"
**Venezuelan Air Force:**
Special Operations Squadron
**Venezuelan Army:**
106th and 506th Special Operations Battalions
**Venezuelan National Guard:**
Grupo de Acciones Especiales (Special Actions Group)
Grupos Anti-Extorsión y Secuestros (Counter-Extortion and Hostage Groups)

### VIETNAM
**Vietnamese Army:**
Dac cong Viet Nam (Vietnam Sapper Force)
**Vietnam Police:**
Canh sat Co dong (Vietnam Mobile Police Force)

### ZIMBABWE
**Zimbabwe National Army:**
Boat Squadron
Combat Diving Unit
Special Air Service

# INDEX

## Picture Credits

© **Getty Images:** 13a, 41, 103a, 103cr, 137al, 154, 167cr, 174bl, 193al; AFP 40a, 53cl, 71c, 77ar, 102, 108bl, 108br, 120bl, 121, 175, 192, 202bl, 217bl; AFP/ Eitan Abramovic 142; AFP/Cris Bouroncle 142al, 143cr; AFP/Mehdi Fedouach 203bl; AFP/Romeo Gacad 161a; AFP/Valery Hachel 203cr; AFP/Marco Longari 12a; AFP/Pascal Pavani 12b; AFP/Joel Saget 4–5; AFP/ Issouf Sanogo 149ar; AFP/Tom Stoddart 277cr; AFP/Vladimir Suvorov 187al; AFP/Yuri Tutov 186; Paula Bronstien 160bl, 166; Check Six 200b; Gamma-Rapha 109a, 206b; Chris Hondros 161br; Hulton Archive 26bl, 26ar, 52bl, 53ar, 53br, 91ar, 96, 120br; Marco Di Lauro 193ar; Peter Macdiarmid 189al; MILpictures by Tom Weber 6–7, 184a; Warrick Page 177br, 221l; Popperfoto 22bl, 23b, 24bl, 24cr, 25ar, 25bl, 27ar, 27b, 77al, 90, 91b; Joe Raedle 13bl, 167a; Juergen Schwarz 59r; Pascal Le Segretain 174cr; Stocktrek Images 188b, 218a; Chung Sung-Jun 10a; The Image Bank/MILpictures by Tom Weber 1, 205a, 205b; Time & Life Pictures 28b; Time & Life Pictures/Larry Burrows 32b; Time & Life Pictures/ John Florea 30bl, 145al; Time & Life Pictures/Greg Mathieson 216ar; Time & Life Pictures/Carl Mydans 29b; Time Life Images/William Vandivert 27al; Roger Viollet 22br.

© shutterstock.com:AISPIX 46; Vartanov Anatoly 2–3, 87c, 132, 141ar; greatpapa 129c; Jaroslaw Grudzinski 140cl; Peter Kim 135c; Michal Ninger 145ar, 145cr; Turnar 98–99; Robert H M Voors 68bl; Whitcombe RD 73a; Luhai Wong 159b.

© **Andrew Chittock:** 72bl, 72ar, 73b, 74–75, 78–79.

☺ **Creative Commons Licence:** Johnny R Aragon 147b; locotenent-colonel Dragoş Anghelache 146cl, 146bl; Azrizainul 8b, 230; Bundeswehr-Fotos 171al, 228; Davric 54a, 139br; Faupel 20cr; Gibnews 131al; Ismeretien 23a; Israel Defense Forces 190a; Edward N. Johnson 14bl; EX13 38b, 39a, 39b; Brian Harrington Spier 47b; Todd Huffman 76ar, 76cr; isafmedia 196–197, 225; Jamesdale10 185br, 201al; Jumpcoach 145bl, 145br; Edward N Johnson 144a, 144b; Roy Lathwell 13br; Leon 187cr; Nenad Martinovic 21bl; Sergeant James McCauley 153cr; Meymaneh 135ar; Mulag 71ar; Nilfanion 67a, 67b, 150b; Panky2sharma 148; John Pannell 131ar; Rama 203ar; Roque Wicker 220cr; Rizuan 141cr; Scheerer (e) 20al; Toni Schneiders 22ar, 22cr; Sfax 124–125; soldiersmediacenter 190b; TourinNicosia 70b; Wiegand 20bl; Oliver Wolters 38a;

**Flickr (Creative Commons):** Calflier001 114bl; neridamano 201cl; PEO Soldier 158b; Scotbot 130.

**Library of Congress (Public Domain):** News & World Report 70br.

**Public Domain:** 8a, 9a, 9b, 10b, 11a, 11b, 14a, 14–15b, 15al, 15ar, 15br, 16–17,18–19, 20ar, 21ar, 24ar, 26cr, 28a, 29a, 30a, 30br, 31al, 30ar, 30b, 32a, 33a, 33b, 34–35, 36–37, 40b, 42–43, 44–45, 47ar, 48–49, 50–51, 52br, 54b, 55a, 55b, 56–57, 58, 59al, 59br, 60–61, 62–63, 64–65, 66a, 66bl, 66cr, 66–67a, 67bl, 67r, 76bl, 80-81,82–83, 84–85, 86a, 86b, 87al, 87ar, 87bl, 88–89, 92–93, 94–95, 97a, 97c, 100–101, 104–105, 106–107, 109br, 110–111, 112–113, 114br, 115, 116–117, 118–119, 122–123, 126–127, 128a, 128b, 129a, 129bl, 129br, 132ar, 132bl, 133a, 133b, 134a, 134b, 135al, 135bl, 136, 137cr, 137br, 138a, 138b, 139a, 140ar, 140br, 141bl, 146r, 147a, 149al,150a, 151a, 151b, 152ar, 152bl, 152–153b, 153al, 153ar, 155al, 155r, 156–157, 158a, 159ar, 160br, 162–163, 164–165, 168–169, 170a, 170b, 171al, 171bl, 171br, 172–173, 176a, 176bl, 176–177b, 177ar, 178–179, 180–181, 182–183, 184b, 191a, 191b, 185a, 185cl, 188a, 189c, 189b, 194–195, 198–199, 200a, 201br, 202cr, 203al, 204a, 204b, 206a, 207a, 207b, 208cr, 208bl, 209al, 209ar, 209b, 210–211, 212–213, 214–215, 216b, 217ar, 28b, 219a, 219b, 220bl, 221ar, 222–223, 227, 233, 235.

The author and publishers have made every reasonable effort to credit all copyright holders. Any errors or omissions that may have occurred are inadvertent and anyone who for any reason has not been credited is invited to write to the publishers so that a full acknowledgment may be made in subsequent editons of this work.